"We throw the word "genius" around too often today, but Brian is the only true polymath I've ever worked with. He understands the necessity of delivering compelling content better than any talent I've ever heard. And he is utterly fearless on the air. All you really have to do is look at a list of the markets – and formats – he's dominated to grasp what a rare talent he is. I know of no one else like him, and I doubt you do either.

Doug Erickson
Erickson Media

"I had the joy of working Morning Drive radio with Brian in DC during the early 1990s. He made me cry… from laughing so hard. How hard, you ask? How about so hard it caused an abdominal hernia. That is something I STILL see every time I sit up in order to get out of bed. It doesn't hurt – certainly not as much as never being able to laugh again."

Bob Madigan
Former partner and WTOP Man About Town

"I too had the joy or working with Brian in DC. Developed the same type of abdominal hernia while constantly laughing. Hey, maybe we have the start of a class action suit…"

Robert Publicover
Official Brian and Bob Laugh Track, WWRC (Retired)

"In my time as 'Officer Vic' on the KSFO Morning Program, I had the magnificent opportunity to co-host with the multi-talented and head-spinningly intelligent Brian Wilson. I'm honored and delighted to have been a cohost with Brian, and the special magic is, that he and I call each other friends.

Tom Benner
30-year San Francisco Bay Area Morning Show Host, Recovering Golfer

"I thoroughly enjoyed every day Brian and I worked together at Z100! A razor-sharp mind, wickedly subtle sense of humor and… obviously… a great memory. Fifty years' worth of stories. Wow! I can't even recall two from last year!

Claire Stevens
News/Original Cast, Z100 Z-Morning Zoo

A hilarious career of legendary proportions!"

John Nolan
Afternoon Drive Host, The Fish, Los Angeles

"Fifty years? Amazing! I met Brian when I was operations director at Baton Rouge's first FM rocker. He was incredibly funny and I had the feeling that he would skyrocket from there, and I was right! Open [this book] up and start reading. You'll enjoy it and may even get a feeling of how great radio was before it died.

George Bonnell
Operations Director, WAFB-FM, Baton Rouge (Retired)

In my nearly 50 years in the business, I've only worked with a couple of people I would work with again in an instant. Brian Wilson has been, simply, one of the funniest and most natural on-air talents of his generation. No mold. His book is a must-read for anyone wanting to know how things really are in the biz; his insight is absolutely dead-on.

Sean Hall
News Anchor B104/Baltimore (Mostly Retired)

50 Stories

50 Years in Radio

Brian Wilson

Book cover design by Cassie Wilson

Published by Myrmidon Press

ISBN: 9781724111173

These 50 Stories, memories, laughs, tears, brilliant creativity, stupid mistakes and scattered temper fits would just be Glory Days in print, loaded with errors, omissions and verbal hair balls if it weren't for all the people who were a part of this project before, during and after I did the scribbling.

So to my long-suffering editor, legal counsel, technical advisor, historian, research assistant, IT director, proofreader, jacket designer, layout artist, public relations director, media relations director, photographer, caterer and transportation assistant -- my profound and undying thanks for everything you've done – most importantly, your patience.

More astounding, all those mentioned above are embodied in one award-winning broadcast journalist, writer, lunch date, partner and beloved bride, Carol Anne "Cassie" Wilson.

Contents

INTRODUCTION

Thanks for reading this far.

Some reading this have been listeners, viewers or readers for most of these **50 Years** and already know to expect droll sarcasm, biting cynicism, ruthless ravaging, heated passions and raw sex on the following pages. There are some who will think this is a new Beach Boy anthology. And some will think it's all about a major league baseball player's notorious beard cultivation. Some could even think this is about any one of several other "Brian Wilsons" sprinkled through the radio business.

The first group got it right.

While there is unavoidably some personal stuff in here, this is not my autobiography. Other than a sure cure for insomnia, who would want to read mine anyway? No, this is more like -- Three! Three! Three books in one!

There is the historical part -- from 1965 through 2015, I was involved in some remarkable broadcasting events. I may only have been Center Stage for some of 'em, but I was *on* stage for all of 'em! Those times made some *great* stories.

Then there is the hysterical part -- a half-century of valiantly attempting to entertain audiences from Red Stick to the Big Peach to the Big Apple along with Baltimore, San Francisco, Dallas-Ft. Worth, Kansas City, Charlotte, Los Angeles and others, and occasionally filling in on some nationally syndicated shows. I must have done *something* worthwhile along the way.

Finally, the half-fast part -- goofy, crazy, tragic, weird, scientifically inexplicable, multi-orgasmic, Machiavellian, even a few antidisestablishmentarianisms. I have no idea what that last one means but big words always add a measure of credibility.

OK? Glad we got that out of the way.

Not surprisingly, a lotta major changes took place in radio during my half-century. Technology made equipment better, faster, easier, smaller, bigger, more powerful or more efficient. It made many parts of the job easier and less time consuming, providing more opportunities for some spasmodic inspiration to create more Wild 'n Crazy stuff for the show.

Going from analog to digital was unspeakably huge. Vinyl records, carts, reel-to-reel decks, grease pencils, razor blades, splicing tape, music selection, program logs, even transmitter readings were replaced by the eventually ubiquitous computer -- as remarkable as going from horse 'n buggy to fuel-injected Corvette.

Along with the techy stuff, deregulation in the 1970s brought an end to limits on station ownership, clunky programming requirements and – The Big One – elimination of the dreaded Fairness Doctrine, opening the door to Talk Radio, the other half of my career.

What does any of this have to do with what's in the book? Only to set the stage, scenery, props and actors through which all these stories played out, how they rippled through the lives from one to millions of people -- at *one time, maybe even you*. Radio had that power.

Then there is that "posterity" thingy.

It's great to be loved and admired but it's more gratifying to know you've produced something unique from within yourself, something of great quality, better than most, maybe the best of all; something that impacted the audience so much, it might be remembered for a lifetime.

Of course, none of that may be on any of these pages! But reading these **50 Stories**, I hope you will at least be entertained, maybe amazed, occasionally even informed. If my writing is good enough and your brain is sharp enough, we just may hit the Trifecta!

Enjoy!

I hope!

-BW

THE READER'S GUIDE TO 50 STORIES

During my 50 years, I was teamed with three other air personalities; twice in Music Radio, once in Talk Radio not counting the historical and somewhat awkward transition when WABC/NY flipped from Music to Talk. One from the other, the teams couldn't have been more different.

Ross and Wilson

In September 1977, I was hired to do AM Drive at WJBO/Baton Rouge. Time and space don't permit a full accounting of how this happened without turning this into some autobiographical tome of little interest to most everyone. Presumptuous, I know, but trust me on this one.

Almost immediately after I started, the new GM fired the PD who hired me and brought in the former assistant PD from WLCS, Baton Rouge's dominant Top 40 station, one Chuck White. Chuck deserves more space than I can give him here. Word is he is deceased, so there is that. Suffice to say, Chuck was the genius or moron (pick one) who introduced me to Ross Brittain, at that time, the midday jock at WLCS. Chuck's lead-in to my formal introduction went like this:

> *CW: I was wondering… have you ever done a two-man show?*
>
> *BW: Not really. Dabbled in it a few years ago on WIBR but the GM killed it. Why?*
>
> *CW: This guy I worked with at WLCS, Ross Brittain, does middays. Have you heard him?*

BW: Nope. I have another life after the show. I own an insurance agency, real estate agency, advertising agency and – you may have seen on TV – just opened a skateboard park. Why? Should I care?

CW: Well, he's a little boring, kinda low energy, but a damn good jock, tight board, good basics. I was thinking, with your energy and humor, you might jack him up a bit and the two of you would make a helluva team!

BW: I do not follow that logic one bit. What do you want me to do?

CW: Meet him. Have lunch. I'll pay. Tell me what you think later.

BW: Hmmph! The elusive free lunch! OK, set it up. Let me know where and when.

Months later, according to Chuck, this is the conversation he had with Ross:

CW: Have you ever done a two-man show?

RB: Not really. More like an ensemble at Georgia Tech when friends would drop by the studio or call in. Why?

CW: Have you heard Brian Wilson, the new AM Drive guy over at WJBO?

RB: Not really. I'm usually doing show prep.

CW: He's really good but he's kinda wild and crazy sometimes. I thought if you could calm him down a bit, the two of you together could have a damn good show.

RB: OK. What do you want me to do?

CW: Meet him. Have lunch. I'll pay. Tell me what you think later. I'll set it up.

RB: OK.

Chuck arranged for the lunch at the Frost Top Inn, a root beer and burger joint a few blocks from the station. "Spare every expense" is a radio rule.

We met, we lunched and we had a damn good time. Back at the studio, I told White that Ross and I were willing to give it a try. *It's Baton Rouge. What have we got to lose?* Ross must have told him the same.

The rest is radio history. For all our successes, both our partings – at WABC and Z100 – were dumb and unnecessary. At least we started off well and made some great waves over seven years. But for all of the time and work we put into those years and for all the success we enjoyed, we should have had a better finale.

Brian and O'Brien

The listening audience wasn't the only source of **Ross and Wilson** fans. Several program directors at heritage stations across the country dreamed of having a Morning Team as magic as R&W. One tried to hire us away from WABC when word got out the station was flipping to Talk. We flew down to DC for the traditional "lunch chat" with the PD and GM. When the GM discovered we were still under contract to ABC, he ran out of the restaurant like a turpentined cat. Tortious interference is expensive and embarrassing. The PD had inadvertently exposed the GM and station's owners to a legally precarious and expensive situation which was fortunately avoided.

That same PD was running B104/Baltimore when the trades reported WABC turned me loose in April 1984, thus ending both halves of the **Ross and Wilson** "legacy." Within 48 hours, I got a call: I'll beat any offer you get from any other station if you come to do AM Drive on B104.

Nice to know, since four other stations had already booked me on flights for the traditional "talk and tour" ceremony.

Eventually, I got to Baltimore for a look-see.

While the PD strangely made every effort to make sure I did not visit the studio or the station, he made his case for the morning gig. Once all the details had been agreed to, a breakfast meeting and tour of Baltimore with the GM was set for the next day, dinner with the PD that night and then we'd see if we would seal the deal.

Two things happened next that should have chased me away.

Over dinner, the PD handed me a "letter of intent," detailing the essentials of their offer. Everything appeared in order until I read down to the compensation line: $10,000 below what we had agreed. I handed the letter back, thanked him for dinner and headed for my room. The GM promptly resolved the problem the next day.

Number two: The PD casually informed me I would be teamed with one Don O'Brien. The PD said he thought *this could be bigger than* ***Ross and Wilson***.

Having been burned by that recent break-up, I was adamantly opposed to taking on another partner. Who was this guy? Never heard of him. What was his background? Where was he working? None of the answers were gratifying:

> *He'll just run the board and do the news and sports. Give it a week. If you don't like it, we'll get rid of him.*

With those conditions, I agreed.

Don met up with us later at Baltimore's Inner Harbor. After some getting-to-know-you conversation, the PD suggested we storm the Control Room (it was 10 p.m. on a Friday), literally break-in and take over the board from Brian Carter, the late night jock.

Sure, what the hell! We did exactly that.

This was my first time seeing the station and studio -- two and three floors over a greasy spoon restaurant, six blocks up from the

Inner Harbor. Holes in the cheaply paneled walls were poorly covered with rock album posters. An old gas lawn mower was parked just outside the Control Room, sitting on a patch of ancient shag carpet. I had to believe this was an old joke left behind by the previous team.

It wasn't.

We barged into the Control Room just as the "On Air" light came on over the door. To say Brian Carter was "surprised" would be an understatement; "terrified" would be more accurate. Two white guys making such violent entrance had to have been unnerving for a young black man – until he saw Don whom he recognized from hanging around the office recently. Then he was just really confused.

Don took the board while I took the mic. I announced that we were the new "cleaning guys" and wanted to come in and have some fun. Hell, it was Friday night, right?

For the next few minutes, we crashed, banged, and raised enough commotion to get the listeners' undivided attention, assured Brian Carter this was all a bit to satisfy the PD and called some early attention to the new AM Drive show that would be starting next week.

Which it did – and it did not go well. At all.

I can't go into all the issues, it just wasn't a good time. Apparently Don didn't get the PD's memo that he was not going to be the new morning "star." Immediately, there was a tug of war over the show's mechanics, content and priorities.

While technical matters were finally resolved, who was going to be the On-Air Lead Dog was another matter. After a frank conversation with the PD, Don mostly dropped it and followed my lead. On those occasions he fell out of character, I had to jerk his chain, even on the air. It didn't take long for the audience to pick up on the growing tension.

This led to a big change in my on-air personality. With Ross, I was the semi out-of-control goof-ball DJ to his steady-as-you-go Radio Announcer. After countess confrontations with Don on and off the air, I could not hide my frustration. With no resolution from management, I was left to deal with Don's "issues."

While the audience noticed the tension, they loved it! They thought it was all part of the act! My verbal put-downs of Don became the "World Wrestling" match of the morning. Ratings went up and up and up; seeing the numbers, advertisers eventually formed a line; B104 became the most listened-to station in Baltimore's AM drive with an audience that had as much of a love-hate relationship with the show as I had with Don.

Our popularity notwithstanding, **Brian and O'Brien** came to an end in 1988, after management caught Don drinking on the air during a station party. Over the next few months, four people auditioned for Don's part but to no avail; even bad chemistry is hard to come by. The show continued as **Brian and O'Brien** in order to maintain name recognition with the advertisers and listeners. But by September, advertisers were pulling out of the premium-priced show. I was informed I had to agree to be reunited with Don. I refused and was fired. Subsequently, I sued for Breach of Contract and won. By then, I had been hired to take Scott Shannon's place on the Z100 Z Morning Zoo, reuniting **Ross and Wilson** back in New York.

For all the friction, the on-air product was genuinely hysterical – much of the time. There's no question the **Brian and O'Brien Show** became and remains a Baltimore Radio Legend. Anyone living there from 1984 to 1988 knew of or listened to us at least once! It was both a great and horrible four years out of my **50 Years in Radio**.

Brian and Bob

In the early 90s, Rita Foley and Bob Madigan, two respected news personalities, were conjoined to form **Mornings with Rita and**

Bob on WWRC/Washington, DC. It would be professionally fair and accurate to say the show wasn't working; there was zero positive chemistry between the players. Professional broadcast journalists rarely make for zesty entertainment; they report the news. From a "showbiz personality" perspective, journalists are the accountants of humor.

The board-op was John Nolan, a rare multi-talented guy who skillfully handled the controls at B104 during the contentious months of **Brian and O'Brien**. Seeing the need for a spark plug, John dropped my name on Tyler Cox, a PD of great repute who was building WWRC into a credible Talk Station, if not for the dysfunctional AM Drive show. John and Tyler hatched a plan for a trial run that might demonstrate how good the show could be – with the right mix of talent.

They arranged for me to be a call-in guest, a "corporate behavioral specialist" who was going to oversee a controversial weekend "seminar" set up by the DC Mayor. Her contentious DC City Council was proving even more unproductive than governing bodies generally are and an Eastern Shore get-away was just the thing to restore conviviality and productivity. How? The "corporate behavioral specialist" would explain.

I'm not certain, Bob may have been in on the gag. I say that because Rita handled most all of the questions. But that would have been the case, regardless.

Through the "interview," I was able to provide sufficient psychobabble to either explain or confuse anyone listening, especially Rita, asking the questions. Unable to make any serious headway with humor, I finally stipulated the seminar would be so fruitful, productive and stress-free that, "I could guarantee the City Council would be so relaxed, the members would be able to *pass wicker furniture.*"

That's when the "gotcha" light went on in the WWRC studio and, **Mornings with Brian and Bob** was born.

With John Nolan running the board and Shelia Jaskot, producer, **Mornings with Brian and Bob** started at full speed. In no small part, Bob Madigan was mostly to blame. His not-just-a-journalist personality plus major market experience at NBC gave me someone I could respect and work with. His sense of humor -- or more importantly, his keen ability to appreciate my warped sense of humor -- made for seamless transitions from "seriously serious" to "reasonably amusing." We did great interviews and covered current issues with his manners, tact, and diplomacy mixed with my recurring lunacy. Bob was the china shop; I threw the bull.

One morning while questioning the need for TV commercials advertising embarrassing products, Bob cited the example of a Massengill spot. It showed a mother-daughter duo walking down an ocean beach with the daughter asking, "Mom… why douche?" On the air, we pondered the worth of whatever instructive answer "Mom" gave. At that point, I suggested, "Why didn't Mom say: Why don't you ask that flock of seagulls that's following us?"

I can still see as clearly as if it just happened: Bob Madigan turning, trying to escape his microphone, slipping off his chair, landing on the floor, laughing so hard. To this day, I still consider that one of my greatest comedic victories -- the gut-busting endorsement of a renowned NY Talent (who then became an even more famous DC Personality)! John Nolan quickly fired off a commercial break.

The End of **Mornings with Brian and Bob** was more tragic than the finales of my previous pairings. This one was absolutely inexplicable and inexcusable. Two years later, senior management literally apologized en masse and in-person at Corporate HQ. Big deal. The damage had been done. Here was a morning show that was growing quickly and organically, tripling the ratings in just six months along with winning the Achievement in Radio (AIR) Award for Best Morning Show in Washington, DC. Why were we terminated? Because of a complaint registered with the Human

Resources Department, charging us with "creating a hostile work environment." The general manager was ordered not to disclose any details to us.

Later we learned the "complaint" was made by an emotionally-challenged overnight board-op. Each morning as we arrived for work, we would dump our headphones and work material in the Control Room and exit until show time. Our lack of effusive "hellos" etc. was reported to HR as "creating a hostile work environment." By itself, that could have been easily dissuaded. However, Corporate HR was run (literally) by a little old lady related to upper management, who allegedly was as psychologically-challenged as the board-op. In those perilous times of growing "political correctness" and Feminist angst, the Corporate Suits panicked and demanded we be terminated forthwith. This *epiphany* is what they apologized for – *two years later.*

Maybe it was all for the best. While I'm certain **Mornings with Brian and Bob** could have quickly dominated the DC ratings and reigned over the market for decades, the insanity of our termination freed Bob Madigan to achieve great things as WTOP's **Man About Town**, the accolades for which cover a couple hundred pages in Wikipedia. To the regret of hundreds of thousands of fans, Bob retired a few years preceding this book and is no doubt enjoying entertaining the lobsters from his oceanfront mansion on the coast of Northwestern Wyoming. Meanwhile, I invented VRINK and continued my nomadic wanderlust, irritating audiences and management across the country, finding my bride hiding from me in Vain, a small village just outside Baltimore.

Special Extra Added Bonus Surprise

Many of these 50 Stories have accompanying pictures. Woo-hoo – everybody does that. My career was focused on doing what nobody else did!

So my combined team of IT and Creative (namely, Cassie) has designed a Facebook page chock full of all sorts of audio and video tracks from some of the **Stories** here, and some that I didn't get a chance to write about for all kinds of miserable, flabby excuses! Bookmark it because we will be adding more as we roll along!

Here's the URL you need: **https://fb.me/50Storiesbook**

Story One

IN THE BEGINNING…

I remember it as if it was just ~~yesterd~~ 53 years ago…

Labor Day weekend, September 1965, Baton Rouge, Louisiana. If memory serves -- and memory will be a big issue going forward -- it was a Saturday, and we were at a baby shower. The "we" here was my wife Sharon, our one-month-old son and guest of honor, and I, the newly-minted father. Sharon's best friend from high school, Barbara Johnson, was the hostess. With everyone our age heading back to college, Barbara thought it would be a swell time to get Sharon's girlfriends together to do what young women do when confronted with a baby, especially when the little munchkin had popped out of one of their peers. Other than driving the car and hauling baby paraphernalia, my presence was purely utilitarian.

Remarkably though, for reasons known only to them, many of Sharon's friends had dragged their dates along, so at least my boredom had company.

It was in this setting, an upper-middle-class home in an upper-middle-class neighborhood in suburban Baton Rouge, I took part in a two-minute conversation which would change my life. My entire life. It happened this way:

Standing in the Johnson living room, talking college-talk with one of the boyfriends, a large, pink young man came into my peripheral vision and, in today's parlance, "entered my space." In a break in the conversation, I turned to acknowledge the portly dude. Not knowing anyone there other than Barbara, Sharon, and my son, the best I could offer was:

> *Hey - how ya doin'?*

His response was nothing I could have predicted or expected.

> *Hi, my name is Bill Loving. Ya know, you've got a really great voice for radio!*

In my entire life, all 20 years at that point, no one had ever told me that. Needless to say, I was a tad puzzled. What could I say?

> *Thanks.*

What I didn't say was, "What's your point?"

> *Have you ever thought about getting into it?*

> *No, not at all. I'm in pre-law at LSU.*

Ever curious about large pink young men coming on to me at baby showers, complimenting me on my voice and asking if my career decisions included radio, I had to ask why.

Large Pink Bill (whose voice rivaled Minnie Ripperton) said he worked at a local radio station. One of the DJs was joining the Navy, so the station needed someone with a really great voice.

> *I heard you from across the room and thought I should come over and meet you.*

Sidebar:

For several weeks prior to this conversation, I had been working as the overnight manager of the snack bar at the only 24-hour bowling alley in town; 10 p.m. to 5 a.m., Monday through Friday. The bowling biz dropped off precipitously around midnight, leaving me the wee small hours for homework or short naps. At the end of the week, I received what remained of a sixty-dollar paycheck after Uncle Sam, the IRS, and FICA took their pieces.

I gave Large Pink Bill a thumbnail summary of the above and ended with the question:

> *How much does the job pay?*

> *We make sixty-five dollars a week.*

Hmmm… an extra twenty dollars a month was significant, even after the ravages of government theft, especially in 1965-dollars, with rent, food, car, gas, tuition and now diaper service.

While I hadn't given it a lot of thought, I imagined a DJ's job amounted to sitting in a small, air-conditioned room for a few hours with a stack of records, a microphone and some complicated electronic equipment. Every now and then he would say something about the song or read a commercial and move on. At least that's what it sounded like back in New Jersey, when I drove home from Wayne High School, listening to Dan Ingram on WABC.

I thought, I like music. Hell, I had played in a band. I can read. I can speak coherently. This had to be better than staying up all night flipping the occasional burger. And there *was* that extra twenty bux!

Large Pink Bill said:

> *If you can come out Monday morning around 10:30, I'll tell the boss, Brad Guarino, you'll be there.*

> *I'll be there.*

> *That's great!*

As he shook my hand and turned to leave, Large Pink Bill squeaked:

> *I think you're going to be really great!*

Large Pink at the WLBI board (1965 Photo: Brian Wilson collection)

Except for dental appointments, I've always had a thing about punctuality. On Monday morning, September 6th, 10:30 a.m. on the dot, I walked into a radio station for the first time: WLBI, 1220 on the dial, "The Voice of Denham Springs, Louisiana."

Whatever I had expected, this wasn't it. I could see the offices through the etched glass -- a large, open room with two desks, two secretaries, a couple chairs and a credenza that supported a Mr. Coffee and a copy machine. The first desk provided the fortress surrounding Mabel Smith, whom I would soon discover was much more than just a receptionist.

At the other desk sat the bookkeeper, Bonnie Crow. Their roles should've been reversed. Bonnie was stunning to the point of distraction, compared to Mabel, who had her own ZIP Code.

After the standard, "Good morning, may I help you?" greeting from Mrs. Smith, I announced myself:

Good morning. My name is Brian Wilson. I have an appointment with Brad Guarino.

Oh yes. (Large Pink) Bill Loving said you would be coming in. Brad's not here right now, but he's on his way and should arrive shortly. Would you like some coffee?

No, thanks. I've already passed my two-gallon limit.

Bonnie laughed out loud; Mabel looked confused.

Well, have a seat if you like. Brad should be here any minute.

I took the opportunity to look around instead. The two rooms to my left each had large glass windows. One was empty except for a table with a microphone in the middle and three chairs. I later found out this was Studio B.

The next room, Studio A, was actually the Main Control Room. Inside, I saw a guy about my age who turned out to be Dick Wickwire, the new Navy recruit. He was sitting in front of a control board with six differently-colored large knobs on the front with several smaller knobs and switches and a VU meter in the middle of it all. Two big turntables were perpendicular to the left side of the board. On the right sat something resembling an eight-track machine; next to it a big reel-to-reel tape recorder and next to it, a tower of metal slots holding plastic boxes that obviously fit in the "eight-track" machine. Along the back wall, eight feet of double-shelving held the station's music library.

As I took all this in, the front door burst open. Brad Guarino, general manager, had arrived. He barely glanced at me as he dumped two handfuls of paper on Mabel's desk and spouted instructions. When he finished, he gave me another glance, nodded a smile to Bonnie and breezed down a short hall, disappearing into what I correctly guessed was his office.

After a moment, Mabel hauled herself out of her chair and made her way to the GM's office. A short time later, she returned to her desk. Five minutes later, out came the boss.

Brad was middle-aged, medium height, medium build, medium Italian looking. He greeted me with a big smile, a salesman's firm handshake and invitation to his office.

In short order, we reviewed what he already knew about me from Large Pink Bill and outlined what I already knew or surmised about the job.

> *Have you ever done any work in radio?*

> *No, but I listened to a lot of it growing up.*

> *I can tell you're not from the South. Where did you grow up? What station did you listen to?*

> *I was raised on a farm in northern New Jersey. Everybody I knew listened to WABC.*

Brad was impressed. Everybody in radio knew WABC was the mecca of every DJ in America.

> *Well, let's see what you sound like.*

With that, he led me out the door and down the hall, paused at the nonstop chugging AP news machine and tore off five or six feet of accumulated news copy.

Just before the rear exit, we came to the door to the station's Engineering Room. There was a workbench loaded with electrical parts and tools, a lawnmower and between them, a rack housing an Ampex reel-to-reel tape recorder. In front of that stood a music stand and a gleaming silver microphone.

Brad handed me the armful of AP paper while he busied himself threading a reel of tape on the deck. Done, he took back the AP paper and quickly ran through several feet before stopping, tearing off the excess and handing me the rest. Then he punched a couple of buttons on the tape recorder, which started the reels turning. To confirm that it was in record-mode, he tapped the microphone to make the VU meters jump.

He told me to stand in front of the microphone and read what was on the paper. With that, he walked out of the room and closed the door.

In my hands -- an Associated Press Five Minute News Summary. Even though I'd never seen one before, it didn't take an LSU pre-law student to figure it out. Fortunately, I have always had a talent for sight reading, to the point of near perfection. Since I'd also listened to radio newscasts, I had a sense of what was expected. So I read. And I kept reading until the door burst open again and Brad came bustling in.

All right. Let's see what you sound like.

And with that, he hit the rewind button and let the reels spin for several seconds. Stop. Play. And my voice filled the room. Most people are unpleasantly surprised when they hear the sound of their own voice for the first time. I thought it just sounded like me.

After listening to ten or 15 seconds of my in-house closed-door radio news debut, Brad hit the stop button again, glanced over at me and said:

You sound pretty damn good! You go on the air at noon.

Kafkaesque as it was, even by 1965 standards, my **50 Years in Radio** began.

Story Two

I CLICKED THE SHERIFF

Even tho you're usually sitting down, you have to think on your feet in radio.

While my multi-tasking TV weather, AM news and mid-morning DJ gig at KPLC-TV, AM & FM/Lake Charles, LA only lasted ten days in February 1966 thanks to a little 18-wheeler incident, it had one memorable moment of adroit adjustment for phonic failure. I'm referring specifically to a New Jersey native's challenge to accurately pronounce otherwise undecipherable Cajun verbiage!

First day, I had less than three minutes to make it from the TV weather set up to the AM radio news booth to rip 'n read the local news. Fortunately this day, the morning man knew I was the "new kid on the block" and had done me the immense favor of executing the time-consuming part -- tearing the news copy from the AP machine, separating out the local stories and stacking them in order.

I hit the door, sat down, yanked on the headphones and nodded my thanks with barely 30 seconds to glance at the copy when the news sounder came on. I read the printed intro and sponsor mention in the copy book and started in.

(As I mentioned earlier, I was an ace at sight reading. That, my tonsils and a modicum of talent got me here in the first place.)

While I can't recall the specifics, the lead story concerned a party over the weekend that had gotten out of hand, far enough for the neighbors to call the sheriff. That's when the trouble began. Not for the rabble-rousers at the party, not for the sheriff and his posse, but for me -- the intrepid news reader. The sheriff had one of those Cajun names, and so did his parish of jurisdiction. The AP copy identified him as, "Sheriff Jessel Ourso of Calcasieu Parish." If you're not from Louisiana, East Texas or speak French, you might not noodle out the proper pronunciation: *Sheriff Jessel Or-soh of Kal-kah-shew Parish.*

I know that now.

What to do? First day! First impressions! Arrghhh!

Only solution -- improvise! And what better improvisation is there when surrounded with sensitive electrical equipment than "equipment failure!" If I cut my mic at the last second, the listener would hear just a slight hiccup and hardly notice the dropout! Or so (no pun intended) I hoped.

This is what the audience heard:

> *Blah, blah, blah subdivision outside Lake Charles Sunday night, residents called Ca.....Parish, Sheriff Jessel.....so, who arrested two attendees on drunk and disorderly charges. No other arrests were made.*

After the news, the chief engineer came rushing in:

> *What happened during your newscast? Did you have a mic failure or what?*
>
> *Dunno Chief, the mic just went out.*
>
> *Dammit. That's the third time this week! Sorry. I'll replace it.*
>
> *No problem, Chief.*
>
> *(Insert huge sigh of relief sfx here).*

I had to use that stunt on a few other occasions before leaving Louisiana, but it worked every time!

Story Three

HELLO, COMRADE

Sometimes, running a radio show in a small market can get boring. This was one of those days!

Early one morning on WIBR/Baton Rouge, a "general interest" news story crossed AP about the current life and times of former Soviet Premier Nikita Khrushchev, now resigned and in retirement. **TIME Magazine** had him on the cover as did several other news magazines. With no particular agenda for the show that day, I talked the audience into this bit: "Let's call Nikita! What the heck! If he will talk to **TIME**, he should talk with the leading radio station in Baton Rouge, right? Right!"

It was 6:40 a.m. when I put the phone on the air (you could do that back then) and called the operator:

OP: Operator…?

BW: Yes ma'am, good morning. I'd like to place a long distance call to Moscow.

OP: Moscow, Russia?

BW: Is there any other?

OP: Well yes… there's a Moscow, Idaho…

BW: Wow! Wait until the John Birch Society hears about that! I just need the real deal in the Soviet Union.

OP: Oh! Well, you will have to speak with the International Operator for that. Hold on and I'll connect you.

BW: Thanks! Will do!

So far so good!

IO: This is the International Operator, may I help you?

BW: Yes ma'am, this is Brian Wilson at WIBR Radio in Baton Rouge. I'm trying to contact former Soviet Premier Nikita Khrushchev in Moscow.

IO: Alright, Mr. Wilson… I only have two lines available to call Moscow and they are both busy. May I call you back when a line comes available?

BW: Only two lines? Does that count all the ones our government has?

IO: No, there are the only two available to the general public.

BW: Well, I'm not "the general public," operator. I am the news media. Don't you have any accommodation for media calls?

IO: No sir, not directly. But I can let you know as soon as a line becomes available.

BW: I understand. Can you give me an estimate on how long this may take? We are live here this morning and need to have some idea of when we may connect.

IO: I'm sorry, sir. I cannot predict when either of these lines may become available.

BW: Uh-huh. OK. I'd appreciate it if you would keep us informed. Do you have our number?

IO: Yes sir, I do.

BW: OK! I'll wait to hear from you.

To her credit, the International Operator called about every 30 minutes. Each time, anticipating success, I answered her "live" on the air. Unfortunately, the message was always the same.

IO: Hello, Mr. Wilson? This is the International Operator. I'm sorry but both lines are still tied up.

BW: Thanks, we'll continue to hold.

Time was becoming a problem. The show ended with local news at 8:55 a.m. With the delays coming in half-hour increments, it didn't take long before I was up against it.

At 8:50 a.m., the International Operator made her regular call – only this time she said:

IO: Mr. Wilson, I have a line to Moscow available now. Would you like to go ahead with your call?

BW: YES! Yes indeed! Thank-you-very-much!

IO: You're welcome. There will be a slight delay to make the connection. Please hold.

BW: Of course!

The thing is – or was – all this time I had been running the show, playing records, taking calls, reading live commercials, running contests, ripping and reading the local news, making coffee – the usual. Which is to say, I had nothing prepared to talk about with Mr. Khrushchev! Now he was minutes from being on the phone and I was going to sound like a complete putz!

The listeners and I remained on "hold" as I blew off the local news, waiting for the Moscow Operator. Small talk ("tap dancing") was getting difficult.

8:55 a.m. -- I didn't dare break for any commercials but I did have to hit the Network at 9:00 a.m.

8:56 a.m. -- You can only repeat the weather forecast so many times.

8:57 a.m. -- Ditto running through the PSA announcements.

8:58 a.m. -- …and get out of the way for the next jock!

8:59 a.m. -- The International Operator was back!

> *IO: Mr. Wilson? I have the Moscow operator on the line.*

> *BW: Thank-you-very-much!*

Now what?

> *Moscow Operator: Yes, this is Moscow. Who are you trying to reach?*

This woman sounded exactly like Natasha Fatale from the **Rocky and Bullwinkle Show**! I thought too late, I should have asked her to say, "Moose and Squirrel!"

And then I thought, this person is a Communist! Am I gonna get in trouble for speaking with a sworn enemy of the United States? Nah, it's just a radio interview. Happens all the time, right?

> *BW: Hello! Yes. Hello, Moscow! I am trying to reach your former Chairman, Nikita Khrushchev. I don't have his contact number. Can you connect me?*

Pause.

Long Pause.

Longer Pause.

> *MO: Yes, I am sorry but Mr. Khrushchev is retired and does not have a phone.*

> *BW: Really? The former head of the entire Soviet Union retires and doesn't even get a phone?*

> *MO: Yes, that is correct. Thank you. Good bye.*

Stunned, I only had seconds to give the station ID "WIBR, Baton Rouge" and hit the network news intro.

I hadn't noticed the small gathering of station personnel outside the big window to the Control Room, watching and listening on the office monitors. They gave me an inaudible round of applause and smiles as they dispersed.

Technology being comparably archaic, I had no clue how good, bad or indifferent the whole bit had been.

But I found out.

For the next hour, the switchboard was flooded with calls from listeners saying what fantastic experience it had been, it kept them glued to the radio right up to the end. Some complained that it caused them to be late for work as they listened in their cars, refusing to go into their office until the call played out. And there were some amazing callers who said I put us on the brink of nuclear war; that they were going to report me to the FCC, FBI, NSA, CIA, Police, Congress, the Senate, even the White House!

Sure they were.

To his credit, the GM/Owner, Bob Earle, said the whole thing was... "OK." High praise, indeed!

Story Four

NOAH!

March 1967. My first firing was behind me along with my first TV job, the latter lost to my Too Damn Close encounter with an 18-Wheeler that put me in the hospital for a few months. I'm now at WIBR/Baton Rouge doing PM Drive 3 p.m. to 7 p.m. and **Night Flight** from 9 p.m. to midnight. The **Night Flight** segment was a local biggie, thanks to the immense popularity of folk music and 22,000 LSU students listening every evening. We were the only station on at night playing what the campus wanted to hear.

I had a lot of leeway in what to play, including occasional comedy cuts from the Smothers Brothers, satirical songs from the Chad Mitchell Trio and stand-up acts, like Bill Cosby. By 1967, he was the new King of Comedy. One night, I aired all three cuts of his **Noah** routine, recorded live.

Stop right here. If you don't know this part of Cosby's career, Google "Bill Cosby Noah" and come back.

As it played through, I could almost hear the laughter from campus – even though it was seven miles away!

The last cut ends with laughter and applause and I segued into a New Christy Minstrels tune -- or maybe it was Bob Dylan. Whatever! Then the hotline lit up. Unusual. I hadn't done anything wrong for the boss to call…

WIBR…

*Hey, Yankee -- Did you just play that n****r again?*

It was Bill Carrigan.

"Catfish" Bill Carrigan was the reigning king of AM drive on WIBR. With his longevity and monster ratings, he was an internal force with which to be reckoned! While I didn't feel intimidated, I was aware of whom I was dealing with and I'll never forget the next two minutes.

Good evening, Bill. Well, I did just play three cuts from a Bill Cosby LP, if that's what you mean.

You're goddamn right that's what I mean. Now listen to me, Yankee boy, I don't want to hear that blasphemy on the air ever again. You got that?"

Well, it is cleared for air, Bill, so I…

I don't give a shit what it is. It's blasphemy and I don't want to hear it. I'm not gonna hear it. You got me? I've been getting calls all night from people in my church telling me about you playing that shit. If it happens again, I'll have you fired.

Well, I think Bob Earle needs to tell me that, Bill. He's the boss and he cleared these records to air.

Alright, Yankee boy, I'm tired of your smart-ass talk. You better clear your shit outta there this evening because tomorrow morning, I'm goin' to Earle's office and tell him it's me or you, got that? Me or you boy. Now, who do you think he's gonna choose? Huh?

Well…

Click.

To say I was scared would be the biggest understatement in this book. I think my hand was shaking despite my death grip on the phone. It was after 11 p.m., but I had to call the boss. The biggest DJ in Baton Rouge said he was going to get me fired. All I could think of was telling my side of the story first. After four months in the hospital with no insurance, bills over $100,000, a wife, a son, college and now -- out of job for playing Bill Cosby? Now that I think about it, I was flat-out scared blank-less! Panicked would be more accurate.

I dialed Bob Earle's home. As was his engrained custom, allegedly from his Hollywood days waiting on agents to call, he picked up before the second ring with an intense, "Hello!"

> *Hi Boss, sorry to wake you. It's Bri…*

> *Yes, yes I know who it is. What's wrong?*

How could he know I was calling? There was no caller ID in 1967.

> *Umm…well…*

I just blurted it all out at once.

> *I just played the Noah cuts from Bill Cosby and Catfish Bill called all pissed off and said he was getting calls from people at his church and they were all pissed off because I was playing blasphemy by this Bill Cosby and this n****r – that's what HE called him, NOT me – wasn't going to be on the air again and I told him you were the boss and he told me to clear out my stuff tonight because he was going to come to your office tomorrow morning and tell you it was him or me and I don't want to be fired. So that's why I'm calling.*

All that in one breath.

After a moment's silence, Earle calmly told me to finish the show and put the Cosby album on his desk.

> *I'll handle Bill tomorrow and you come see me before you go on the air. You're not going to be fired.*

Instant Relief!

> *Right. OK. Thanks a lot. See you tomorrow.*

The next afternoon's meeting with Earle was a nothing-burger. Other than not playing "Noah!" till further notice, nothing changed. With Catfish long gone before I came in, an uncomfortable confrontation was avoided. In fact, I left for my next job (voluntarily this time), without ever seeing him again.

Fast forward 20 years.

It's now February 1987. WIBR, Z-93/Atlanta, WABC/New York and **Ross and Wilson** are all in the rearview mirror. It's the third year of the enormously successful **Brian and O'Brien** AM Drive team on "Baltimore's Best B104." Along with a local TV station, we were hosting a Bill Cosby appearance at the downtown Baltimore Arena. **Brian and O'Brien** would welcome and entertain the audience; a warm-up of sorts while two of the TV station's personnel would introduce Cosby. Strict orders had gone out from Cosby's people through station management that Cosby would not do any interviews; in fact, everyone was to steer clear of him. I remember thinking -- how stupid is that? If he comes down the hall, are we supposed to run, scatter and hide? *Don't even look at him!* Seriously? Why? Would you turn into stone? Was Cosby a latter-day Medusa?

Fifteen minutes before we were to go on stage, I was wandering the empty chambers of the arena, away from the sold-out audience, getting some ideas of what to do on stage and wound up in what appeared to be a cafeteria. It was dark except for the ambient light from the windows. Over at a corner table, an orange glow that could only be a cigar; Bill Cosby smoked cigars.

Rather than turn and *run away! run away!* I walked directly to the orange light.

The Man spoke first:

Good evening.

Not, get the hell outta here?

Good evening, Mr. Cosby, how are you?

I'm OK. I'm good. Who are you?

I'm Brian Wilson. I'm part of the team introducing you this evening.

Is it a good house?

Packed. SRO. Your show has been the hottest ticket in town for weeks.

How would you know that?

My partner and I do a morning drive radio show. People have been ragging us for tickets pretty hard.

He chuckled.

Well, that's nice.

I know you couldn't possibly know this, but you almost got me fired 20 years ago.

Where was that?

WIBR in Baton Rouge.

And without the slightest pause…

Noah?

I was surprised by his quick guess.

Yes sir, it was!

Was it your boss or the audience?

Actually, it was the AM Drive guy. I was doing a night show. After I played all three segments, he called the hotline and told me to clear out my stuff; he was going to have me fired in the morning. In a panic, I called the boss, woke him up and dumped it all on him. Basically, he said he'd take care of it and hung up.

Pretty good boss.

Yeah, pretty much. Not many of them around.

Yeah, a lot of that was going around in the South with that piece back then.

I never met anyone – Baton Rouge or anywhere else -- who didn't think it was a riot!

Another chuckle from Mr. Cosby.

Well, it's just a few minutes before we go on. I know you'll be great. Sorry if I disturbed you.

Not at all. I enjoyed the chat. Sorry about what happened!

My turn to laugh.

Not me! It scared the hell out of me but it was a great lesson and a great experience. Thanks for the time.

He stood, leaned across the table, and shook my hand.

Brian, It was a pleasure meeting you.

That's the only Bill Cosby I ever knew.

Story Five

GORILLA H-Q

Back in the "old days" of radio, things could get downright silly for no apparent reason. In this case, lack of sleep may be the best explanation, but situational apathy works as well.

In the early 70s at WIBR/Baton Rouge, we got a new morning man -- Bob Tyler, whose real name is Bob Mooberry. The boss, Bob Earle, in all his brilliance, wanted something more "generic" than Mooberry, so "Lucky Bob Tyler" was created. To me, that was one of Earle's dumber moves. Name recognition or branding is a big deal in radio, TV and advertising – in all areas of showbiz and marketing. If the audience or market can't remember who you are or what you're selling, big-time failure is guaranteed. Who would forget a name like Mooberry? Occasionally, just to yank the boss's chain, I'd refer to Bob on the air as "Bob Cowfruit." Bob got it; Earle never did!

But I digress…

We both worked a six-day week. While it might not seem so to someone who does *real* heavy lifting, 30-36 hours per week playing DJ is exhausting. OK, *mentally* exhausting but exhausting nevertheless. To fix it – or at least make it more palatable, I sold the boss on the idea of Bob and me doing a two-man show on Saturday mornings. He'd still squeeze the hours out of us but, working together, we would at least have a better time doing a new show. Remarkably, he said OK – to a one month trial.

Predictably, by the end of the month, Earle was sending strong signals of disapproval. Not that he said anything specific, but that was the indication -- he never said anything good or bad about what we were doing. And honestly, we had done some damn good shows! I thought we might actually make this permanent! But no!

So came our last Saturday show. What were we going to do to go out with a BANG? The answer came from the most unanticipated source ever: Ringling Bros. and Barnum & Bailey Circus.

The circus train was passing thru town Friday night/Saturday morning when one of the cars derailed. Nothing serious – but it was an item for **WIBR Action Central News**.

As we talked off the air about what had happened, Bob wondered aloud, "What if some animals escaped?" And there it was! In a matter of seconds, we concocted a story about the escape of a trained gorilla!

> *Circus handlers have been combing the area of the derailment for hours overnight without success. Circus management contacted us here at WIBR for help, asking you to be on the look-out for this escaped, trained gorilla. If spotted, please call Gorilla Headquarters at 348-6272 and report your sighting. If that line is busy, call the Gorilla Hotline here at 348-WIBR and we'll pass the information along to Gorilla Headquarters.*

348-6272 was Bob Earle's unlisted home phone.

At 6 a.m. we started the show with **WIBR Action Central News** and the lead story of the escaped gorilla. Of course, the phone exploded; all five incoming lines lit up simultaneously.

And of course, we put the callers on the air:

> *WIBR Gorilla Hotline, hello? How big is the gorilla? About seven-foot-four, 662 pounds – ya can't miss him! In fact, he's the*

only escaped gorilla in town at the moment – but check in with Gorilla H-Q immediately at 348-6272.

WIBR Gorilla Hotline, hello? What should you do if you see the gorilla? Call Gorilla H-Q immediately at 348-6272… then arm yourself with a bunch of bananas and get up on your roof!

And so it went for the next two hours! People just waking up and tuning in, hearing the story for the first time, kept the spoof alive. As the audience caught on, the Q&A became downright hysterical.

By 8 a.m., "Lucky" Bob and I were in physical pain from laughter. Maybe the calls weren't *that* funny, maybe it was exhaustion and a lack of sleep mixed with general silliness. Eventually, everything anybody said was hysterical. Maybe there was a nitrous oxide in the a/c vents!

Around 8:15 the WIBR hotline lit up; Moo (my off-air nickname for him) was sitting at the news desk and closest to the phone: "WIBR Gorilla Hotline… Yes? Oh, OK… hold on… it's for you, Brian." With an inscrutable look, he handed the phone across the desk.

WIBR Gorilla Hotline…

GORILLA MY ASS! WHAT ARE THE HELL YOU DOING THERE? THE PHONE STARTED RINGING HERE TWO HOURS AGO! I WAS ASLEEP AND IT WOKE ME UP! I'VE BEEN TRYING TO CALL OUT FOR TWO HOURS BUT EVERY TIME I PICK UP THE PHONE, SOMEONE IS THERE ALREADY, ASKING ABOUT SOME DAMN ESCAPED GORILLA THEY HEARD ABOUT ON WIBR! WHAT THE HELL IS GOING ON? HOW DID THESE PEOPLE GET THIS NUMBER?

Obviously, this was an incensed Bob Earle.

Oh, good morning boss! How ya doin'? So you've... um... heard about the gorilla?

YOU'RE GODDAMN RIGHT I HAVE – NOW GET ON THE AIR AND TELL EVERYONE THIS IS JUST ONE OF YOUR STUPID JOKES! TELL THEM THERE IS NO ESCAPED GORILLA! AND TELL THEM TO STOP CALLING THIS NUMBER! AND BE IN MY OFFICE MONDAY MORNING AT 9. GOT THAT?

Tell audience... stupid joke... no gorilla... your office...Monday at 9... Is that about right?

YES!

One question – should I tell Bob Cowfruit to join us?

Click.

Of course, the audience had gotten into the joke early on. So rather than spoil their fun and ours by calling it a "stupid joke" as instructed, I announced the all clear: the gorilla had been captured in Bocage; found by the trainers while helping a well-known broadcast executive improve his management skills.

(Bocage was the swankiest of the swanky subdivisions in Baton Rouge and home to Bob Earle; it may be "Section 8" by now.)

You'd never get away with anything like that today. Not only are audiences too sophisticated for such sophistry, lawsuits would pour in and the FCC would be sending out fines by the truckload.

Bob and I still laugh about **Gorilla H-Q**, back in a simpler, less litigious time when there really was a circus on and off the air.

Story Six

SUICIDE

Strange things happen in radio -- things you never could imagine happening in any other (normal) job.

In 1967, I worked noon to seven on WIBR/Baton Rouge, Monday through Saturday. If you think sitting in a room, playing records for seven hours straight, occasionally interrupted by three-minute commercial clusters or five minutes of news is *the most fun ever*, try it for a few months!

I had pleaded with the boss for a reduced shift. By the time the all-important Afternoon Drive officially started at 3 p.m., I had already done three hours, the average length of a "regular" show. By 5 p.m., the Golden Hour when everyone leaves work and drives home, I needed to be at the top of my game; instead, brain-dead was fast-approaching. No matter how much you love your job, you can be "tight and bright" for only so long before "tired and dull" sets in. Such was the case in the summer of '67.

I don't recall the exact day. With that shift, they all just flowed one into another. Because Baton Rouge was a much smaller market then, the streets were empty by 6 p.m. It made continuing my usual high-energy, New York-style Afternoon Drive show difficult. At WIBR, jocks had the autonomy to select our own music from the "approved" record library, so I made certain the records I chose for the 6 p.m. hour featured some of the longest cuts on LPs at the time. Invariably, I'd throw in some comedy or "in-concert live" tracks; that usually ran about seven to ten minutes. The audience, such as it was at that hour, got a kick out of hearing Bill Cosby, the Smothers Brothers, Frank Sinatra, etc. while I got to relax.

On this day, coming out of the 6:30 p.m. Mutual News, I made the customary time check, promoted Jim Irwin's **Let's Talk It Over** show coming up at seven and fired off a three-minute commercial set; an 11-minute cut from a Smothers Brothers album was ready to go. At that moment, one of the studio lines lit up. Whenever possible, I made it a point to always answer them.

> *WIBR…*
>
> *Hi… Is this Brian Wilson?*
>
> *Oh my God! Is this the IRS?*
>
> *It is Brian Wilson!*

The caller's voice sounded young.

> *Yes, I'm afraid so... How may I help you in some small insignificant way?*
>
> *My name is Edie and I really love your show and WIBR and I was calling so you could have the story first.*

Hmmmm.

> *OK… that's very considerate of you. Exactly what story are we talking about?*
>
> *I'm going to commit suicide.*

Pause here. First of all, Edie sounded as she was 12. Second, prank calls have always been common on personality-driven radio stations. They're right up there with legendary comedic beauties like, "Do you have Sir Walter Raleigh in a can?" or "Is your refrigerator running?" And "I want to dedicate a song to Dick Hertz." So here comes a 12-year old doing the usual, "how much I love you and the station," followed by a real attention-getter:

"I'm going to commit suicide." While I had never heard that one before, I took these calls with my usual sarcasm and cynicism; it tended to take the fun out of it for the caller.

> *Suicide huh? OK, let me get a pencil. Alright, when exactly are you planning on doing this?*
>
> *Right now.*
>
> *Oh, OK. Well if you want this on the news, I need to get some more information. What did you say your name was?"*
>
> *Edie. Edie Hébert.*
>
> *And where do you live Edie?*
>
> *1234 Choctaw Road, Apartment A.*
>
> *Oh, you're right down the road then! Well, that's convenient.*

Silence.

> *How old are you, Edie?*
>
> *I'd rather not say.*
>
> *I agree, that is a little intrusive. I'll get it later from the coroner's report. Now Edie, have you ever committed suicide before?*

More silence.

> *What I meant was… why exactly are you committing suicide?"*
>
> *I'd rather not say.*
>
> *Well, it would really help the credibility of the story but, OK, we can fly without it.*

Again -- silence.

Her silence was beginning to concern me. Usually, prank callers wound up giggling or getting angry at not being taken seriously and hung up. Not Edie, not yet.

OK, I think I have everything -- name, address, motive unknown... Oh, one other thing... How exactly do you intend to pull this off? Knives? Spears? Grenades?

Rather matter-of-factly, she said:

I'm going to shoot myself.

OK, got it. Gun. Noisy, a little messy but definitely efficient. I think I have all I need now Edie. There is one thing...

What's that?

Well, as you know, WIBR pays ten dollars for the best news tip of the week phoned into our Studios at Dickens 2-4411. I think your story just might be this week's winner. With you committing suicide, what should we do with the money?

I don't care. Give it to whoever comes in second.

Under the circumstances, that was a pretty good line!

OK, got it. Well, that's about it. Thanks for the call and thanks for listening to WIBR, Edie. Go ahead...

OK.

Silence.

BANG.

Honestly, at that point, I was not concerned. Some of these prank callers went to DefCon Two to troll the DJ. I figured Edie would likely hang up in a moment or two, blowing the cover on her "suicide" story. But just to be on the safe side, I put her on hold. I needed one more record to make it up to news time and then Jim Irwin would take over.

OK -- last record on the turntable cued up, all set to sign off and make room for Jim. I still had seven minutes before the Smothers

Brothers piece would end and the Frank Sinatra cut would start. But technically, I was done for the day.

What about Edie?

The hold light was still blinking. If she really was a prank call, she would have hung up and the light would be out. Since it was still blinking, the line was open and Edie was still there. Or was she?

I punched the button, "Hello? Edie?" Nothing. I could tell by the ambient noise at the other end of the line, the phone was off the hook.

This was not good.

I put Edie back on hold and called the unlisted media number for the Baton Rouge Police. It always was answered, and fast.

> *Baton Rouge City Police, Sergeant Strickland.*
>
> *Hi Sarge, Brian Wilson at WIBR.*
>
> *Yeah Brian, what's up?*
>
> *Possible suicide, Sarge…*

I proceeded to tell him the short version of what had happened. Sounding as skeptical as I had been, he said he would dispatch a unit to check it out anyway.

Edie's line was still blinking, and I started thinking there was a real problem.

I called the station engineer, Herb Coussou, who was puttering back in the Transmitter Room and gave him the police version of what was going on.

> *Her apartment is just a couple miles down the road. I've got everything set in here. If you'll start the Sinatra record, I'll head down there and meet the cops. If there's anything to this, tell Jim I'll call it in for the news.*

Let me add at this point in my budding career, I had zero news-reporting experience beyond the "rip-and-read" local newscasts that were part of the show. "On-the-scene" reporting had managed to elude me.

I was driving the severely underpowered model '63 VW Beatle at the time, yet managed to make it to Edie's address just as a City Police squad car pulled into her driveway; her apartment was above a garage. Naturally, the two cops went up the stairs first and knocked on the door. I walked past the two officers and looked in a window. It was the bedroom and, sure enough, there was a woman, phone in one hand, revolver in the other and blood all over the sheets.

I called out to the cops:

> *She's in there and she's shot.*

With that, the officers "encouraged" the door open. In four steps, they were in the bedroom. One officer checked her pulse, pronounced her alive and made the call for an ambulance; the other officer ran out to the squad car for the first-aid kit. The clock radio on Edie's nightstand said it was almost news time.

I grabbed the phone and called the station hotline. Jim Irwin answered immediately, the news open started playing in the background.

> *Do you have something?*
>
> *I do.*
>
> *All right, I'll be going right to you.*

Short pause.

> *Good evening, it's 6:55 -- WIBR News Director Jim Irwin reporting. We go immediately to WIBR's Brian Wilson with this late breaking story… Brian?*

What the hell do I do now? Wing it!

> *Jim, I'm standing in the bedroom of Edie Hébert who just attempted to commit suicide.*

At this point, you should know that Jim Irwin positively hated doing **Let's Talk It Over**. *Hated it.* In fact, Jim hated it so much he would usually arrive at the studio half lit, carrying a brown paper bag that contained the remains of a pint bottle of Jack Daniels. On most nights, that bottle would be empty before 9 p.m.

This was one of those nights when Jim had already achieved lift-off by the time he arrived. How do I know? Because after I delivered my poorly worded opening line about standing in a bedroom where a woman attempted suicide, News Director Jim Irwin totally lost it, laughed uncontrollably over the rest of my bungled report until he or the chief engineer cut his mic and hit a commercial.

Frankly, I wasn't doing much better at my end. I hadn't considered the mental picture or insinuation of my opening line. It took me a couple seconds, but once I heard Jim's uniquely raucous laughter, the picture popped into my head. It was all I could do to retain enough composure to intelligibly get through the rest of the story!

Needless to say, this treatment of a tragic news story received more attention than Edie's attempt to end her life.

However, I am pleased to report Edie survived and the story has an even happier ending -- although it took a couple of years to get to it.

By then, I had moved on from WIBR to WAFB-FM, a brand new Top 40 station in Baton Rouge, with long-time radio pal, George Bonnell.

Walking into the front office one afternoon, our secretary, Jennifer Pasqualetti, told me I had a call waiting on line two. She said the caller didn't give her name.

Brian Wilson…

Brian? This is Edie Hébert, do you remember me? I called you on WIBR one afternoon two years ago and tried to commit suicide. You had my name and address and called the police. After I got out of the hospital, I was in therapy for quite a while. The doctor says I'm going to be OK now and the first thing I wanted to do was to call you and thank you for saving my life.

I certainly couldn't tell her what had been happening at my end of the phone reporting her story that evening or Jim Irwin's unique participation back at the station. I accepted her thanks as graciously as I could, wished her well, said goodbye and hung up.

I never heard from her again. I hope she lived a happy and healthy life.

Story Seven

BRUSLY AND OTHER SORROWS

Shortly after the **Ross and Wilson Show** was born on WJB0/Baton Rouge, October 1977, I learned a basic truth about radio listeners that would serve me very well in the years to come.

One morning, yapping about local events, Ross came upon a story from Brusly. Still fairly new to the greater Baton Rouge area, he stumbled over the name and, after correcting his pronunciation (it's BREW-lee), he asked where it was and what did it mean. I explained Brusly was Coonass for "Burnt Tree;" that it was just a wide spot in the road across the river in West Baton Rouge Parish. With that, we moved on to other things.

As soon as we got off the air, General Manager George Jenne, newly arrived from the Miami market, paged us to his office; his voice agitated.

Where is Brusly?

I gave him the same answer I had given Ross.

What was it you said this morning about Brusly?

What I said had been so inconsequential, it took me a moment to remember and reconstruct the dialogue for him.

Why? What's the problem?

Jenne said he'd received a call from some little old lady who was incensed that we'd ridiculed Brusly.

> *This is a nice little town! You don't live here so just who do you think you are?*

Jenne told her he hadn't heard the comments but would look into it and get back to her.

I explained I had visited Brusly on several occasions; my insurance agent's office was there and, no question, it was a one-horse town and the horse and seen better days. Its big tourist attraction was a tree, the Brusly Oak.

Jenne laughed -- more of a snort -- and waved us out of the office.

That someone could become so exorcised over a snarky little reference to their microscopic town to complain to the manager gave me an idea: why not keep doing it? Everybody knew where and what Brusly was. Having some fun at their expense could get people talking. And there is no better publicity in radio than word-of-mouth. Being the new act on the air, we could use all the free publicity we could get. WJBO ownership wasn't buying any advertising, despite owning one of eight AM stations, one of four FM stations, the two daily papers and one of three TV stations in town.

Around the same time the next morning, I went on the air and apologized to the residents of Brusly:

> *Brusly isn't a "wide spot in the road," it's a booming micro-opolis! The pending grand opening of the new earwax recycling plant has the town all abuzz! Not only that, Brusly Mayor John LaBouve announced just this morning, the new College of Incidental Wart Removal and Memorial Clinic is breaking ground north of the traffic light, even as I speak. So congratulations to all the finally-employed citizens of Brusly, Mayor LaBouve and the Brusly Chamber of Commerce and Extortion for a job well done.*

As soon as the show was over, we were again paged into the GM's office. This time, he was laughing his butt off. Not only from what I had said on the air, but also because the same little old lady called again, this time apoplectic over my comments.

For the rest of our seven months at WJB0, Brusly's people and alleged events became a regular feature of the show. We celebrated the opening of the new Q-tip refurbishing factory that was located conveniently adjacent to the earwax recycling plant. This kind of economic symbiosis was something Baton Rouge and larger metropolitan areas should strive to emulate! And the gold medal won by the Brusly Olympic Nose Hair Braiding Team couldn't have arrived at a better time!

Eventually, the little old lady from Brusly stopped calling. Her regular morning screech fest to the GM was replaced by calls to the sales department from various Brusly businesses wanting advertising information. When the local newspaper and Baton Rouge TV stations broke the news **Ross and Wilson** were leaving for Atlanta, Mayor LaBouve and the village of Brusly invited us to a black-tie farewell party, thrown in our honor at the Brusly Country Club! I think all 1,927 residents showed up, with the possible exception of one little old lady.

A good time was had by all! The mayor, business owners and members of the Chamber of Commerce (and Extortion) all gave appropriately short speeches thanking us for putting Brusly on the map; since its founding in 1901, no media outlet had ever paid so much attention to tiny Brusly. As for **Ross and Wilson**, I made a few sincere, complimentary comments, predictably followed by a few insincere, sarcastic, snarky comments which were raucously appreciated and followed by a standing ovation as we exited stage left. The next day, **The Baton Rouge Advocate** gave the festivities a nice spread.

The take away from the Brusly experience was: why wouldn't this work in Atlanta or anywhere? All we had to do was find a suburban town with a strange name and put it in the **Ross and Wilson** comedy spotlight.

Flying back to Baton Rouge after signing our new Z-93 "employment agreements," we found the new town on a roadmap (remember those?). There, near infamous Stone Mountain, fairly leaping off the page was *Snellville.* While the population has exploded since our 1978 arrival, back then Snellville truly was just a wide spot in the road.

Shortly after we arrived and got comfortable, we started in on Snellville using some of the tried-and-true lines that worked on Brusly. The audience reaction was instantaneous: the Atlanta metro audience got it and, thankfully, so did the residents of Snellville. The town actually sported a Pizza Hut! And the big buzz was the pending arrival of a McDonald's, right across the street. There was a gas station or two and some mom and pop shops, the prerequisite public schools and that was about it. At the time, Gwinnett County was dry. One of the first things I noted was -- if anyone could use a stiff drink, it was a resident of Snellville.

As an extra added attraction, we discovered the mayor of Snellville was perfectly named Emmett Clower and the Sheriff, J. D. Hewitt.* We had lots of fun with those guys! Over the next three years, we became the Snellville spokesmen. Before we left for WABC/NY, we had been guest speakers numerous times at the Chamber of Commerce, Rotary Club and the growing high school student body's Career Day with "How to Starve to Death with a Career in Radio." We did a TV feature, **Snellville Night Fever**, a video tour of Snellville on a Saturday night that included visits to the Pizza Hut, the new Mickey Ds, plus a ride-along with Sherriff Hewitt in his Model A "squad car," visiting the "seedy sides of Snellville." Ultimately, we were co-grand marshals of the Snellville Day Parade with the magnificent Clayton Moore, the original **Lone Ranger**.

Our departure for WABC happened so quickly and with a studied lack of organization, Mayor Clower and the citizens of Snellville could not give us the black-tie treatment we received from Brusly – assuming they wanted to! But cards, letters, and phone calls of congratulations poured into the station, noting our move to the Big Apple, while mourning Snellville's loss of the limelight. Even a couple of **Atlanta Journal-Constitution** columnists wrote about it.

Moss Creek, NJ was the next town. The details are in another **Story** in this book.

At the end of the long slide down the razor blade of WABC, I found myself doing mornings on B104/ Baltimore. I was shotgun-married to another partner and not very happy about it. But the show must go on and here was a new show in a new town that needed a successor to the Brusly/Snellville/Moss Creek heritage. On the east-side outskirts of Baltimore, I found Dundalk, an incorporated area with nearby U.S. Steel and GM plants, predominantly blue-collar workers, an accent all its own and a town name that sounded like the mating call of a Blue Heron. The most popular activity in Dundalk: bowling. It doesn't get much better than this!

While the people of greater Baltimore caught on quickly, it took the Dundalkians a little longer to get the joke. The calls came fast and furious:

> *B104 Brian and O'Brien Show, hello…*
>
> *Hey, why are youse guys always crackin' on Dundalk?*
>
> *Sir, you just answered your own question. Thank you so much for bothering us.*

Eventually, these calls morphed into:

> *B104 Brian and O'Brien Show, hello…*

> *I think the Brian & O'Brien Show is rude, crude and obnoxious… and I love it!*
>
> *Well, thanks. Obviously, there is no accounting for taste!*

And so it went. When the **Brian and O'Brien Show** disintegrated in October 1988, Dundalk's days in the radio limelight were over.

But not for long.

In a tragic twist highlighting the accelerating descent of the public's sense of humor, I briefly returned full-time to the Baltimore airwaves in January, 1995, firmly ensconced in Talk Radio with a regular show on WCBM. The unrivaled success of the **Brian and O'Brien Show** was still familiar to the Baltimore audience (now six years later). Of course, I returned with a fresh supply of Dundalk material.

It was a disaster.

Over the intervening years, Dundalkians had started to believe their own lousy self-image. The closing of the steel plant and the pending shut-down of the GM plant wreaked havoc on the Dundalk economy, and killed Dundalk's miniscule sense of humor with it. When I started lofting my customary one-liners about the Dundalk Overhand Bowling League and similar pastimes, the phone calls to the program director were vicious.

Obviously, I grossly overestimated the longevity of Dundalk denizens' self-inflicted deprecations of the mid-80s. By the time this became clear, a number of Dundalk residents had quickly organized a sponsor boycott against WCBM; to management's credit, they didn't believe it either. For a while. Then the sales department started getting the calls usually reserved for the program director or general manager. The message was clear, "lay off Dundalk -- or else." The unsophisticated Dundalk business owners cum advertisers did not know and would not take the risk that these "boycotters" could not be serious. There was only one heating oil company that serviced Dundalk. *Were you really going to let your family freeze to death because that company ran commercials on a show poking fun at your town?*

No one wanted to find out. So Dundalk was left to its own devices.

It was a funny bit that ran from Baton Rouge to Atlanta to New York to Baltimore back to New York and back to Baltimore where Dundalk killed it.

But it sure was fun while it lasted!

**J.D. Hewitt was a great sport and a class act. As a caricature of the stereotypical Southern sheriff, he played along with our antics about Snellville, took our calls on the air and contributed to the overall good times. We got to be good friends just about the time the call came in from WABC. Sadly, J.D. died before I could get back to Atlanta to spend some more meaningful time with him. RIP, Sheriff.*

Story Eight

DUMB RADIO CONTESTS

As much as I was thrilled to be on WIBR/Baton Rouge, a top medium market station in a drive-time slot, that station should have a special place in the Broadcasting Hall of Shame for running two of the dumbest on-air contests ever (and they ran for *years*). One was called the **Sorry, Wrong Number Game**.

On the altruistic bandwagon of "encouraging everyone to drive safely," management made arrangements for the Baton Rouge City Police Department to call the WIBR hotline every time there was an accident within city limits. The on-air jock or our receptionist would dutifully answer the phone and record the location. The jock then had to immediately hit a God-awful Klaxon auto horn sound effect (sfx), announce the location of the wreck, the new total number of accidents for the day and "Remember the total for our next **Sorry, Wrong Number Game**." The truly asinine part of this "game" was that we had to hit this irritating sound and recite all that crap, *regardless of what was on the air at the time* (except of course, news or commercials). The only thing to interrupt -- MUSIC! The main reason people were listening! So here you are, singing along with your favorite hit tune when all of sudden:

> *BWAAA-WAAA-BWAAA-WAAA... Baton Rouge City Police have just informed WIBR of another accident, this one at the*

corner Dumb and Dumber Streets. This brings our total to XX for the day. WIBR reminds you to please drive with greater care. And remember our total (insert total again here)! Right now, we have XXX dollars in the jackpot if you know the correct number of accidents the next time we play the WIBR Sorry Wrong Number Game, coming up soon!

After reciting all that bull, you would return to whatever was left of that spiffy tune you just interrupted, supremely annoying a huge number of people who flat out didn't give damn about some fender bender.

Then there were the mechanics of the **Sorry, Wrong Number Game** itself. Here's how this exercise in nitwittery was played:

SFX: BWAAA-WAAA BWAA WASS

Female Voice: Sorry, Wrong Number!

Jock: Yes, it's time once again to play WIBR's Sorry Wrong Number Game! I'm going to call a phone number chosen at random from the Greater Baton Rouge telephone directory. If this is your number, just answer your phone with the correct number of accidents we have announced on WIBR so far today, and you will win all the money in the Sorry, Wrong Number jackpot, which right now totals XX dollars. The correct number of accidents reported in Baton Rouge so far today is XXX, XXX. Remember you must answer your phone with that number.

I'm now dialing that number, chosen at random from the Greater Baton Rouge telephone directory.

Place call on air.

Jock: The phone is ringing… (DUH).

Let phone ring five times. If no answer, hang up.

Jock: There was no answer at (telephone number) so no one wins all the money in the Sorry, Wrong Number jackpot. Stay tuned for the next time we play the Sorry Wrong Number Game with XXX dollars in the jackpot, and remember to drive with greater care.

If the caller answers with anything other than the correct number of accidents:

*Jock: Sorry, Wrong Number (and IMMEDIATELY HANG UP)! As you heard, the party at (telephone number) did not answer with the correct number of accidents. So now we'll add (ready for this?) **TWO DOLLARS** to the jackpot, making the new total XX dollars the next time we play WIBR's Sorry, Wrong Number Game. And remember to drive with greater care!*

If the caller answers with the correct number, play Party Music Cart 100, congratulate the winner, get the name and put him/her on hold.

*Jock: Congratulations to Furd Douchnozzle on Road Apple Road! He answered his phone with XX, the correct number of accidents we've had in Baton Rouge so far today and wins all the money, XXX dollars, in the Sorry, Wrong Number jackpot. Listen again for the next Sorry, Wrong Number Game when the jackpot total will start over with (here it comes) **TWO DOLLARS**! We'll increase the total two dollars every time we get a wrong answer on WIBR's Sorry, Wrong Number!*

(Jingle out or segue into stop set.)

The only radio game on the air that highlights stupidity and carnage!

Hopefully, I've managed to convey the marrow-deep sense of how tedious, insipid, boring and stupendously counterproductive this "game" was. Throw in morbid while you're at it. It was ridiculous to believe a dumb game was somehow going to inspire the average moron driver to change his/her ways. I used to say on the air that those involved in accidents were listening to other stations and all this "encouragement" to "drive with greater care" was a monumental waste of time. But the boss/owner, Bob Earle, got the idea from a small consortium of station owners in similar markets. The group met to trade or steal ideas from each other that were (allegedly) creating great ratings. Personally, I never saw or heard anything from anyone that supported the notion the listener or advertiser gave a rat's ass about the number of accidents; even less having their favorite tunes interrupted. The only people who got excited were the rare winners who got checks for $100-$200. At $2 per answered call, it took forever to build the "jackpot" to an amount the average person would find sufficiently attractive to listen through all the bilge in the hopes that his/her phone would ring.

But wait! There's more!

If the **Sorry, Wrong Number Game** wasn't cringe-worthy enough, there was the other WIBR brain-dead classic: the **Meet Your Neighbor Game**. It went like this:

> *MEET YOUR NEIGHBOR SFX (mercifully I have forgotten what it was…)*
>
> *Jock: And now it's time to play the WIBR fun game (we actually called it that), Meet Your Neighbor! I'm going to read a commercial message from one of our Meet Your Neighbor sponsors. Then, I'm going to call a phone number chosen at random from the Greater Baton Rouge telephone directory. If the person who answers the phone can tell me the name of the sponsor I just mentioned, they'll win all the money in the Meet Your Neighbor jackpot – which right now stands at XX dollars!*

Our Meet Your Neighbor sponsor right now is Roadkill Restaurant (blah blah blah…) from the middle of the road to the middle of your plate, unidentifiable but guaranteed-fresh at Roadkill Restaurant!

(Dial phone but do not put caller on the air.)

This what the listener heard:

Jock: I'm calling the Dumbass family on Lobotomy Lane in Baton Rouge…. the phone is ringing….

OK…there's the third ring, two more before I have to h… Hi! Is this Mr. Dumbass? Great! This is Brian Wilson at WIBR Radio with the Meet Your Neighbor Game, Mr. Dumbass. If you can tell me the name of the last sponsor I just mentioned, you'll win the XXX dollars in the Meet Your Neighbor Jackpot. Can you give me that name, Mr. Dumbass?

Ohhhhh… that's too bad, Mr. Dumbass! It was the Roadkill Restaurant on Squish Road. Right... well better luck next time, Mr. Dumbass, and thanks for playing Meet Your Neighbor here on WIBR!

*Well, as you heard, we didn't get a winner this time so I'm going to add (hang on now) **ONE DOLLAR** to the jackpot, bringing our total to XXX dollars the next time we play the Meet Your Neighbor Game!*

(Jingle out.)

If the above wasn't enough to kill-off the most dedicated listener, there are a couple other things that made this "game" an insult to any sentient being. First, with the caller kept off the air -- for fear s/he would mention some OTHER business -- what you *didn't* hear often went like this:

Jock: Hi! Is this Mr. Dumbass?

Caller (Sleepy, grouchy voice, probably a shift worker): Yeah?

BW: Great! This is Brian Wilson at WIBR Radio with the Meet Your Neighbor Game, Mr. Dumbass, and if you…

Caller: Who? Beat Your What?

BW: …if you can tell me the name of the last sponsor I just mentioned, you'll win the XXX dollars in the Meet Your Neighbor Jackpot.

Caller: What the hell? Is this one of those stupid radio games? Who is this waking me up?

BW: Can you give me that name, Mr. Dumbass?

Caller: I'll give you more than that, you bastard! Who is this? I'll come down there and beat the crap outta you.

BW: Ohhhhh… that's too bad Mr. Dumbass. It was the Roadkill Restaurant on Squish Road. Right… well better luck next time, Mr. Dumbass…

Caller: You're gonna be roadkill, asshole. Who the hell is this?

BW: …and thanks for playing the Meet Your Neighbor Game here on WIBR!

Caller: Your neighbor? What? Why I…

(CLICK)

BW: Well, as you heard, we didn't get a winner this time so…

This happened more times than you could reasonably guess, or believe. On top of that, with no winner, adding a whopping

ONE DOLLAR to the jackpot sounded cheap and silly. Which it was. Because Bob Earle (RIP) was cheap but never silly.

As you've probably guessed, when we *did* have a winner, the jackpot went back to one dollar. Imagine the thrill of waking up someone and telling them if they get the answer right, they'll get a buck! I implored Earle – at least start it at ten dollars! Nope. Not happening. Didn't happen. Never happened.

I hated that game.

Maybe it all worked out. After numerous ownership and format changes, WIBR has been off the air for years!

Story Nine

THE BIRTHDAY DESSERT

This story has little to do with 50 Years in Radio - other than it happened during that time! It's just a great story with a great ending! I actually have two of these! This is the first one…

One of the best dumb things I've ever done was "buy the farm" -- literally. One hundred eighty-five acres in Upstate New York, north of Elmira, south of Ithaca, east of Watkins Glen, just a short drive from Corning. Regardless of a number of pesky inconveniences, I loved the place! Woods to hunt and roam with our two Goldens, Stoby and Katie, open land to plant and mow -- mostly in that order -- and a great place to get married! The fact an ISDN line for my VRINK business ran right up to the creek alongside the house was *the omen* that sealed the deal! All of this really has nothing to do with the story per se. It just got me thinking how we came to have dinner one evening just before Christmas in a little restaurant on the outskirts of Elmira.

Like many eateries far from major metropolitan areas, the entire dining experience was typically underwhelming. Once you accept that as your new normal, it ain't so bad. The problem was: we both grew up in the NYC metro area *and* with Cassie's stunning culinary expertise, we never could quite make it to that Nirvana of acceptance.

But I digress…

Whenever possible when dining out, we've made a point of going early. Waiting and patience have never played well with my other charming attributes, plus we are terminally allergic to paying for a lukewarm meal served with a side order of screaming kids, crying babies or large groups of adults who don't believe in volume control because after all, they are the only people on earth and can blithely ignore any semblance of courtesy, manners or social grace. In addition, when you are only one of three or four couples in early for dinner, it is remarkable how service improves and the food is almost hot-on-arrival.

Again, I digress…

Against this background, we were one of four couples in this modest eatery festooned with holiday decorations; strategically seated to ensure maximum conversation isolation. Nevertheless, over coffee at the end of the meal, we began hearing a growing animation of the conversation at the nearest table.

A mother and her young son also had finished their meal and with great excitement, decided on dessert. The waiter had just arrived and the slightly raised voices of the waiter and mother caught our attention. Something was amiss.

As we pieced the situation together, the mother had a discount coupon for a "dinner for two," won from a local radio station promotion. It was her son's birthday and this was his party -- just the two of them. Did I mention the child, about 10 years old, was autistic? It also was clear this was their first time out in quite a while. Mom was thrilled to be able to provide this extra-added dinner-date surprise attraction despite the obvious fact she was not swimming in discretionary income. There was a certain tone to the conversation between Mom and the waiter. The waiter was telling Mom in no uncertain terms the discount coupon did *NOT* include dessert. Condescendingly he added, "*That* would be an extra charge."

While the waiter hovered, the mother searched every nook and corner of her purse but was unable to come up with enough cash to cover two pieces of German Chocolate Cake. Absent any holiday spirit from the waiter, Mom ordered the one piece she could afford. With Scrooge-like indifference, the waiter dutifully marched off, as clouds of disappointment gathered over what had been this festive birthday bash. The mother tried to put the best spin on the situation, telling the boy she was sorry she didn't have the money, but everything was OK because she wasn't that hungry, and wouldn't it be fun to share? The son may have been autistic, but he seemed to do his best to put on a happy face. Regardless of their mutual efforts, neither fooled the other. Mom's best laid plans had been harpooned by the fine print, lack of funds and a waiter void of empathy, awareness, human kindness or the Christmas spirit. Probably all four.

Meanwhile, back at the Wilson table, we were having none of it. Before he could retrieve the single piece of cake, I caught the waiter's eye, and he promptly came to the table that had ordered that expensive bottle of wine with their steaks. As sotto voce as possible, I said:

> *If you'd like to actually receive the substantial gratuity I planned to leave you, please do the following -- return to that table with the mother and son with two very generous pieces of your German Chocolate Cake, with whipped cream. Apologize to the mother -- you made a big mistake, the coupon does indeed cover dessert for both of them and, since you happened to pick up on the fact that it was a certain young man's birthday, the restaurant would also like to present him with a scoop of ice cream and a candle. Put it all on my tab and say nothing about this conversation to the mom. OK?*

With a grin only raw capitalism can create, the garcon zoomed off, setting a new land speed record, arriving at the table with two ginormous pieces of cake piled high with whipped cream. In sufficiently audible tones, he recited his heartfelt apologies to both mother and son, offered the Birthday Ice Cream Special to a squeal of delight and left two very happy people with their desserts, which included a generous serving of chocolate ice cream. With whipped cream. And a candle. The waiter had outdone and redeemed himself.

With laughter and giggles from those two party animals, we left a very happy mother and son and headed back to the farm.

See? A great **Story** -- and one of my favorite memories.

Story Ten

DANCING

When **Ross and Wilson** set up shop at Z-93/Atlanta, it didn't take long to realize we'd have to smarten up the act, both on and off the air. Atlanta was booming! People in their 20s and 30s were pouring in from all over the Deep South to grab great gigs at Southern Bell, Delta, Eastern, IBM -- just about every business of every size was growing big time! Natives and Newbies were handsome or beautiful; Disco was hot and everybody was making good bux! There wasn't a better place to be in radio than Atlanta, 1978!

Many of the big discos in town hired DJs from various radio stations to work the tunes 'n turntables. Who else knew the music and equipment better? Who else was totally comfortable behind a mic? Who else brought real personality along with them? Most importantly, who else had a fan base that would come out to see The Dude on the Radio and stay awhile?

I was hired at Tingles. Great name for a disco! I did my thing but disco DJ wasn't my forte, regardless of the very nice $$$ paid in cash at the end of the evening. But the act was **Ross AND Wilson** – so our budding fan base naturally wanted to know, "Where's Ross?" Simple answer -- ownership wouldn't spring for double bux just for spinning records and tossing in a few one-liners.

As the radio show grew, one club did -- Harlow's. And it only took one night to realize our Baton Rouge "nightclub act" wasn't gonna cut it at an Atlanta disco. Something new had to be developed that was totally different from anything else in town.

Enter the **Ross and Wilson Dance Lessons** and the **Ross and Wilson Kissing Contest**.

If you are too young or old to know/remember, disco dancing was way different than just standing in one place and waving your arms around like in the 50s and 60s. Who couldn't do The Twist? Hand Jive? Watusi? Fly? **Saturday Night Fever** showed there was an elegance to disco. People who came to Harlow's to dance really danced well! Others sat, drank, eyeballed the opposite sex and waited for the slow dance tunes. With so many people on their butts, we would take advantage of the situation with our new **Ross and Wilson Dance Lessons**!

> *Here's your chance to learn bona fide disco dancing, guaranteed to open the door to romance – and burn some tonnage while you're at it! Which wouldn't hurt busting open that door to romance!*

There was only one song perfect for the bit -- the Village People's **YMCA**. If you are one of the eight people still living who have no clue what this involved, Google it. Watch YouTube! All will be revealed! Naturally, we had to use the eight-minute and 56-second "Disco Mix" version to have enough time to pull this off.

The opening set-up was the only part that remained consistent every week. The DM-LP cut starts out with an acapella "Y-M-C-A!" followed by a 20-second instrumental/bongo bed leading up to the familiar brass intro from the hit version, then four "Y-M-C-As!" and the lyric.

I would announce the "lesson" was about to start and everyone who wanted to learn needed to come down to the dance floor, "Where my partner, Ross 'Disco Dementia' Brittain will be your disco instructor this evening."

After we did this a couple weeks, there was no mystery what was happening. **YMCA** was such a great tune and big hit, everyone knew the drill and swarmed the floor with the first "Y-M-C-A!" shout. The simplicity of it also made the "group dance" a great way for people to meet 'n greet and… whatever developed later.

The 45-second intro gave me time to roust everyone into line while Ross took his instructor's position in front of the "class" where he would demonstrate the proper way to get arms and body to make the proper Y, M, C and A. Invariably there would be a doofus who'd get it wrong. While I excoriated the man/woman from the DJ perch, Ross would see to it special attention was given to the rhythmically challenged "student." This provided a target-rich environment for all sorts of comments which livened up the crowd – as if they needed any at this point!

All this was timed to hit the post, "Young man, there's no need to feel down…" And the class was off and dancing even though the "dance" pretty much consisted of marching in place as the Village People performed it! Everything else was improv until the chorus when everyone would face Ross and do the required Y-M-C-A arm/letter/spelling thing.

And something usually went wrong. Someone who had been "overserved" would screw up the spelling; others would be laughing so hard they'd collapse on the floor and the occasional wardrobe malfunction had its own special needs. But you couldn't have packed more fun, laughs, and exercise into just under nine minutes anywhere else! There were awards for Best Dancers, Most Illiterate Couple, Most Revealing Wardrobe and anything else inappropriate for the session!

It was a great time!

While the **YMCA** dance lessons were a big hit and got everyone into a good time, we were paid to fill *three* hours per night. Dancing and our occasional commentary took up most of it, but after **YMCA** killed 20 minutes, we had to come up with something else…

Story Eleven

...AND KISSING

Everyone knew why everyone else was at the disco. It was only logical we should do something to encourage Mother Nature along. So after the **YMCA Dance Lessons** and another 45 minutes of non-stop music, we took charge of the dance floor to announce it was time for the **Ross and Wilson Turgidly Erratic Kissing Contest**!

(Note: Sarcasm, innuendo, double entendres and overbearing intimidation all were necessary ingredients for the success of this bit. Fortunately, they also were everything we did really well whether on or off the air!)

Here's how it went:

> *If you'd like to be in the Ross and Wilson Kissing Contest, we need two couples – preferably of opposite sexes -- although that is not an absolute requirement in these modern times. Neither age nor sobriety are qualifications either – in fact, the older and more sloshed you are usually works out best for all of us! Singles are not necessarily excluded but the rules will cause considerable difficulty regardless of how limber you may be.*

While I ran through this, Ross lined up the contestants for the sorting and interviewing process.

> *OK, everyone… first, we have to divide you into the proper category -- Vets or Virgins. So, how long have you two known each other?*

Based on their answers, two couples who had known each other the shortest time would be the Virgins; the other two couples would be the Vets. Obviously, the Q&A provided lots of opportunity for ribald, demeaning, sarcastic and lurid comments from R&W.

> *Alright, it appears we have our suckers… um… contestants all together. Let's find out where they really are and who they've done…*

Ross occasionally would step in to correct my Spoonerism.

Names, towns and occupations provided even more raw material for fun comments. Once everyone was questioned, Ross announced the rules, accompanied by my running commentary.

Here's a sample:

> *BW: Now before we get started, you must first know our official Kissing Contest rules – here is my partner, Ross "Osculation" Brittain, with tonight's rule review!*

> *RB: OK, tonight we'll be playing by college rules so listen carefully. First, at all times both hands must remain above the waist…*

> *BW: …on the back! There can be no anatomical explorations during the contest!*

> *RB: I will give you a "three-two-one-go" countdown. Do not start kissing before I say GO!*

> *BW: Correct! Our judges will take points off for any premature osculation so guys especially, control yourselves!*

> *RB: I will then give you another countdown – "three-two-one-stop." Do not STOP kissing before I say STOP!*

BW: Correct! Judges will deduct points for early withdrawal. It's just like a bank. Women especially lose interest with early withdrawal...

RB: *Alright, couple number one, assume the position... and three-two-one-GO!*

Depending on the couple, anything could -- and often did -- happen next. Most couples would kiss as enthusiastically as their familiarity and sobriety permitted. We would do our best to crack them up.

BW: *Ross! I think I hear some rooting around going on there!*

I would hold my mic close to the juncture of the kissing contestants while Ross would turn away and make grunting, heavy breathing, moaning noises while I expressed my surprise and outrage. The crowd went nuts.

BW: *Oh my God! Ross -- do you hear that? What animals! They're damn near devouring each other.*

Usually, the couple would catch on to things by now and just lose it! The audience was always into it. Even if they had watched the routine a dozen times, it always was a hoot.

When the second couple finished, the audience was informed they were to be the judges; their applause would decide the "Big Weiner." Without fail, the "most enthusiastic" couple won with a thunderous ovation, hoots, hollers and whistles.

This was repeated with the second pair. Then with one winner from the Virgins and one from the Vets, we would proceed to the "Kiss Off" where both couples would kiss simultaneously to the final countdown, then the audience applause. The grand prize was two beers and a complimentary condom.

The **Kissing Contest** was easily the most popular part of the act.

While couples generally did not go beyond "enthusiastic smooching," there were a few occasions when things got out of control. One was during an **I Love You, Atlanta** party at the notorious Atlanta Omni. At the time, the ground floor featured a skating rink, shops, food court and all the touristy things that welcomed visitors once attracted to the remarkable but ill-fated **World of Sid and Marty Kroft** indoor amusement park. With the park de-commissioned, there was plenty of space at one end of the still functioning skating rink to set up our Z-93 **I Love You, Atlanta** stage.

The **I Love You, Atlanta** parties were held weekly during Happy Hour at different venues around the Big Peach and featured *free* beer! Obviously, for maximum promotional effect, there had to be some sort of attraction beyond free beer, hanging out with your buds and favorite DJs! What better time, place and audience for the now-notorious **Ross and Wilson Kissing Contest**?

This occasion, there was a larger-than-usual crowd for the Omni party. Downtown, summertime and Z-93's huge popularity with young professionals provided the "perfect storm" when the prize included our highly-coveted, limited-edition **I Love You, Atlanta** Z-93 T-shirts. You couldn't buy these anywhere -- they were *only* available to Z-93 contest winners. Since we had promoted only having *two* T-shirts to award to the "Big Weiners" of the **R&W Kissing Contest**, it contributed mightily to the crowd size. After 90 minutes of music, dancing, and free beer, we took the stage -- the crowd was pumped!

The eight contestants were way more… *enthusiastic…* than our nightclub folks. Considering the time and location, we hadn't anticipated inhibitions to fade that quickly! When we got to the "Kiss Off" finale, things were barely in control, but in a good way. There was no fighting or cursing or anything anti-social. Everyone was having a great time with their peers and beers.

We counted down the start of the "Kiss Off" and our Vets and Virgins promptly got out of hand. As they kept an eye on each other, competition set in. Hands started finding their way to buttons and clasps and zippers "on the back" in strict accordance with the rules. This may have lasted 30 seconds. With increasing crowd encouragement, a blouse flew in the air, then one guy's T-shirt, then a gal's T-shirt. By the time we thought it best to start the final countdown, one couple was on the floor and a bra had been launched! The couple standing up was attempting the same wardrobe adjustment from their position. The crowd went berserk!

With the distinct possibility of the Boys in Blue with Shiny Badges showing up, we did our best to break up the passionate pairs, retrieve the wayward clothing and return things to some semblance of order. Difficult to believe, but we pulled it off (no pun intended).

The crowd enthusiastically applauded for a tie. Fortunately, we had an extra pair of the highly-prized T-shirts to award our over-heated contestants. During the "Award" ceremonies, I offered each couple a hotel room in lieu of T-shirts. Big laugh -- no takers. The T-shirts were *that* popular!

The **Kissing Contest** stayed in Atlanta when WABC brought us to the Large Apple – except for one last encore at the **Ross and Wilson Fifth Anniversary Bash**, taped in Wayne, New Jersey before a live audience in 1982. Only one copy of that never-seen in-public tape exists today! Well, maybe two. You have to check with Ross!

Ross & Wilson Z-93 Studio, Kinda cramped! (Photo: Brian Wilson collection)

Story Twelve

IRON CHEF WILSON

Before leaving Atlanta and Z-93, the Benihana restaurant there threw a fund-raiser, inviting a representative from each of the top radio/TV stations and the **Atlanta Journal-Constitution** to be a Celebrity Chef for an evening of cooking competition on their hibachi grills. Station personnel and invited guests (listeners) would sit at each media outlet's table to cheer the efforts. Of course, **Ross and Wilson** were chosen to represent Z-93. No one had a noodle's worth of experience doing this beyond watching the timpani and juggling acts that were part of the Benihana dining experience.

With a modicum of cooking experience compared to Ross, I took the lead and he backed me up. Literally. After the guests were seated, the cooks were introduced and cheered. Ingredients were scattered across the cooking area, and the clock started. Beyond knowing that the meat had to be cooked, I could only guess what to do with whatever those *other things* were.

So with great flourish, rhythmic riffs of the giant salt shaker and peppermill, I tossed and scattered the pieces around the cooktop, beating out a tattoo of sorts with the various utensils while keeping up a steady chatter of genuine Japanese gibberish, supposedly describing what the hell I was doing. When I finished with the peppermill, I tossed it over my head behind me where Ross fielded it and handed it back when prompted. It was all noisy, messy and funny. The food itself actually turned out pretty tasty! Amazing what a little soy sauce can do!

Iron Chef Wilson demonstrating his Chaos Cooking Technique at Atlanta's Benihana Celebrity Cook-Off (1979 Photo: WZGC)

Our theatrics got the attention of the guests at competing tables and they jilted their competitors and joined in the fun -- a great time was had by all! At the end of the competition, the Z-93 table was judged the Big Winner by virtue of Original Choreography, Uninhibited Rhythm and Utensil Juggling!

I later learned a certain unnamed talk show host was supremely ticked off at our success. Reportedly, he had gone to great lengths to learn and practice everything hibachi, incorrectly assuming *expertise* would win over *entertainment.* He may have done better if he had understood -- *Radio is showbiz!*

By 1981, there still was some fun to be had in radio for both listener and performer.

One morning on WABC, we got to talking about cooking, and Ross complimented me on my excellent lasagna. The irredoubtable Joe Nolan/Shadow Traffic (who occasionally played along with our shenanigans), jumped in with the contention that *his* lasagna would put *my* lasagna to shame. This escalated to a full-blown on-air battle that could be resolved only one way: a lasagna cook-off.

Remarkably, we actually got support for this from management. Ultimately, it was decided the big event would be held in the yet to be completed talk studio, 8C. Listeners were invited to apply as guest judges with the usual card-name-address-phone number entrance rules; 12 people with dubious qualifications beyond "taste buds" would be chosen at random to come to the ABC Building Saturday morning in two weeks.

With much bravado and appropriate on-air sparring, the big day arrived along with our 12 judges from the WABC listening area. With everyone appropriately assembled and seated, we announced the entire event would be recorded for later broadcast. After some semi-appropriate comments from Ross, Joe and me, every judge received two paper plates -- one red, one blue – each with a hearty portion of lasagna. The judges were instructed to taste each sample and vote for their favorite by placing one paper plate on top of the other. Projectile vomiting was discouraged. Of course, the judges had no idea whose lasagna was on which colored plate.

During the tasting, Joe, Ross, Rasa Kaye, Jay Clark and I made inappropriate remarks about the judges and the proceedings: questioning the greenish complexion of one, taking bets on the survival of another, and other allegedly entertaining comments.

When the final plate was placed, there were 11 red plates and one blue plate. If you have a keen sense for the obvious, you know what color my lasagna was served on.

As the final insult, the one judge who voted for Joe Nolan with his blue plate said he actually *preferred* mine but felt sorry for Joe when he saw all the red plate votes. He switched his vote to blue so as to not hurt Joe's feelings!

It was all great fun. Lots of great lines and great laughs. I wish the tape was still available. It would be funny, even by today's standards.

The lasagna judges (1981 Photo: Brian Wilson collection)

A couple years later, after WABC switched to Talk and Ross had been fired, former WLS/Chicago newsman Harley Carnes became part of **Brian Wilson and Company**. It was Harley who introduced me to "real" chili. After getting the list of essential ingredients, I gave it a try. With my wife and kids as the control group (see also: Guinea pigs), after several attempts I came up with a unique recipe* that always received lots of compliments whenever served.

Jose Cuervo's sponsorship of the **Maryland State Chili Tournament** was my first venture in competitive chili cooking. Representing B104, I won the Celebrity Division. When the news made it up to the people who sponsored the annual Corning New York **Chocolate and Chili Festival and Competition**, they sent the station a formal invitation requesting my participation. I was as surprised as I was impressed! Naturally, I accepted. What was unnatural -- I won! Out of 15 competitors from around the country, including two from Canada, it was a big surprise (for everyone) I came out on top!

The chefs lined the Corning footbridge with elaborate cooking gear, custom staging, fancy costumes, and attractive assistants; competitive chili cooking obviously was a major part of their lives. There I was with a rickety card table, a folding chair and a Coleman propane two-burner camping stove, adding the final touches to my barely gurgling cauldron. I didn't even have a sign! The David and Goliath contrast made the win even more surprising -- especially to the guys with the huge, expensive displays. The following year I was invited back to defend my title. With the competition and my recipe mostly the same, I somehow only managed to come in third. At least I didn't get skunked!

The crowning touch came in 1987.

The annual **March of Dimes Gourmet Gala** was a black-tie event in selected major markets around the country. Hyatt hotels along with a major local appliance dealer and a leading local home decorating firm hooked up to stage this event; the hotel provided the venue while the appliance dealer and home decorator collaborated and constructed a variety of kitchen sets, complete with countertops and functioning ovens. The March of Dimes sent invitations to all the media outlets in town -- radio, TV, newspaper -- to send a representative to cook for guests and a panel of celebrity judges. Tables of ten were sold at a hefty price, mostly to the participating media; strips of tickets were sold to be redeemed for sample tastings at the various "kitchens." B104's GM "volunteered" me to represent the station with my award-winning chili.

My wife and I arrived as scheduled, toting an extra-large sampling of my **Authentic Hot Damn Chili**. As an added attraction and an added incentive for guest votes, we also brought a blender and fixins for frozen margaritas. My on-air partner was of no use in preparing the chili for the presentation to the judges, so he worked the room, glad-handing, while we got the chili into the fancy presentation dish and handed out samples to unsuspecting courageous ticket holders. A March of Dimes representative arrived to take servings to the three judges who would decide its fate and mine. Next, the formal presentation to the judges was made. This involved **Brian and O'Brien** toting the large and tastefully decorated serving bowl of **Authentic Hot Damn Chili** up to the judge's table for our introduction and their visual review.

I have forgotten the two local judges, in part due to the blinding light coming from the third: **New York Times** Food Editor and Restaurant Critic, Craig Claiborne!

After all the dishes were presented and judged, the winners were announced in each category: Best Appetizer, Best Entrée, Best Vegetable, and Best Dessert. Sadly, I didn't win any of them (and here I had been holding out for Best Dessert)! Oh well. I had received many compliments and a bunch of requests for the recipe.

But then there was one more announcement.

The master of ceremonies told the assembled multitude: "the judges had a problem with one of the dishes in that it didn't really fall into any one of the definitive categories; it was so unique and so excellent that Mr. Craig Claiborne insisted some sort of recognition be given to B104's Brian Wilson for his **Authentic Hot Damn Chili**. And so, for the first time, we have created an entirely new category, Best Dish, to be awarded this evening to Mr. Wilson."

I went on stage to accept the award amidst a thundering standing ovation (since most people were standing already). Coming back, I passed the judges table, shook hands and thanked each one for the honor. When I got to Mr. Claiborne, he shook my hand with both of his, smiled and said:

> *Congratulations! Most excellent, best I've ever had!*
>
> *Thanks very much! I'll send you the recipe!*

Coming from such a culinary luminary, that comment made the evening!

Brian Wilson and Craig Claiborne March of Dimes Gourmet Gala (1987 Photo: Brian Wilson collection)

A few year later for a surprise birthday present, my wife had the Gourmet Gala plaque and a copy of the stained original recipe framed. To this day, it hangs in our kitchen.

**As an extra-added surprise bonus for investing in this book, I've included a copy of the original recipe to try. At your own risk, of course!*

BRIAN WILSON'S AWARD-WINNING AUTHENTIC HOT DAMN CHILI

Parts:

3 lbs Venison* plus Secret Ingredient (revealed later)
2 lbs Ground Round
9 oz Kraft BBQ sauce (Original Flavor)
16 oz Tomato Sauce
10 oz Water
1/2 lb Mushrooms, sliced
2 Red Bell Peppers, sliced
2 Green Bell Peppers, sliced
2 Tomatoes, large dice
2 Onions, large dice
5-6 Jalapenos, sliced
1/2 bottle Chili Powder
(see notes)
1/2 bottle Cayenne
(see notes)
1-2 Tbs Cumin
5 shakes of Oregano
5 shakes of Garlic Powder
Several Tbs of Flour
Sharp Cheddar Cheese
Scallions
Sour Cream

Notes:
**Stew beef if deer season is closed, you missed your shot or you're a wimp-a-zoid about eating wild game.*

McCormick Chili Power and Cayenne, use ½ of the large bottle size.

Assembly:

Two days before assembly, cut meat to bite size chunks and layer in a Pyrex baking dish or similar. Add Secret Ingredient (equal parts of Worcestershire, Soy and Teriyaki sauces) to nearly cover the meat. Cover with plastic wrap and refrigerate.

The Big Day:

Slice Tomatoes into eighths
Slice Red and Green Peppers and Onions into bite-sized pieces
Slice Jalapeno Peppers to quarter-inch pieces

Secure a LARGE pot. Set burner to Medium.

Add water, tomato sauce, BBQ sauce, all the spices and all the peppers, tomatoes and onions. Stir and ignore.

Cover the bottom of a large fry pan with a light coating of olive oil. Set burner to Medium High. Scoop enough meat and marinade into pan to cover bottom. This is just a quick sear, you're not cooking the meat.As soon as most of the sides are brown, dump everything into aforementioned cauldron. Repeat. If there is any marinade left, pour that in, too.

Brown/drain Ground Round and add to pot. Do a quick sauté of the mushrooms in some butter and add to the mess.

Cover and bring pot to a rolling boil, then reduce heat to Medium Low. Go find something to do for an hour or so. After about 30 minutes, one good stir is permissible otherwise, no peeking.

Cut the heat to Off and let stand for 10 to 15 minutes. Skim off any excess oil/fat from surface.

Mix sufficient flour and water to make a paste and stir in to thicken. This is a subjective determination. We're not creating

Super Glue here but the finished product should not have the consistency of soup either.

You're done, but it's not ready to eat. For best results, let it sit covered for 3 to 4 hours.

Serve in bowls. Top with Shredded Sharp Cheddar Cheese, Chopped Scallions and Sour Cream.

Story Thirteen

FANTASY ISLAND

As I've mentioned in other stories, phone calls from listeners used to be spontaneous and exciting, like the original **Candid Camera** show -- no one knew what to expect. This story combines all the excitement of unscreened phone calls with the pre-recorded but still wild world of radio promotions.

No doubt you've heard a DJ say, "Be the tenth caller at 555-WOO-HOOO and you could win ten billion dollars and the backstage passes!" Of course, all this hype is meant to attract as many listeners to the station as possible during the all-important semi-annual Arbitron rating periods, lovingly referred to as the fall and spring "Books." The numbers generated by these ratings serve as a guideline to time buyers at ad agencies. In the bigger markets, your favorite DJ or talk show host could also see a nice bump in the old paycheck if he was smart enough to get a "ratings bonus" in his contract – and actually *increase* the ratings!

Over the years I was a part of some of the dumbest contests and radio promotions to ever hit the airwaves. The **Meet Your Neighbor** and **Sorry Wrong Number** games are just two of the beautiful losers that come to mind (see **Dumb Radio Contests**).

In 1977, the **Ross and Wilson** radio missile achieved lift-off, moving from AM Drive at WJBO/Baton Rouge to AM Drive at Z-93/Atlanta. At the time, Z-93 was owned by the Marriott folks of hotel fame. Despite their big bux, they were notoriously cheap when it came to station promotion. Why? I have no clue. Certainly, it was in their financial interest for the station to do well, yet typical promotional items such as billboards, TV spots, T-shirts, even the lowly bumper sticker were assiduously eschewed by the Suits at First Media, Corp.

Here's an example of just how cheap the company was: the big promotion to announce our Atlanta arrival involved the rental of a Winnebago, hoisted about 100 feet over a 24-hour Burger King parking lot, with **Ross and Wilson** inside. On air, we invited listeners to come by, say hello and buy something from Burger King. A portion of the proceeds would go to the Make-A-Wish foundation.

Even in 1978, this was pretty damn stupid. First, the *only* place the promotion was heard was on Z-93, so those listening to our competitors were not challenged to leave their customary station and come to Z-93 to hear us! That's the whole idea of a "promotion" – *get new listeners.*

It also was dumb to think people would be motivated to come by to see a Winnebago dangling in the air with two idiots' heads poking out a window, yelling down to people in the parking lot. How exciting is that? Mostly it was just embarrassing.

By the way, we had to stay in that damned Winnebago from Saturday morning until Sunday afternoon. The answer to all the questions you're asking right now is, "YES!"

Along with receiving *zero* television coverage or any mention in the in the Atlanta newspapers, it's safe to say the dangling Winnebago promotion ranks right up there with **WKRP in Cincinnati's Turkey Drop**.

Another Z-93 promotion which actually worked out really well was the **Ross and Wilson Bunch for Lunch**. The station traded-out a lunch for 12 with a local restaurant. Monday through Wednesday, we would take the names of callers selected for any variety of weird, dumb or funny things they said, and award the caller and a companion lunch with us on Thursday. This gave us the opportunity to meet and greet listeners upfront, close and personal and chat with them. This can be a great way to keep a listener for life -- assuming you're not a slobbering moron.

In the spring of 1979, our GM, Bud Polacek told us the Mother Ship had actually given him some money to spend for the Spring Book! All we needed was a promotion! By then, Top 40 listeners in major markets had become accustomed to hearing about winning a new car, a trip to Disney World or some other big cash prize. All you had to do was "be the tenth caller…." etc.

I always had a big problem with contests like these. They were boring. And they only attracted what DJs lovingly called Contest Pigs, people who only listened to win prizes. Statistics showed only ten percent of the most active listeners participate in a radio contest, unless it was something truly unique or they really wanted. Despite the attraction of a new car, a trip to Disney World or big money, audience-attracting results were not getting the bang for the buck. Plus, listeners found them boring, too. Their chances of winning were the same as today's lotteries.

I came up with a different idea -- unique, compelling *and* subsequently so successful -- the GM praised it as the biggest, best and most original radio promotion he had ever heard. The spike in numbers we received in the Spring Book was superb, because we trounced our cross-town arch rival.

I called it the **Fantasy Island** contest. I don't know if we violated any copyright laws with the name, but the essence of the idea came from the TV show. Why not borrow the name? As popular as the show was, it would make the contest damn near self-explanatory!

Here's the way it worked:

Listeners had to write, in 25 words or less, the fantasy they wanted us to fulfill for them. We'd choose the winners, read the fantasies on the air and call them with the good news for a rousing reaction. What the audience didn't know was those phone calls would be pre-recorded for a spontaneous response – the high point of the contest – *then* we would read the fantasy on air and play back the recording. Even "passive" listeners not participating in the contest would want to hear how **Fantasy Island** played out when we called.

In my pitch to the GM, GSM, and PD, I told them we could use the company's promotional money along with trade-outs to get 20 or so great prizes. It was a slam-dunk that we would receive lots of requests for trips to Walt Disney World and new cars, along with less glitzy items for those who would surely write in with stories about parents who never had a honeymoon, grandmothers who never had a washing machine or an uncle who never had clean underwear.

Management went for it big time. The next Thursday morning on the show, we kicked off the **Ross and Wilson Fantasy Island Contest**, telling listeners to get their 25 words or less in the mail immediately if not sooner (remember, we only had snail mail in 1979).

On the Monday morning after that show, we were disappointed to see a whopping 18 entry letters had trickled in. Actually one of them was not too shabby. The sales weasels immediately started having second thoughts. The next three days changed their minds. On Tuesday, the USPS delivered an entire duffel bag of entries. Wednesday, two more arrived. Thursday three more were dropped off.

There was so much mail to go through, everyone in the station was recruited to sit in the conference room, open envelopes, read the "25 words or less" and save the best.

One of the first winners was a guy who wrote how he had been a total loser in high school but had since done pretty well for himself in the insurance biz. His high school reunion was coming up and he had asked his old high school girlfriend, still single, living in Nashville, to be his date. His fantasy was for us to rent a Mercedes for him to pick her up at the airport, and reserve a suite at the Hyatt Regency Hotel in case things went better than expected!

When I called him off the air to tell him his fantasy had been granted, he damn near blew out the station phone system! He was beyond ecstatic. And LOUD! But that's what you want on a phone call to the winner!

Here's what the audience heard on the air: Ross introducing the **Ross and Wilson Fantasy Island Contest**, my reading of a winning letter and, "Let's give old Furd Burfal a call and tell him we are granting his Fantasy!" Then we hit the recording of the earlier call. The audience heard me dialing, the phone ringing, the winner answering and receiving the good news. Since the audience didn't know the call was pre-recorded, it sounded as if it was happening in the moment. And that's what made the promotion exciting and compelling for the listener who might rarely play a radio game but would listen for the fun of it.

The most memorable call -- and the reason I've included this story -- came as a result of a letter from a 14 year old girl who said she was writing for her little sister, ten years old, who wanted a bicycle. Not just any bicycle -- a *special* one that could be peddled with her hands. Her sister was born with spina bifida and her legs didn't work well enough to pedal a bike.

I knew we had to do this. The trips to Disney World, the Mercedes for the dude's reunion, etc. were all grins 'n giggles, but this one was special. Regardless of showbiz shtick, performers are occasionally human, too -- even Top 40 DJs. The **Fantasy Island** promotion and this girl's letter gave us the opportunity to show the station and ourselves in a different light doing something great for this ten year old.

The fact that my parents' first child, Katharine, was born with spina bifida and died two days later played a small part in getting this done.

There were only two companies in the world that made hand-pedal bicycles in 1979. One was in Germany; the other in Arizona. Unfortunately, time, money and red tape were against us. Even big-time DJs in Atlanta couldn't do everything, like getting a bike shipped from Germany in less than two weeks. But the good news was that we sometimes had connections with people who *could.* In this case, it was Phil Niekro, the famous knuckleballer for the Atlanta Braves. Phil, whom we had gotten to know from appearing together at various functions around Atlanta, was the celebrity chair of the Atlanta Spina Bifida Association. I called him with our problem and bingo! One hand-peddled girl's bike with all the trimmings was on the way!

The morning came to make the call to the 14 year old who wrote her little sister's fantasy. When she answered the phone I was immediately disappointed. After two weeks, other winners had gone ballistic when they heard me say, "Good morning! It's **Ross and Wilson** at Z-93..." Immediately they knew they had won and the fireworks began. Not this morning.

Hello…

Good morning! May I speak with Mary, please?

A soft voice answered.

This is Mary…

In my typical DJ basso profundo:

Mary! Good Morning! This is Ross and Wilson at Z-93!"

In the same soft voice:

Oh… hello.

I was bummed. Of all our winners, I had expected a 14-year-old girl to go screaming and yelling and laughing and dancing for at least a couple of minutes!

Not Mary.

I thought maybe she hadn't understood me.

> *Yes Mary, this is Brian Wilson at Z-93 with the Fantasy Island Contest! I'm calling to tell you we got your letter and we're going to make your fantasy come true! We're getting your little sister the bicycle you asked for! How about that?*

In the same soft, nonplussed voice:

> *That's nice. Thank you.*

I guess this wasn't going to be the big dramatic radio phone call event I had hoped for.

> *OK Mary, well, we have your address and phone number and as soon as the bicycle arrives in the next couple days, we'll call you and your folks to arrange delivery. OK?*

In that same soft voice:

> *OK. My sister, Tamara, is right here. Can she ask you something?*

> *Sure, yes, of course!*

She had her sister's voice.

> *Hello?*

> *Hi – is this Tamara?*

> *Yes.*

> *Well this is Brian Wilson on the Ross and Wilson Show at Z-93, Tamara – and, I don't know if you know, but your sister Mary just won you that special bicycle you wanted, the one you can pedal with your hands. How about that?*

> *That's nice. Can I ask you something?*

> *Sure, anything…*

> *Could I please get a basket on it so I can carry my crutches?*

That was the last thing I expected. It took a couple seconds to manage a response.

> *Of course! A basket! A basket it is, Tamara. We will most definitely take care of that.*
>
> *OK. Thank you. Goodbye.*

And she hung up!

I found out later the only dry eyes in Atlanta that morning belonged to those who were not listening. The audience response was overwhelming. Even the sales weasels were thrilled! The **Atlanta Journal-Constitution** gave it a mention, even one of the TV stations ran the audio in their evening news.

I've made or taken thousands of calls in 50 years, but this one had everything that showed how Radio makes *Magic.*

Story Fourteen

THIS WAS CNN

You would think that with more than 50 years in broadcasting in some of the nation's largest markets on some notorious heritage stations, I would have been part of at least one memorable event that had a major impact on the world of showbiz. As a matter of fact, I did -- not just once but three times! The first happened on May 23, 1980, in Atlanta. As **Atlanta Journal-Constitution** columnist Dick Williams dutifully reported under blazing headlines:

> **Ross and Wilson Joining in Turner's Cable News**
>
> *Ross and Wilson, Z-93's sassy and pointed morning men, will join Cable News Network as teen news jockeys every afternoon. Reese Schonfeld, CNN president, said: "Brian Wilson and Ross Brittain will appear each half-hour between 3 p.m. and 6 p.m. reviewing records, talking to kids about their favorite music and reporting personality items on rock stars and teen idols." It's "American Bandstand" come to the news channel. News jockeys will pump out the headlines while Ross and Wilson pump out the hits. Cable News Network starts services June 1 at 6 p.m.*

To say we were stoked would be an understatement!

Here's the way it worked:

Every Wednesday afternoon, Ross and I would meet at CNN HQ, still under construction in the basement of an old country club, the birthing chamber for CNN (sometimes referred to as "Tara on Techwood"). While carpenters and electricians banged and drilled in the background, the writers, producers, cameramen, videotape editors and news anchors all would scurry about amongst makeshift cubicles and anchor desks. For anyone watching in those early days, it would not have been unusual to see two guys in overalls carrying 2x4s right through the set where two anchors were *live* with the latest news. Old-school TV news types were shocked SHOCKED! to see such travesties! The rest of us took it in stride, actually appreciating the air of spontaneity that came with being the new kid on the block and, under the circumstances, we could get away with it! Ah, the Ted Turner entrepreneurial spirit writ large!

But I digress…

Prior to our arrival, we assembled the essentials of whatever was happening in pop music, movies, concerts and pop culture in general. Our job was to tape ten five-minute segments of this stuff; each one new, different and remarkably entertaining.

Not a problem.

I think it was our reputation for never doing anything "straight" that impressed head honcho, Reese Schonfeld. In our initial chats, he made it clear he understood and, therefore we understood, we were under no obligation to act anything like the seasoned "news anchors" who surrounded us. But whatever we did, it had to be over in five minutes flat.

Of course, we didn't have a "set" per se. Two three-legged bar stools in the middle of a rare empty space, more or less alongside the enclosed Control Room with something resembling a cocktail table between us screamed NO FRILLS or, maybe NO BUDGET! We were allotted one teleprompter-equipped camera, a cameraman and a floor director. With that, I think we were costing more than Reese had budgeted! My name for this new feature: **Ross and Wilson's Music Notes**. Cutting-edge humor in 1980!

Once we had all our topics and relevant information kinda/sorta typed up for the teleprompter, we would assume our positions perched on the barstools and proceed -- all ten segments, back-to-back, all in one sitting.

And don't fail to remember, we were subject to the same traffic of carpenters, electricians, dead trees and interns that plagued the hard news folks.

So now we were ready to roll, except for one thing -- that secret ingredient, that unexpected, indefinable whatever-it-was "thing" that would convert a boring, vanilla reporting of showbiz news into something irreverent, scintillating and spontaneous; something uniquely **Ross and Wilson**.

I took care of that with a red telephone, sitting on the table between us. This would become known as the Rumor Phone, our "hotline for breaking news from an anonymous source, deep inside the record business." Of course, the phone wasn't connected to anything, had no wires and couldn't ring. Nevertheless, even though we weren't technically-advanced enough for sound effects, through the wonders of "Theater of the Mind," a call would manage to come in the middle of almost every segment, interrupting the flow of fluff news. Of course, unheard by the audience, our anonymous source -- code name Deep Note -- provided us with the rumor du jour. I would always answer the phone while Ross continued reciting the minutia of the day's news.

Depending upon time remaining in each segment, after a sufficient number of off-mic "WHAT?" "NO!" "REALLY?" "WHERE?" comments, I would hang up the phone and interrupt

Brian on Rumor Phone with Deep Note (1980 Photo: Brian Wilson collection)

Ross with the urgent, late-breaking, inside, totally confidential rumor involving some famous recording star and some nonsensical, improbable rumor; the more outrageous the better. Of course, there had to be an element of truth in every rumor for credible humor. Creating this controlled insanity was never a problem; it was just an extension of the same type of chaos that peppered our Z-93 morning drive show. Eventually, a small crowd would gather behind the camera for our taping sessions and provide a much appreciated spontaneous laugh track to the Rumor Phone segment.

Unfortunately, our most popular-running gag proved to be the demise of **Music Notes**.

If you were around in the late 70s, you may recall recurring real-life rumors about a Beatles reunion. Hardly a week went by without some aspect of the negotiations in the news. Invariably, however, something happened that caused one or more of the Fab Four, in many cases John Lennon w/Yoko Ono, to call it off. After days or weeks of silence, rumors again would begin surfacing that some reconciliation or accommodation had been reached and plans for the concert were on again. More days or weeks and another rumor would surface, torpedoing the latest efforts. Naturally, this provided a target rich environment for **Music Notes**, the Rumor Phone, and Deep Note. Every week or two, Deep Note provided interruptions about the "oft-rumored, on-again-off-again Beatles reunion concert" to keep pace with the real news.

Remember, all ten **Music Notes** segments were recorded on a Wednesday afternoon, *one week in advance of their airing.*

Then came December 8, the Monday evening John Hinckley murdered John Lennon. If you were in Music Radio at the time, there was no other story anywhere else in the world. On Wednesday, when we went to record **Music Notes**, we were handed our termination notice. No explanation. Just the note and a severance check.

It was weeks before we found out why.

Remarkably, John Lennon and Yoko Ono were big CNN fans. If they were awake, CNN was on, or so the story went. Knowing this, one of the senior CNN editors with some serious connections had arranged to tape an exclusive interview with Yoko Ono on that Wednesday. All the preparations had been made: lights, two cameras, director and reporter in the Lennon apartment with Yoko. CNN was on; no mention had been made to anyone other than the necessary technical people this taping was taking place.

Mere minutes before the interview was to begin, **Ross and Wilson's Music Notes** came on the screen. Shortly into the segment, what should appear but the "spontaneous" interruption of Deep Note on the Rumor Phone with news of the "oft-rumored, on-again-off-again, Beatles reunion concert." This time, the concert plans had been canceled due to an objection from Yoko Ono, complaining she didn't have a big enough part. In the silence of the apartment, preparing to tape the exclusive interview, the segment was heard loud and clear by all. Ms. Ono was not amused -- unless "furious" could be considered amusing.

That was the end of the exclusive interview that never happened; a giant coup of an interview that would have helped propel CNN from relative obscurity to worldwide notoriety. Of course, we were blamed for the debacle and summarily dismissed.

Prior to sealing the WABC deal, on a couple flights I made from the Big Peach to the Big Apple, Ted Turner was on board; we sat together in first class and discussed -- or rather he discussed -- the state of affairs in the world of broadcasting. Based on those times along with some other occasions (and our hosting of his celebrity roast) I didn't hesitate to put in a call to him to clear our names. Not surprisingly, he did not take or return my call -- or any of the other three I made later.

In the beginning, all the independent contractors supplying programming elements for CNN were called "Contributors." We were in good company: Barry Goldwater, Dr. Joyce Brothers, Ralph Nader and Daniel Schorr. Several years ago I saw a book on the history of CNN that listed the names of all the anchors, reporters, directors and contributors. It must have been edited by Winston Smith inasmuch as **Ross and Wilson Music Notes** was not listed. But we *were* there and made a serious mark on CNN history – just not one approved by certain historians through no fault of our own.

With apologies to Paul Harvey, now you know the rest of the story.

Story Fifteen

ANOTHER ONE BITES THE DUST

Everyone in this business wants to be famous. We want big audiences, big ratings and big recognition from our peers and everyone else for our talent, performances and accomplishments. Recognition and admiration are our currency. If we get them at all, we get them the old-fashioned way: *we earn it.* But sometimes all that notoriety can be inflicted upon us, and not in a good way. This story is a true, perfect and immortal example of a bad joke that morphed into fake news that would never die.

The "Atlanta child murders" as they came to be known, occurred from mid-1979 to 1981. It was a huge, grisly story that dominated the news for the last two years the **Ross and Wilson Show** aired on Z-93. Due to their hard-core content, other than part of our regular newscasts, we didn't deal with them; we were there for music and good times.

I first heard the "joke" one evening in November 1980 when the WABC/NY deal was warming up behind the scenes. I had gone to Timothy John's, a hot little nightclub in Sandy Springs. **Banks and Shane** played there regularly, as they were that night. A listener recognized me at the bar, came over and said:

> *Hey! Did you hear that song* ***Another One Bites the Dust*** *was written for all those black kids who were murdered? Ha-ha-ha!*
>
> *Yeah, that's a real knee-slapper.*

And I left him with his beers.

Four months later in Manhattan, relaxing in the ABC Suite at the Waldorf Astoria, basking in the glow of our rise to the number one station in the number one radio market in the entire world, the phone rang. I answered:

> *Waldorf Astoria, Ross and Wilson suite, how may I help you in some small, insignificant way?*

That got a laugh on the other end from Bill King, a media columnist for the **Atlanta Journal-Constitution**. Bill had written several complimentary articles about us during our Z-93 years.

Our conversation went something like this:

> *BK: Hi Brian, Bill King. How are things in New York City?*

> *BW: It's a lovely day in the Big Apple, Bill! How are things in the Big Peach?*

> *BK: Nice day here, too. Listen, I'm calling to find out if you're aware of the rumor that's been going around town about why you and Ross left Z-93.*

> *BW: Rumor? What rumor?*

> *BK: People say you guys were fired from Z-93 for playing Queen's* ***Another One Bites the Dust*** *and dedicating it to Atlanta's murdered and missing kids.*

I came out of the chair on that one.

> *BW: WHAT? Who is spreading that bullshit?*

> *BK: Well I don't know who started it, but everybody's talking about it. For the record I have to ask you, is it true?*

> *BW: Bill, you know us better than that!*

> *BK: Yes, I do. But as much as I loved you guys, I didn't listen to every minute of every show every day, so I guess it could have happened and I just didn't hear it.*

BW: Well, thanks for that personal endorsement. I would've thought you'd have known automatically. That's hardly our brand of humor.

BK: Look, Brian, don't shoot the messenger; I'm just calling to get you guys on the record for the story.

BW: OK, here's everything I know: I heard that crap from some drunk at Timothy John's; he told it to me as a joke back before Thanksgiving. I made it clear I didn't share his bigoted sense of humor. And that was it. I never saw him or heard the comment again. You're the first person to mention it since then.

Also, our debatable on-air taste and maturity aside, it would have been absolutely impossible for that to happen on our show anyway. ***Another One Bites the Dust*** *was day-parted out of Morning Drive so it wasn't even available to us to play. Second, remember that John Young was not only our news guy but the program director. Had we pulled a dumb stunt like that, he would have -- and should have -- fired us on the spot and done the rest of the show himself. And finally, does anyone with half a brain really think we would've been hired by WABC to do Morning Drive in the largest radio market in the world if Z-93 had canned us for a tasteless, bigoted stunt like that? You can quote me on all of that, Bill. It never happened.*

BK: Brian, I didn't believe it for a minute but you know I had to call and ask.

BW: Got it. Thanks for your diligence and professionalism. I hope you get it printed in all caps.

He laughed.

BK: I'll see what I can do. Good luck. Bye.

I gave Ross the gist of Bill's end of the conversation. We talked about it for a few minutes, speculating unsuccessfully on who may have connected us to such a racist joke -- and came up empty.

Everyone in the media who made a comment was both complementary and supportive of our success. Even the GM at the "other station."

I believe the story ran in the **AJC** the very next day and that was it, for about a day. After a flurry of calls from reporters in and out of the broadcast biz, Atlanta friends and acquaintances, even a gentle inquiry from WABC's GM, Al Racco who heard about it from the head of an ad agency in Atlanta, the story died a natural death.

Or so I thought.

For the next several years -- *yes, years* -- you would be amazed and astounded at the number of times and remarkable circumstances that story came back to haunt me. Here's one example:

In 1991, after reuniting with Ross at Z100 for the **Ross and Wilson Z-Morning Zoo**, a full ten years after the Bill King interview, I was flying back to Manhattan from Atlanta and got into a conversation with the guy sitting next to me. It didn't take long before we got around to the "What you do for a living" questions. He was Ted, a purchasing agent for Georgia-Pacific. My colorful career in radio taught me at times like this, it's best to shy away from telling people my full name or occupation, especially when confined to an airplane or other close quarters where immediate escape was impossible. I told him my name was Brian and I was a backward electronics engineer of sorts. It was mostly true; I occasionally operated electronic equipment. I just left out the *broadcasting* part.

Over the next hour or so, we talked about living in Atlanta, restaurants, SEC football, the Braves, the Varsity, CNN and Ted Turner. As we started the final approach into Newark, out of nowhere the guy says:

> *T: So you live in New York City now?*
>
> *BW: Yes, I do.*

T: Did you ever hear of Ross and Wilson on WABC? They used to be on in the morning in Atlanta on Z-93.

BW: Yeah, I heard them a few times down there; I catch them once in a while here on Z100.

T: Did you know they were fired from Z-93 for playing ***Another One Bites the Dust*** *and dedicating it to the murdered and missing black kids back then?*

BW: Really? How did that happen?

T: I don't know all the details exactly, but I was listening one morning and they played ***Another One Bites the Dust*** *and at the end, the one guy says, "This is dedicated to all the murdered and missing kids here in Atlanta!" And the other guy laughs and the next day they were gone. Then there was the story in the newspaper that they had been hired up here at WABC.*

BW: Really? Wow. So you actually heard them play the song and make the dedication when it was over?

T: Yep. I damn near drove off the road!

BW: Yeah… I'll bet.

By now, we were at the gate and people were starting the scrum to collect themselves and de-plane. Having the aisle seat in first class, there was a bit more room to maneuver. I stood, retrieved my briefcase from the overhead and looked down at Ted.

BW: Well, Ted, I enjoyed our chat.

T: Yeah, me too.

BW: Except for that last part -- you know, the bullshit about Ross and Wilson getting fired for playing ***Another One Bites the Dust****.*

T: What do you mean bullshit?

> *BW: I didn't mention my last name. It's Wilson. Brian Wilson. As in Ross Brittain and Brian Wilson. And I was there for every show we ever did. You never heard it because it never happened. It's all a lie. And you know it.*

Like the old MasterCard commercial line, the look on his face was "priceless."

And that's just one example. Despite repeated confirmation in subsequent media interviews with PD John Young, GM Bud Polacek and several Z-93 sales weasels all there at the same time, the story would not die. As of this writing, it's been 37 years but I would make a sizeable wager you could easily find 100 people in Atlanta who would say they remember it! Heard it with their own ears! Or they knew someone who knew someone who knew someone who said they heard it! Just Google **Ross and Wilson** and **Another One Bites the Dust**!

Everyone in this business wants to be a legend, immortalized in the annals of radio for (insert accomplishment here). Actually, I have some of those "merit badges." They just haven't achieved quite the same notoriety as the outright lie about **Another One Bites the Dust**!

Story Sixteen

BEING BRIAN WILSON

It can be fun having a famous name when you're only nearly-famous.

Sometimes.

It shouldn't be hard to imagine with the huge popularity of the Beach Boys in the early 60s. Still, after landing my first radio gig in 1965, it was another four years before anyone – including myself! – made the connection.

1969, and my third day on KXYZ/Houston.

ABC had just purchased the AM/FM combo. Most staff members were new to the station and the market. After our first air staff meeting, the AM Drive guy (whose name must remain anonymous) came up to me:

> *Say, you're Brian Wilson, right?*
>
> *That's me!*
>
> *Love your show, man! You are really good!*
>
> *Thanks.*
>
> *And I really love your music!*

I said thanks again, thinking he was referring to my on-air mix of tunes.

> *Ya know, I was wondering… I don't want to be an idiot… you probably get this all the time, but I have to ask you… I've written a few tunes myself and I was wondering if one day after your show, would you come over to the house for dinner and give a listen? Whaddaya think? Would that be OK?*

It took a second to hit me. Wait! He thinks I'm *Brian Wilson* – as in Brian Wilson of the Beach Boys! Then a second thought -- *what an idiot*! What the hell would the Beach Boy Brian Wilson be doing as a DJ in Houston? In money alone, *that* BW was making more in a week from concerts and royalties than I made in a month. Maybe a year!

But, all of us were just getting started here and to laugh in his face would have been rude. Radio was hard enough on the ego to go around making enemies out of simple mistakes. Even not so simple mistakes!

> *Yeah, sure. We're still unpacking, but we'll work something out.*

You would have thought he had finally gotten his pony for Christmas!

> *OH WOW! GREAT! Thanks! My wife will freak out!*

Because of our AM/PM shifts, we didn't see each other for a few weeks until the next regularly scheduled staff meeting – where he avoided me like the Plague! Guess he did a little research or had a chat with his wife and discovered there was more than one person on the radio named *Brian Wilson*.

The incident gave me the idea, though, to take advantage of sharing the name of a superstar. Whenever I did play a Beach Boys record, I would intro or back-sell it with: "**Good Vibrations**, me and the Beach Boys! Wrote that one back in '66 just before the sandbox days -- always been proud of that one!" or something similar. Eventually, some people in the audience who were paying attention caught on and the legend grew!

Despite some great reactions from listeners calling in, nothing stupendous happened between Houston, Baton Rouge and Atlanta; it was on WABC/NY when it came around again.

I was still doing the occasional, "Wrote that song back in…" bit after a BB tune; Ross played his role to deny it and we'd make it through to the next big thing, not wanting to beat the bit to death. And "death" is what almost killed it when Dennis Wilson drowned at Marina Del Rey in 1983. The morning it was on WABC news, a woman from Brooklyn called in. After the usual pleasantries, she said:

> *I just wanted to call and tell you how sorry I am, hearing about the death of your brother, Dennis and to let you know I'll be saying a novena for him today.*

Uh-oh.

> *Well… um… that's… ah… very kind of you. I know the family will appreciate that. Thank-you-so-much-for-calling-goodbye… we'll-be-right-back.*

No more callers!

Nothing more was ever said about it – not management, the news department or any subsequent callers. It wasn't a disaster, just a moment that could have been embarrassing to the caller who was just making a kind gesture.

Humor can be dangerous!

Some weeks later, I took a few out-of-town friends to lunch at Tavern on the Green which is always crowded. As I approached the hostess's station, she smiled and said:

> *Good afternoon - How many in your party?*
>
> *Four.*

Do you have a reservation?

No, we don't.

They'll be a short wait… may I have your name?

Brian Wilson.

As she wrote my name down, a waiter standing nearby snapped a look in my direction, stepped briskly up the young woman, leaned over and whispered in her ear with a noticeable head-jerk in my direction. The hostess looked up with that deer-in-the-headlights look, did a double-take at the list, flashed a bigger than big smile and said: I'm so sorry, Mr. Wilson – I see your table is ready and waiting… will you follow me, please?

Celebrity Privilege.

These things happened with irregular frequency as markets came and went, but none measured up to that time in Sacramento.

After several fill-ins for Tom Sullivan on KFBK, the station suddenly had a full-time opening. The PD flew me out for the big interview, tour of the station, the town, dinner and the Really Big Talk.

He sent a limo to pick me up at the airport, always a nice touch. I arrived at the "hotel," not far from the iconic State Capitol building. I put "hotel" in quotes because it didn't look much like a hotel; more like a large and very classy B&B. Suitcase in hand, I went it in.

A short hall led to the front desk. Behind it, a 30-something guy with "Jeffery" on his name tag, greeted me:

J: Good afternoon, sir; welcome to the Bltzcsfx Hotel. May I help you?

BW: Yes, I have reservations -- they're under KFBK Radio.

J: Yes – for two nights. Would you mind filling this out? I'll also need a credit card for any incidentals the station may not be covering.

I put my American Express gold card on the counter. Jeffery glanced at the card as he started to turn – then froze, turned back and stared at me…

J: You're… Brian Wilson?

BW: If that's the name on the card, I guess that's me.

He was clearly flustered.

J: Are… uh… are you here… uh… for a radio station function at KFBK?

BW: Well, yeah. That's why they flew me in.

J: Oh! Of course! Well… I… um…. it's a GREAT pleasure to have you staying with us!

I had him at the credit card freeze -- another one who thought I was *THE* Brian Wilson. And this was California!

He handed my card back without running it, saying the hotel would gladly comp anything the station didn't cover. He then whipped around the counter, grabbed my bag and headed for the sole elevator across the lobby:

J: Please let me show to you your room.

BW: Sure, thanks.

J: I can't tell you what a pleasure it is to finally meet you. Will you be doing something with KFBK?

BW: Well, let's hope so. That's what I'm here to discuss.

J: Will you be doing a concert here?

BW: It wouldn't be prudent for me to discuss anything like that at this point.

> *J: Oh, yes, I totally understand! Totally! I wasn't trying to pry! Please forgive me!*

As we arrived at the room, he opened the door and led me into perfectly acceptable accommodations, then froze again.

> *J: Oh, my! Oh no! This can't be right. This can't be your room. I do apologize, Mr. Wilson. I must have been distracted. Please, follow me!*

Off we went, down the hall, around the corner to a short hall to a door.

> *J:* ***THIS*** *is your room, Mr. Wilson!*

The door opened to a room the size of small airplane hangar; the bed could have qualified for foreign aid. Jeffery busied himself adjusting the curtains, revealing the courtyard view; I checked out the bathroom. The enclosed shower must have been a carwash in a previous life.

> *I do hope you'll be comfortable here, Mr. Wilson and I apologize for the earlier mistake. If there's anything you need, Mr. Wilson, my name is Jeffery, just call the Front Desk. I'll be here all day today and tomorrow.*

How could the entire Osmond family not be comfortable here?

I slipped him $10 for lugging the suitcase and the gratuitous simpering as he bowed and scraped his way out the door.

When I checked out two days later, Jeffery avoided me as if my middle name was Ebola.

Easily the most remarkable and embarrassing incident took place during one of my regular trips to KSFO/SF. PD Jack Swanson would fly me out two or three times a year for promotional Meet & Greets, etc. to demonstrate to sponsors, audience and station personnel there actually was a body that went with the voice from the Right Coast. I'd also get to hang with immortals Lee Rodgers,

Melanie Morgan, Officer Vic (Tom Benner), Geoff Metcalf and producer extraordinaire, Sheri Yee.

Cassie and I took advantage of being on the Left Coast to pay another visit to a few of our favorite Napa Valley wineries and renew an old acquaintance. A guy with whom I attended prep school in Connecticut had heard the show and emailed me: "Could you be the same Brian Wilson I went to school with back in the Dark Ages?" In fact, Bruce Gammill and I had rooms in the same dorm! Small world.

After we established contact, I learned he was in some lofty area of international finance, living in Napa and just for grins and giggles, had a part-time job as a "greeter" at the Beaulieu Vineyards Tasting Room. What great news! BV is one of our all-time favorites grape juices!

Arrangements were made to meet at BV Saturday afternoon. I recognized him immediately and vice versa despite the years in-between; Laurel and Hardy handshakes all around! After a brief catch-up and agreement to have dinner that evening, Bruce invited us to the Heritage Room where one could sample BV's premium wines.

The posh surroundings were reserved for those who would regularly enjoy and purchase substantial quantities for large dollars. This was *heaven* for your amateur oenophile!

While enjoying sips of reserve chardonnay, Bruce said he had mentioned our visit to a high-up manager. Not only was she "thrilled to have a celebrity visiting BV," she also had mentioned it to her husband who went bonkers! She said her husband was the "ultimate Brian Wilson fan" and had invited himself along to meet The Great He.

OK, it happens. Some of the beauty of radio (now passé) is it often created ardent followers. The anonymity of the person behind the personality produced the perpetual curiosity, "What does he look like?" For some listeners, a radio personality could be close to god-like.

Bruce relayed the "fan" information mere minutes before the BV manager arrived with hubby in tow. Things quickly became uncomfortable.

She gave an effusive welcome and introduced her husband. If Mrs. BV manager had been excited, this dude was orgasmic! "*SOOOO* happy to finally meet you! So much an admirer of your work! Been a fan for years! Always dreamed of the opportunity to meet, etc." ad nauseam.

Every DJ, talk show host, news anchor, weatherman and on-air talent enjoys recognition and compliments. Approval and appreciation for work done invisibly with little opportunity for standing O's magnifies the value of the compliment. But this guy was over the top. OK, I was a talk show host on a very popular San Francisco station, but this was getting out of control.

Then I found out why:

> *May I ask you a question?"*
>
> *Absolutely not! This is a no-questions zone!*

He was immediately taken aback, totally missing my often-missed sarcasm.

> *Oh, I'm so sorry…*
>
> *Hey! Chill! I'm just yankin' your lariat. What's the question?*

He was visibly relieved.

> *Oh! OK, thanks! Well… I've always wanted to know how you do it! How do you come up with those great songs, like* **Good Vibrations, Surfer Girl, Little Old Lady from Pasadena** *– how do you do that? They're all so wonderful and yet so different! It's an amazing talent! How does it happen?*

His wife's face had the same wide-eyed look of eager anticipation of the answer.

Whoa! These folks *also* thought I was the *OTHER* Brian Wilson.

Bruce's face was showing signs of embarrassment, along with a tinge of fear and a soupçon of dread!

As noted earlier, over the years I had developed a glib immunity to the mistaken identification, but the stakes were never this high. I didn't want to embarrass Bruce; he had no idea his uber-boss and her mate had so screwed the pooch! It was logical they should have thought I was just who I was -- a KSFO talk show host. After heaping such a welcome upon us, correcting them would have made them look like adolescent groupies and adult fools. My only choice was to play along as I always did, figure they would miss the sarcasm (again) and we could move on to wine talk.

> *Well, that's hard to say, exactly. The source of creativity is as indefinable as any other intangible. Sometimes it's a memory; other times a fantasy; still other times a hangover!*

Laughter all around. The big question asked and answered. Let's move on.

After several more fawning compliments, that's exactly what we did.

Except…

The BV manager asked:

> *Where are you staying this evening?*

> *Oh, we'll drive back to town after dinner with Bruce. The station has a room for us at the….*

She interrupted in major-management tones:

> *No! I won't hear of it! I insist you be our guest at the Beaulieu Vineyards guest house. We will have dinner and you won't have to subject yourself to the time and traffic back to San Francisco.*

Now things had *really* gotten out of hand but I couldn't see a viable win-win solution, so we accepted.

After a little time chatting and arranging for dinner, we all left. Bruce, Cassie and I went right to the restaurant while Mr. and Mrs. Management went home to "freshen up" and would meet us shortly.

As luck would have it, they didn't! In all the excitement, someone had forgotten a previous engagement and so…

Hooray for us! Sustaining an entire evening as faux Beach Boy was not my idea of a swell time. When did perpetuating fraud become a great way to pass the time?

Relief alone provided for a great dinner. The BV Rutherford House was sumptuous, the accommodations bordering on royalty; the availability of several bottles of open Reserve Cab was noticed.

Cassie and I beat a hasty retreat Sunday morning, fearing our mistaken identity might have been discovered and we would be presented with a bodacious bill for the snooze! Nothing of the sort happened; we escaped unscathed!

Back in New York several weeks later, a note from Bruce advised that the manager had been replaced. (No clue if it was connected to our visit.)

The Cases of Mistaken Identity still happen – although these days those making the wrong connection are old enough to realize the *other* Brian Wilson would not likely be offering his credit card to pay for a bag of fertilizer at Smith Mountain Feed 'n Seed, wearing a worn-out Bassmaster T-shirt and a grubby pair of cut-offs. Still, it comes up and I reply: "Shhh! Not so loud! People will be wanting an autograph and a few verses of **Surfer Girl**…"

Story Seventeen

WABC – THE CALL

From 1960 thru 1980, Musicradio 77 WABC/New York City was *the* biggest thing in Top 40 radio. Ever. Period. You can argue markets, stations, owners and DJs forever, but for those 20 years, WABC was *the* mecca, *the* King Kong, *the* undisputed heavyweight champion of Top 40 radio. DJs everywhere dreamed of having a show alongside Big Dan Ingram, Ron Lundy, Cousin Brucie, Harry Harrison, Johnny Donovan and the rest who made up the small, exclusive club of the station's monster Talent. If every one of the jocks who worked those glory days was gathered together, we could fit around one large table at a decent restaurant; the lineup was that exclusive. The egos, however, would need a separate building!

My WABC adventure could be a book in itself. There are so many stories within stories within stories, huge personalities, corporate politics, great times and stupid decisions, each related to the other -- to understand the one previous and the one that followed and the tragic conclusion. At this point, I'll just quote that old cliché, "I wouldn't take one million bux for what I went through there, but I wouldn't go through it again for a million bux either."

Here are some of the highs and lows from my tumultuous years.

<u>The Call</u>

The day arrived most disc jockeys only get to dream about.

Mid-October 1980 at the Z-93 studios in the C&S Bank Tower in downtown Atlanta. As usual, **Ross and Wilson** performed our signature "closing credits" sign off and turned the studio over to the seriously-talented Randy Reeves. If you remember the days before voicemail, you will recall phone messages were delivered on pink slips of paper with "While You Were Out" in bold letters across the top, and stuck via receptionist in an appropriate receptacle with your name on it.

Sure enough, as we passed the receptionist's desk, there were pink profusions blossoming from the **Ross and Wilson** slot. As I flipped through them, nothing unusual presented itself until the last one, a call had come in just as we were coming out of the studio:

Jay Clark - return call – ASAP.

I turned to Ross.

Do we know a Jay Clark?

Ross almost achieved liftoff!

Jay Clark? He's the new PD at WABC!

Well, well. Jay Clark wants to talk to us ASAP.

We knew at the time something was happening at WABC; the trades had been filled with rumors and stories about how the mighty WABC, was getting its butt seriously kicked by one **Imus in the Morning** with his "irreverent mix of talk and music." With the departure of the gentlemanly Herb Oscar Anderson and then Harry Harrison from WABC's Morning Drive, the King of Afternoons and all of New York City radio, Big Dan Ingram insisted he be moved up from his years ruling Afternoon Drive to take over the vacant morning slot. With his years of rating dominance, WABC management wasn't about to turn him down.

Reportedly, it took one day for reality to settle in -- Dan Ingram and AM Drive were not made for each other. Dan hated the hours. Despite a chauffeured limousine to and from the studio, he wanted his old PM Drive slot back. The negative effects of programming inconsistency on the audience notwithstanding, this put management in the difficult position of finding someone to fill radio's most important daypart in the nation's number one market on the market's number one station -- and fast. Complicating it all was programming genius Rick Sklar, the PD who made Musicradio WABC a stupendous success, had announced his retirement some months earlier. Despite interviewing many of the nation's top Top 40 PDs – including our own John Young at Z-93 -- no one wanted the gig. The NABET and IBEW union contracts strapped programming types in too many ways to make for efficient operation; AFTRA on-air talent had it almost as bad but worked around it.

Rumor had it that Jay Clark was somewhere around 43rd in line when he was called in to interview. While he had little major market Top 40 programming experience, coming from a talk station in Hartford, he landed the job. First assignment: find an AM Drive act good enough for NYC so Ingram could head back to afternoons.

We suspected The Search was the reason for The Call.

Off we went to the seclusion and privacy of the station conference room to find out what Jay Clark had to say; he was staying at the Hyatt Regency, just a few blocks down the street.

As I recall, our conversation went like this:

> *Jay Clark…*
>
> *Good morning, Jay. Brian Wilson and Ross Brittain at Z93 returning your call.*
>
> *Well hi, fellas… I've been in town for a few days listening to your show. I'm sure you're aware of what's going on at WABC; I'd like to get together for lunch and talk about Ross and Wilson possibly*

doing Morning Drive in New York City. Where would you like to meet?

(Note: If you have yet to read the history of **Ross and Wilson** elsewhere in these pages, a brief background: by the fall of 1980, we had been in Atlanta for almost three years and were near the top of our game. Our ratings were going steadily upward; we would beat our crosstown rival in that fall's Ratings Book. We were mentioned regularly in the **Atlanta Journal-Constitution**; our shenanigans often were covered on Atlanta TV, usually for something outrageous we had done on or off the air. We were doing three nightclub acts per week and countless birthdays, bar mitzvahs, weddings and corporate events. It is not an exaggeration to say we were making three times our salary with these off-air non-station self-promotion efforts. By actual count, in our last 12 months on Z-93, we made 376 of these appearances. Life was good – personally, professionally and financially! And, because I grew up in Wayne, New Jersey, 28 miles west of Times Square, listening to WABC, I knew this could be *The Call* for that Crowning Achievement of a radio career.)

Back to The Call…

Lunch? Today? Hmmm… I'm afraid lunch won't be possible, Jay. We have an appearance scheduled for noon to speak at one of Atlanta's biggest high schools; it's their Careers and Occupations Day. We're slated to explain to the combined junior and senior classes how they, too, can starve to death with a career in radio. But we should be finished up by 1:30 and could meet you in the lobby there at the Hyatt around two. How's that?

It sounded to me as if Mr. Clark was somewhere between peeved and astonished that I was putting him off, even for a couple hours; in the chair across from me, Ross didn't appear too keen about it either.

I'm afraid that won't work; my flight back to New York leaves at 2:30.

Frankly, that got me a little frosted. Back in 1980, getting from Downtown Atlanta to the airport, through check-in and out to the proper concourse for a 2:30 p.m. flight would require leaving the Hyatt not a second later than 12:30 p.m. Even that was cutting it close. I thought, what kind of conversation about a major career move were we going to have over a 30-minute lunch? If you've been in town "a few days," why did you wait until the *last* minute of your *last* day to call? Did it really take "a few days" to decide whether you liked the act?

But my reply was different:

> *Gee that's too bad, Jay. Maybe we could make it another time when it would be more convenient for both of us.*

Silence from Mr. Clark, although "exasperated" seemed to waft through the phone receiver. I suspected he wasn't accustomed to this response when he was offering the Ultimate DJ Wet Dream -- AM Drive on WABC, New York!

> *Well, I don't exactly know when I can make it back to Atlanta...*

Right.

> *OK, well we will likely be here whenever you can make it. Give us a day or two's notice and we'll make sure some pesky personal appearance doesn't get in the way.*
>
> *Okay, fellas. I'll be in touch. I enjoyed listening to your show.*
>
> *Thanks, Jay. So did we.*
>
> *Click.*

If Ross achieved lift-off when first learning Jay Clark had called, he was in orbit when I hung up the phone.

> *I don't believe you! The program director of WABC calls to offer us AM Drive and you put him off! Are you crazy?*

Like a fox. Look, if there's one thing I've learned in this business -- when they want you, they come get you -- and they don't let anything stand in the way. Just like when Bud and Chris came to get us in Baton Rouge; they weren't going to leave town without signing us. I guarantee you he will call again within two weeks. Maybe he will have his act together by then. He said he's been in town for a couple of days listening to the show and likes it so much and wants to talk to us so badly, he's arranged to give us a whole two hours' notice for a 30-minute lunch to talk about the biggest move of his and our careers! What bullshit. If talking to us was that important, he could have called yesterday or changed his flight. And let's not forget, John Young interviewed for that same PD job just three months ago and turned it down cold. Where did they find this guy?

Ross always kept up with the latest radio scuttlebutt.

He came from WTIC Hartford.

A talk station?

Yup.

Well, personally, that doesn't build a mountain of confidence in me considering him as our next boss. But whatever, maybe he's a genius. But I gotta tell ya, aside from not being impressed with his approach, I'm not really all that excited about going back to New York City. Times Square, Broadway, Yankee Stadium, Empire State Building, Central Park - been there, done that since kindergarten. We're doing great right here. The station's great. The money's great. The city's great. The people are great. And, hell, we're great! We're gonna be number one in the Fall Book, knocking off what's-his-name! Why would we want to leave now to start all over at a station that's having some serious issues -- even if it is WABC? But, I could be dead wrong; I have been before. Let's see what he has as to say when he calls again, and he will call again – or my name isn't Howard Cosell.

Your name isn't Howard Cosell.

I know that.

Story Eighteen

WABC – THE DEAL

And now, back to our story… about two weeks later. Once again, our heroes are passing the receptionist's desk after another high-energy New York style morning show…

Sure enough, a pink "While You Were Out" slip was protruding from the R&W spot: Jay Clark calling. This time, the return number had a 212 area code: New York City. We again headed to our "safe space" in the conference room to dial the number.

Jay Clark…

Jay usually skipped such pleasantries like, "Good Morning."

We had him on speakerphone and gave him our patented…

Hello! We're Ross and Wilson!

Fellas, I have a two-hour layover at the Atlanta airport day after tomorrow along with my Assistant PD, Stephen Goldstein. Any chance you two could meet us there?

Entirely possible, Jay. Do you have a specific time in mind?

We should be off the plane by one o'clock. Let's meet in front of the Delta Sky Club on the B Concourse.

Got it. See y'all there!

Okay great. Look forward to speaking with you then.

Click.

The warmth and excitement were positively underwhelming!

The Big Day of the Big Meeting arrived -- as did we -- 1 p.m. sharp: Delta Sky Club, B Concourse. Of course, air travel being what it was and is, Jay and Steve were fashionably late. Steve was introduced and we trooped inside for the Big Chat.

I won't bore you with all the details; quite frankly, I only recall the ones relevant to getting the job: compensation, length of contract and other vital tidbits. Typical of cat 'n mouse negotiations, despite agreement and handshakes, Jay did his best to soft-pedal any actual commitment on WABC's behalf, repeating several times, everything we discussed ultimately had to be reviewed and approved by ABC Upper Management. (I thought, yeah, right, fine… not likely an official representative, with assistant, would fly to Atlanta just to talk glittering generalities and happy hypotheticals. *We've got the gig!*)

The big take away from this meeting that made this one of the **50 Stories** was an off-hand comment Jay made that would return later like a steel boomerang. It was the last thing he added while heading to the gate for the return flight, almost like an afterthought:

> *Oh, one other thing, fellas. ABC does not move talent -- except between ABC properties. If you were working at WLS, we'd pick up the entire tab for your move. So that's all on you. However, what we will do is put you up in the ABC suite at the Waldorf Astoria and provide you each with a limo to look for a suitable apartment. And don't worry, we will cover all your expenses until you find a place.*

He chuckled.

Now that doesn't mean you can stay there for six months! But we will give you a reasonable amount of time to find something. OK?

Sure. That works.

Good. Enjoyed the chat. If you have any questions give me a call. In any case, I'll be getting back to you with the final decision in a few days.

And off they went.

As it turned out, it wasn't a few days, but more like a few weeks. Seems Jay may have gotten ahead of himself thinking ABC Upper Management was just hanging out, waiting to give their final approval to the new WABC morning show. Meanwhile, not being a business known for its confidentiality, various radio trade publications were floating names up for consideration for this coveted AM Drive slot. The story, with our names on it, even appeared as a rumor in the **Atlanta Journal-Constitution**. Needless to say, that didn't help around the station, with management asking pointed questions like, "So are you two going to WABC or not?" or "When are you guys leaving for WABC?" It was difficult to keep tap dancing since GM Bud Polacek and I had gotten to be pals.*

Ultimately, the word leaked out. It was messy and mildly unpleasant but fait accompli: **Ross and Wilson** were off Z-93, heading for the Big Apple. Sadly, but typical of radio, we never got the opportunity to say goodbye to our very loyal audience and express our appreciation for all of what Atlanta was becoming, the places and events where we had such great times and were so good for our career. Fortunately, the **Atlanta Journal-Constitution** media dude called and I was able to tell him the things we would have preferred to say on the air. To his credit, he printed almost every syllable.

**I didn't find out until years later, Bud, via PD John Young, was kept up to speed on the ABC "developments." As mentioned above, John, a well-known and respected PD in radio, had turned down the PD opening to replace Rick Sklar. Colleagues at that level tend to chat. Even after Sklar left the PD's office, he had a strong hand in guiding the replacement and selection process. Learning that someone of his stature and reputation had "smiled" on our hire, I saw it as one hell of an endorsement of our work.*

Story Nineteen

WABC – THE BILL

We now return to the exciting conclusion! Fast-forward to February, 1981.

We left Atlanta and hit the road for the drive up to Gotham. After an overnight pit stop at my parent's farm in Wayne, New Jersey, I led Ross down the highways and through the Lincoln Tunnel for his introduction to Manhattan… the Big Apple… the City That Never Sleeps! Even though Ross was well-acquainted with large cities (he was raised in the Chicago 'burbs), maneuvering the concrete canyons, the masses of traffic and people, the long-suffering patience and mannerly considerations of the cabbies, driving through legendary Times Square, across Broadway and Fifth Avenue to the iconic Waldorf Astoria may have been Ross's first major-motorized trauma. Watching him in the rearview mirror taking it all in was a hoot! We and our matching Toyota Celicas arrived at the entrance to the parking garage unscathed.

The world-class professionalism and courtesy of the Waldorf Astoria staff was still in existence in 1981. From the parking garage to the check-in desk to R-42 on the door to the ABC Suite, we were treated with deference and efficiency.

The suite was a large comfortable living room area, tastefully furnished, complete with fireplace. Down a short hallway to the master bedroom was a small kitchenette. At the end of the hallway, a door opened into a smaller adjoining room. I promptly claimed the MBR with raised king-size bed, another fireplace, large TV, bookcases, appropriate furniture and door that led to the master bath, itself only marginally smaller than Ross's adjoining quarters.

Once unpacked, we settled into two of the comfy, overstuffed chairs in the living room, turned on the fireplace and made the first of what would be countless calls to the Waldorf's vaunted room service. In mere minutes, a knock on the door heralded the arrival of our first lunch -- drinks, a bottle of wine and six jumbo shrimp cocktails! For dinner that evening, we made reservations at the Waldorf's legendary Peacock Alley where we dined for the next seven weeks. After eating our way through the menu – twice – Carl, our waiter and Boris Badenov look-a-like winner, each night would tell the chefs "just make something good for the boys."

Sidebar:

Before we moved into our West Side apartments, Ross made a weekend trip to see his folks in Chicago. Quite nicely, that coincided with my parents' 50th Wedding Anniversary. For the occasion, I had them, along with their matron of honor, limo-ed in from New Jersey to their rooms at the Waldorf; I had the Peacock Alley chefs cater dinner. "Impressive" would be appropriate here. Not only did we dine with light from the fireplace, the Waldorf staff laid out dinnerware with gold highlights in honor of the occasion. The final touch: gold boxes of Godiva chocolate.*

(OK, OK, this little Wilson family sidebar isn't a radio story per se, but going to WABC provided the great and only opportunity I would have ever had to pull off something like this.)

But I digress…

By the middle of May, seven or eight weeks after saying auf wiedersehen to Carl, the Waldorf chefs, bartenders and our room service people, we've each settled in to our apartments near

Columbus Circle and Lincoln Center. One morning, at the end of the show, we exited the famous Studio 8A, to find GM Al Racco's secretary, Jane, waiting to greet us.

> *Good morning boys!*

Everyone had taken to calling us "the boys."

> *Good morning, Jane. How are we today?*

> *"We" are just fine, thanks. Al would like to see you both in his office.*

> *Great!*

Without further ado, we fell in behind Jane and marched down to Big Boss Al Racco's large corner office.

Jane announced us:

> *Oh, fine! Fine! Good morning boys! Come in! Come in! Have a seat! Great show this morning! You guys are something else!*

> *Thanks, Al! That's our job -- keep the boss and the customers satisfied!*

Al guffawed appropriately and picked up some papers. He glanced at them for a moment and then looked at us.

> *I'll only keep you a minute. I got your bill in from the Waldorf yesterday. Looks as if you really enjoyed yourselves there!*

> *Yes, we did Al! What a great place!*

> *Yes, yes, indeed it is! I'd like to know how you boys want to handle the bill. As you can see, it comes to $10,928 for the Rooms and Dining Room, and car parking fees were a flat $1000 each. Now we can handle this any number of ways. You can put it on a credit card. You can write a check. We can even arrange for payroll deduction. How would you prefer to handle this?*

To say we were momentarily stunned would be a gross understatement. While seven weeks (including meals, drinks, wine and tips) at the Waldorf for $11,000 may be a bargain today, in 2018 dollars it has to be at least three times that. While we were each making reasonable salaries, this would take quite a chunk out of what was left after Uncle Sam, FICA, New York State, New York City and AFTRA took their slices!

But what came next is why this story one of the *top three* of my entire **50 Years in Radio**. After a moment of what was supposed to be studious consideration, I said:

> *Well, Al, to be honest, we'd prefer to not handle this at all.*

Al let out a big laugh from his prodigious Italian belly.

> *I can certainly understand that, boys! This is quite a tab! You must've really enjoyed yourselves!*
>
> *We did, Al. We did. But when I say we would "rather not handle it," what I mean is we have no intention of handling it -- at all.*

The big smile vanished from Al's face, his eyes narrowed and he reverted back to his standard serious GM self. His look was more sinister, his voice almost threatening.

> *What exactly do you mean you have no intention of handling this at all?*
>
> *Well Al, when Jay Clark and Steve Goldstein flew down to Atlanta to hire us back in January, the last thing Jay said to us before getting on the flight was it was ABC policy to not move talent unless they were already ABC employees and that the cost of our move would be our responsibility.*

Al was slightly taken aback.

> *Yes, well… yes, that is correct. That is ABC policy.*
>
> *And then Jay went on to tell us -- and I think I'm repeating this verbatim -- ABC will put you up in the company suite at the*

> *Waldorf Astoria and provide each of you with a limo to find suitable apartments. And don't worry, we will cover all your expenses until you find a place. That doesn't mean you can stay there for six months. But we will give you a reasonable amount of time to find something.*
>
> *So with that understanding, handshake and agreement, I really don't think we have any obligation to compensate the Waldorf or reimburse ABC for these expenses. Do you?*

A blind man could have seen the blood rising in Racco's face. The veins and capillaries on his bulbous nose were visibly pulsating; for a couple moments, he said nothing. Then, calmly, he leaned forward in his chair, riffled through the papers once again and looked up at us.

> *Well, fine… alright, boys. Listen, thanks for coming in. Keep up the good work. We're all very happy you're here on WABC.*

We said "Thank you" in unison, I added, "Great to see you," reached over his desk, shook his hand and we left his office. We said goodbye to Jane and made our way down the short hall out to the main corridor. Just before we got there, we heard the intercom on Jane's phone buzz. There was no need for her to pick up the receiver… Al Racco's thundering voice could be heard throughout the building:

> *JANE! WOULD YOU ASK JAY CLARK TO COME IN HERE PLEASE?*

Uh-oh!

We headed down the corridor toward our lockers, which happened to be directly across from Jay's office door. Just as we got there, out popped Jay, buttoning the top buttons of the vest to his three-piece suit, a big grin on his bearded face and spring in his step.

> *Good morning boys! Good show this morning! Al wants to see me!*

Smiling serenely while exercising the ultimate in self-control, I said:

Yes, we know.

Moments later, Al Racco's vocal evisceration could be heard through the flimsy walls, almost throughout the eighth floor!

You may be asking yourself, "Why this is one of his all-time favorite stories?" If you've been reading elsewhere or between the lines of the myriad of events surrounding the WABC Experience, you likely noticed my relationship with the PD went from fair to bad to worse in less than six months.

Program Director said this was a really good picture! (1981 Photo: WABC)

My thoughts were: This is New York, the number one market! This is WABC, the number one station! Everyone working here is supposed to be at the top of their game! What should have been the most exciting and exhilarating part of anyone's career was corroded by the ineptitude, and inexperience of Management, coupled with a program director, who should have been our Biggest Fan, not a micro-manager. To have witnessed his earlier gaff so appropriately rewarded was truly gratifying! Maybe there is something to that Karma thingy!

Post WABC, Jay had a notable radio career. At one point, I heard he received a tugboat captain's license, was out of the business and moved with his family to Florida. Cassie and I ran into him ten years later in DC at a **Radio & Records** convention, unemployed and "looking" as we all have done in similar circumstances. Considering our history, I was initially uncomfortable but Jay bore no grudges and we had a pleasant conversation. Cassie and I invited him to dinner, in part to see if we could help him find a new gig. His tenure in management at Sirius Satellite Radio began shortly thereafter.

**One other thing for any vestiges of the WABC Accounting Department reading this -- I personally paid for the 50th Anniversary dinner!*

Ross & Wilson in WABC Studio 8A Where Musicradio 77 WABC Legends lived (1981 Photo: Brian Wilson collection)

Ross and Wilson taping TV spot (Photo: Brian Wilson collection)

Story Twenty

BOSTON, GYPSIES AND MOSS CREEK

Lots of big-time radio stars had signature bits 'n quips they made famous— and helped make *them* famous. Remember Arnie "Woo Woo" Ginsburg? If you answered YES, you are one old fart! If you answered WHO? you're an unfortunate child who missed out on great radio on WMEX/Boston! Or you could just be someone who never hung out around Boston in the 50s and 60s. For one semester, I was an exchange student at a Cambridge prep school and listened every night, allegedly doing homework. You'll have to Google Arnie to hear the shtick that made him number one.

In major markets around the country, one DJ usually reigned supreme, known for his outrageous act.

That would be my role model, later my nemesis -- WABC's Big Dan Ingram. BDI perfected the long-forgotten radio principle: talk to one person – you -- whenever the mic was open. And for Big Dan, "you" had the name "Kemosabe." Age, sex, race – irrelevant. Everybody was Kemosabe; every show ended with "Bye now, Kemosabe!" It was his signature line.

Ross and Wilson had a few of our own. Remarkably, they all came into existence through the rarified ether of *spontaneous combustion*; the one inexplicable but consistently magical aspect of our show.

Boston, There's That Name Again! -- 1977

Within weeks of arriving at Z-93, we got a call from the PD at KFMB-FM/San Diego. His morning team was leaving for WRKO/Boston and with the fall book coming up, he needed a "killer morning show" by yesterday. Would we be interested in flying out that weekend for a chat? Despite not having finished unpacking from the move from Baton Rouge, ya gotta be ready if you wanted to move up in radio. We jumped at it! That was on a Tuesday. On Friday, the same PD called: our round-trip tickets which had just arrived were cancelled. The wives of his exiting team absolutely hated Boston and the guys had called, begging for their old jobs back. The PD plaintively wailed:

> *What could I say?*
>
> *Yeah, right, OK... we understand. No problem, we'll tear up the tix. Fine... bye.*

Oh well... Atlanta was still nice!

Not ten minutes later, another call, this one from the PD at WRKO! Maybe we should have seen this one coming. He told us of a certain San Diego AM team which had just "dropped him in the grease." They had had a deal! In fact, the station had just finished a total makeover of the control room with specific accommodations for a two-man show. At the last minute, they backed out because they "missed San Diego." He said he originally intended on calling us first, but read in the trades that Z-93 had scooped us up. Now, between the proverbial rock and hard place, he was desperate. Before going any further, he asked:

> *Have you boys signed a contract?*

(Attempting to hire someone with an employment contract is "tortious interference" in court and can cost the offending defendants big, big bux!)

Nope, no contract. The GM told us First Media (owned by the famous Marriott family) doesn't believe in them.

Excellent! Well, I know it's really short notice but would you boys be interested in spending this weekend in Boston? I can have the tickets waiting for you at the American Airlines desk.

What the hell? We were still packed to go to San Diego.

Sure, why not?

Everything in the WRKO studio was dazzling! New everything – including face-to-face control boards! While everyone was amazed at how well we performed without the benefit of eye-to-eye contact; this would make things infinitely better!

We were introduced to the general manager, general sales manager, chief engineer and several other happy, friendly folks – always a good sign inside any radio station. We talked money and bennies, possible start dates, all the usual stuff. Upon leaving, the RKO Suits said they would put a package together and send it down for our perusal, and off we flew back to Atlanta.

The possibility of going from Baton Rouge to Atlanta to Boston in a matter of weeks was pretty heady stuff! The facilities alone were fantastic; the money, bonuses and benefits damn near overwhelming. Needless to say, upon our return, we said nothing to no one nowhere! We just waited for the mail to arrive!

After the Tuesday show – and before the mail arrived – we were called into GM Bud Polacek's office. In radio, a page from the GM is rarely a good thing. But Bud and I had become racquetball partners and even socialized a bit with his wife and my dates. Bottom line: no worries.

That is until we walked in and saw PD John Young also standing by. Still, things had been going quite well since we arrived. Overall, the shows had been among our best, sales weasels were happy, callers to the front desk were positive. So?

Bud asked Ross to shut the door. Oh-oh…

> *Well, boys, how did you like Boston?*

Gulp. I replied:

> *Boston? How did you know we were in Boston?*

Bud, with his charming, smart-ass smirk:

> *We got a call. Actually, Martin Sherry in Sales got a call from a media buyer friend who was visiting WRKO when he spotted you two with the GM and PD. Knowing you had just gotten here, he called to ask what the hell was going on. John didn't know either, so we thought it would be a good idea to ask you guys.*

Oh.

Strategically, I decided it might be in our best interest to lay it all out. I went from the surprise call from San Diego to the surprise call from the jilted WRKO PD to a brief description of the magnificent studio to vague, unspecified details of the anticipated huge offer to the conversation we were having at the moment.

As things turned out, the "spill the Boston beans strategy" worked quite well. Before the RKO package arrived, Bud persuaded First Media to agree to an actual contract, complete with a very nice raise, superb ratings bonuses and a few other goodies, which he presented just in time to head off the envelope from Boston that arrived the next day.

OK, so now you know the "Boston" background. Here's what happened the very next day after signing First Media's first-ever air talent contract.

Along with being the PD, John Young had assumed the duties of AM Drive rip 'n read news guy for our show. His "news booth" was the studio adjacent to ours with a small window through which we could confirm he was at the board, ready to go – after one of our usually unusual intros.

On this particular morning, after the intro, John started the news with "This story out of Boston…" With our mics still open, Ross and I looked over at John and said -- in unison and with virtually no preparation:

BOSTON! There's that name again!

That was the end of the news.

John lost it. In our own surprise at what we had just done out of thin air, we lost it, too. All the audience heard was off-mic laughter until one us managed to hit the button for a commercial. Still not recovered to professional broadcaster status 60 seconds later, someone also hit the top-of-hour-ID and the next tune.

For some long-forgotten reason, Boston was in the news intermittently for several days. Every time it came up, Ross and I would jump in with "*Boston*! There's that name again!" and it quickly became one of our signature bits. Weeks later, after Boston no longer frequented the news, listeners would call and work "Boston" into their call just to see if it would bring the anticipated response. Still, no one really knew what the hell this was all about!

When we arrived at WABC, "*BOSTON*! There's that name again!" was ingrained; any mention got that response. Naturally, New York area listeners had no clue about any of this either, so a flurry of calls would always come in:

What's with BOSTON?

What's this thing you have about BOSTON?

Why do you guys have a problem with BOSTON?

There was no way to explain something as convoluted – and downright silly – on the air.

So, for everyone reading this who ever wondered what "*Boston*! There's that name again!" was all about, now you know! Trust me – it was a lot funnier to hear than read!

Story Twenty-One

BOSTON, GYPSIES AND MOSS CREEK
Part Two

Gypsies -- 1982

1982 brought a huge infestation of gypsy moths to the NYC Metro area. Not exactly rare, they had been around since way before I grew up in New Jersey. But this year there must have been a gypsy moth **Woodstock**! The damn things were everywhere – especially and eventually on your windshield. This required on-air discussion, ultimately involving our intrepid Shadow Traffic reporter, the now-legendary Joe Nolan.

As with most any bit that "just happens," the details of how, when and where it started tend to be fuzzy at best; "Boston" (first in this trilogy) was an exception. In this case, the details are waaaay less important than the overall bit, but still informative.

Let's take it in parts.

You already know about the Gypsy moth epidemic. In some rambling discussion at some long-forgotten point in time, Ross mentioned a line from a song that went:

Through the forest, wild and free,

Sounds our gypsy melody;

Ever dancing, as they say,

None so merry, and none so gay – HEY!

Ross credited **The Pirates of Penzance** as the source. No one within earshot had ever seen the show. So for years when anyone asked where it came from – and someone always asked – we would say, "It's from **Pirates of Penzance**, and everyone always said, "Oh... OK."

During one of Nolan's reports, he again mentioned the dreaded gypsy moth, and we were ready. How we were ready, I do not know. But as soon as Joe said, "gypsy," we crashed his report with our rousing a capella rendition of **The Gypsy Song**. Joe lost it; we were cool. But then, we knew it was coming!

From that point on, Joe knew saying, "gypsy" would immediately get our over-modulated acapella response; ditto weather wench, Rasa Kaye. And just as with "*BOSTON*? There's that name again!" callers would try to bait us into the bit. Only Art Athens, John Mahar, Palmer Payne and the rest of the stoically indomitable WABC newsmeisters were immune. After all, news is sacred. You never know when that "credibility" thingy may come in handy!

But I digress…

Writing this from a memory 35 years ago, I thought I should provide some serious background demonstrating the lengths to which we went to provide unique program material as well as answer the timeless question, "Where do you guys come up with this #@%*?"

Well… our little "gypsy (moth) song" is sung nowhere in **The Pirates of Penzance**, because it's really called **Romany Life**, performed in the never-popular 1898 operetta, **The Fortune Teller**. The lyrics aren't exactly those we tortured the audience with either. The actual words are:

Through the forest, wild and free,

Sounds our Magyar melody;

Ever dancing, as they say,

None so merry, and none so gay -- HEY!

"Magyar" being the historically, technically and now politically-correct term for those folks once grossly referred to as "Gypsies." Regardless, even in Gotham, the bit wouldn't have worked nearly as well if we had sung about "our Magyar melody!"

Sadly, this is like explaining a joke: once done, it's difficult to find where the humor is. Or was. Or went. You had to be there. Still, for the millions of listeners who laughed (or suffered) through this plosive performance whenever someone (in)advertently uttered "Gypsy!" this is everything you ever wanted to know, or not, about "that Gypsy thing."

Further diligent research* revealed an antique **Andy Griffith Show** segment where Andy comes upon some interloping gypsies who promptly break out into *our* version of the song! I strongly suspect Ross somehow confused **The Andy Griffith Show** with **The Pirates of Penzance**.

For a Georgia Tech graduate, that's totally understandable.

**Thanks to Pop Culture Contributing Research Editor Carol Anne Wilson, B.S., Syracuse University, S.I. Newhouse School of Once Spectacular Broadcast Journalism.*

New and improved Talk Radio publicity shot (Photo: WABC)

Story Twenty-Two

BOSTON, GYPSIES AND MOSS CREEK
Part Three

Moss Creek – 1981

Even with its roots in Atlanta, we kept the *Boston!* bit in the act when we moved to WABC/NY. It didn't take but a few "*BOSTON*? There's that name again!" pops to get people talking, "What the hell is with *Boston*?" Maybe it was a Red Sox thing.

When you're new in town, the audience wants to know where you've settled in; nothing like having a celebrity living down the street! As you can imagine, that didn't always work out well. Having an apartment on the trendy West Side was a good starting point. But being a Country Boy, even by NY standards (New Jersey is the boonies to City dwellers), I just couldn't take city living. Even on the 34th floor, the 24-hour Tenth Street Ambulance Races and 4 a.m. Dempsey Dumpster Tympani Recitals came through loud and clear. A move to New Jersey became a daily topic of conversation with Ross as well as callers.

New York callers ridiculed me for "giving up" on the City; New Jersey callers put out the welcome mat and lobbied for their town as a great place to live.

With a little help from some friends, I found a quaint little place in lovely Alpine, just up the Palisades Parkway from the George Washington Bridge -- 28 miles from my garage to the ABC Building. Glenn Goin was a former Artists Colony -- the artists and their patrons long gone left the collection of stone studio houses available. Shortly after moving in, I discovered Stevie Wonder was a down-the-street neighbor. Much of Woody Allen's **Midsummer Night's Sex Comedy** was shot around the house next door -- and, no, I wasn't invited to be an extra. Damnit!

But I digress…

Once I found the new place, talking about it on the show became a little bit of a problem. I didn't want to spotlight tiny Alpine, but needed to give some indication where I landed to keep my new "New Jersey" connection with the audience. That caused the founding of "Moss Creek, one of the last cute little towns in the Garden State."

Not more than ten minutes passed after the on-air announcement when the first of many calls came in:

> *Where the hell is Moss Creek? I've lived in Jersey all my life and never heard of Moss Creek.*

Some New Jersey callers could be just as pleasant as City folks.

For the next few weeks, I would take a few "Where is Moss Creek?" calls. Dodging the specifics got to be a big game:

> *Do you know where Ridgewood is? OK. It's a couple miles east of Ridgewood as the crow flies…*
>
> *Near Emerson? No, you're too far north…*
>
> *Outside of Paramus? Paramus? That's a whole 'nother country! Waaaay too far south…*
>
> *What's the nearest exit off the Garden State Parkway? I dunno. You can never get off at the same one. But it's on the west if you're going north; that would be the left side if you're going southeast…*
>
> *HEY! You just told some guy – it's on the west side if you're going north and…*

...sorry, I'm outta time. Hey - just check the map -- it's right there!

And so it went.

It didn't take long for the audience to figure it out and start playing along. I was invited to throw out the first mallet for the **Moss Creek Mixed Doubles Croquet** season, judge the **Moss Creek John Galt Look-a-Like** contest, lead the **1982 Annual Moss Creek Snipe Hunt**, MC the **Moss Creek Senior Ladies Wet Sweatshirt Contest, Moss Creek Bring Back Palisades Park Charity Ball** and other "events." Humbly, I accepted them all. Of course, Fate would foil their plans or mine and the festivities would have to be postponed.

A tad hokey today, maybe even for 1982, it was still a great running gag through the WABC years. Today, there are *real* Moss Creek Golf Clubs, apartments and housing communities all over the country. Go figure.

Never fail to remember our motto – "Moss Creek had moss before Lake Wobegon had water!"

Story Twenty-Three

GOIN' DOWN?

The only experience most people outside the biz ever had with ABC's infamous sports broadcast legend, the late Howard Cosell, was seeing him in the broadcast booth with "Dandy" Don Meredith and Frank Gifford on ABC's wildly popular **Monday Night Football** or hearing **Speaking of Sports** on WABC/NY Radio. That's where I met him.

From our perfunctory introduction one morning to our last "conversation" two years later, I can tell you with all candor -- everything you ever heard about Howard was true, assuming everything you heard included: "arrogant, pompous, obnoxious, vain, verbose, prima donna," words he actually used to describe himself in a **New York Times** interview. I would add: "petty, egomaniacal, condescending, selectively hypocritical and legally unethical." And I mean that with all due respect.

I believe everyone who worked in the ABC Tower had at least one "Cosell Encounter of the Weird Kind." Those involving female engineers/board ops were lewd, crude and salacious. Mine was just "typical Cosell."

Before I get to the details, we did have some fun with Howard. More accurately, we did have some fun with Howard at Howard's expense!

Howard recorded **Speaking of Sports** at various times and studios around the ABC campus. When he recorded at the ABC Tower at 1330 Sixth Avenue where WABC Radio was located, the original tape, complete with outtakes, somehow came to our attention. One of two very attractive engineer/board ops would run his board, much to Howard's lecherous distraction, which led to a cornucopia of these rich on-mic outtakes. Like magic, many of those coveted quips, outbursts and flubs made their way to the **Ross and Wilson Show** where they were sprinkled liberally throughout the program as opportunity warranted.

You can imagine hearing Howard intoning: "And it's a big, big, story" or "But NO!" or "…and he did it despite the fact that his shoelace had come untied," or the very popular "lab results prove he was using anabolic steroids to aid his performance." Any one of our board ops -- Kiki Hooper, Carl Carl of the Chicago Carls, Mike Mamone or Debbi Iacovelli would pop-in one of those at appropriate moments while Ross and I were yapping it up on the air.

Good times!

That is, until Howard was listening one morning and went ballistic, calling down from his 36th floor office to bellow at GM Al Racco, who then bellowed at the PD, who then caved and specifically prohibited us from using Howard's voice on the show outside of **Speaking of Sports** or without HC's "express written permission." (As if!)

Another sitting ovation for Creativity.

That's a good story, but no! Not good enough to be one of these **50 Stories** -- like this one:

High atop the ABC Tower, the company maintained a private restaurant for the Big Empty Suits. It could be partitioned to simultaneously accommodate multiple lunch meetings. On several occasions, **Ross and Wilson** were invited to meet with ad agency honchos to chew the fat – literally and figuratively.

After one meeting, several of us lingered to finalize some pesky details and then drifted to the elevator; I was the last to leave, heading back to the eighth floor.

As soon as the journey down began, the elevator stopped. The doors parted like the Red Sea to admit The Great He: Howard Cosell himself, gussied up in an overcoat, fedora and… a lighted cigar.

He entered. I nodded, "Howard." He glanced at me but did not return the greeting despite our several meetings. The doors closed; the journey continued in silence. Howard didn't have a habit of speaking to Lesser Beings, even when spoken to unless it was official business or a camera was pointed at him.

Did I mention Howard also was a lawyer? NYU Class of '40, Phi Beta Kappa.

Posted on the elevator wall was the required "No Smoking" sign. I could just make it out through the smog from Howard's glowing stogie.

> *Say, Howard, I'm sure you're aware of the No Smoking provisions of this elevator. As a member of the bar and officer of the court shouldn't you report yourself for violating them?*

Did I mention Howard stood about six-foot three in his orthopedic brogues?

He peered down at me with a soft glare of disdain the elite reserve for us serfs.

> *I ride this elevator every day. No one complains.*

Wow! I wonder why?

Oh well, first time for everything.

Bailing on the eighth floor, I went to an empty desk, filled out and submitted the first "Smoking Violation Complaint" against Howard William Cosell.

The next morning, just before the show was over, I thought I saw the blurred image of Howard's toupee fly past the door of our studio heading in the direction of GM Al Racco's office. As we were gathering our stuff to leave, the great Ron "Hello Love!" Lundy swung the door open wide and gave us his customarily cheerful, "Good morning, boys!" And right behind him was another blur of the Cosell rug and person zooming in the opposite direction toward the exit.

Chuckling as the door air-locked behind him, Ron looked at me with his big, infectious grin and said: "OK, what did you do to Howard?"

I hadn't shared my elevator experience with anyone, so I related the gory details to Ron, Ross, Kiki, Carl and Art Athens; laughs and raised eyebrows ensued, with a cautionary note from News Director Athens.

A few minutes later, in accordance with "the rules," an amused GM and our not-so-amused PD called me into Al's office to "advise me of the results of my complaint." Howard "Scofflaw" Cosell was fined $150 for his arrogant indulgence – and he was not happy.

Days later, during a nearby function, rumor had it a certain broadcast legend had some vile things to say about me, my lineage and limited future in radio at WABC. But that was OK – by that point in my career, I had been insulted by pros!

Howard Cosell – the smartest man in the room when he was the only man in the room!

Story Twenty-Four

THE TWO DANS

Only two groups of people would ever deny Dan Ingram was the best DJ ever: those who never heard him, or those with an ax to grind.

From the rural confines of a poultry farm in Wayne, New Jersey, I spent most of my teenage years listening to WABC/New York. There were those who preferred WMCA or WINS (before it flipped to all-news). Some thought WMCA played better songs more often; some like WINS for the same reason. But most everyone in the New York City listening area came to WABC between 3 p.m. and 6 p.m. weekday afternoons for the hilarious comments, impeccable timing, "adult" innuendos and unique wordsmithing of Big Dan Ingram. Even my dad, who was way out of the demo by then, would get a chuckle about some Ingram Thing whenever we happened to ride together and I had charge of the station. True, there were others legends: Bruce Morrow, Scott Muni, B. Mitchel Reed, Alan Freed, Peter Tripp, Murray the K, Herb Oscar Anderson, Harry Harrison – I heard 'em all! But Monday through Friday, three hours per, no one could touch Big Dan. And he had the ratings to prove it.

Prior to that fateful day in September 1965, I never had a thought about becoming a DJ. It was law school for me, a decision I made after seeing **Inherit the Wind**, reading up on Clarence Darrow and started following the exploits of a young F. Lee Bailey. But

September '65 arrived and with it, the beginning of these 50 years in radio.

My first station was WLBI/Denham Springs, a Baton Rouge suburb. We had "block programming" -- different music for different day parts. From sign-on to 10 a.m. it was **Country and Western**, then from 10 a.m. to noon -- **Music Especially for You** hosted by the general manager (his daily attempt to pick up a lunch date). From noon to 1 p.m. -- **Music for Daydreaming**, a commercial-free hour of Mantovani/Percy Faith-esque LPs (both sides). From 1 p.m. to 4 p.m. there wasn't a "theme" per se, but the industry knew it as MOR, Middle of the Road: Pop, Adult Contemporary and crossover hits. From 4 p.m. to 5 p.m. it was **Radio 'A Go-Go** – the station's one-hour indulgence in Top 40 hits, and then from 5 p.m. to sign-off whatever was popular, minus anything that might be "Rock 'n Roll." Since my shift eventually became noon to sign-off, I pulled the **Radio 'A Go-Go** gig.

With virtually no radio experience beyond "listener," when 4 p.m. rolled around, coming up with what to say and how to say it was daunting. Prior to that, any "tight and bright" blather from me about the music, lost dogs or current events was acceptable, but having listened to all the Giants named above, **Radio 'A Go-Go** required something different. So I tried a few of the Big Boys shticks on for size!

First, Cousin Brucie. Not comfortable with the yodeling voice changing, I switched to control panel-pounding B. Mitchel Reed. That didn't go over well with my audience (mainly Bonnie and Mabel out in the office) so I slid into the more comfortable wise-cracking, smart-ass-ness of Dan Ingram. I played-off the song lyrics just as he did. Played with the commercials just as he did. Played with callers just as he did – and had a damn good time doing it. The wordsmithing came naturally; the NYC sarcasm was in my DNA. Most of that didn't play very well in Deep South Louisiana. But, like Babe Ruth who struck out more than he homered, we all know what made him famous. Eventually, I managed to perfect the art well enough to crack up the audience inside and outside the station, get away with it and make it a building block of my budding career.

With all that, you might be able to imagine what it was like years later, not only to be hired to go to WABC, the station of my formidable years, but to be replacing my teenage idol, Big Dan Ingram as well! And in Morning Drive! For all the not-so-good times that permeated the "WABC Experience," being in the shadow of Dan Ingram was the biggest and best thing about it.

Almost.

In February 1981, we had only been on the air a few weeks; Dan was back on his old throne-dominating PM Drive. One morning, sitting in the PD's office for yet another interminable micro-managing aircheck critique, who walks by the open door but *the Man himself*: Big Dan Ingram! Since we were on and gone by late morning and he arrived just before 3 p.m., seeing him in person was unlikely, barring some special station occasion. But there he was! "Big" Dan, himself! I'm exactly six feet tall, so that made him somewhere between six foot four and 12 foot eight!

I couldn't help it. I excused myself from the meeting before Big Dan could get away to wherever he was going. This could be my best and only chance! Sure enough, there he was, maybe 20 feet down the hall toward the GM's office, but instead of turning in, he did a sudden about-face and started walking right back to me!

He was reading something, probably one of the incessant "programming memos" we received daily. As the distance between us closed to about ten feet, I blurted out:

> *Hi Dan! I'm Brian Wilson from Ross and Wilson. I can't tell you how great it's going to be working with you!*

Dan didn't miss a beat. He gave me a sideways glance as he walked past, ignoring my outstretched hand and mumbled:

Yeah. Right. Good luck with your career.

Whoa! I was stunned. How snarky, unprofessional and downright hostile was that? I didn't expect a bear hug or autograph request – but pro-to-pro (we *were* working at the same station, right?) I figured some mild pleasantry, "congrats," "yeah-me-too" wasn't too much to expect.

Not so much. Hell, not at all.

I thought: OK. Screw you, Dan. Good thing your name isn't Dick. We work for the same company in the same studio in the same market. You've got the years, ratings, reputation and money. I get it. You earned it the old-fashioned way. Well, I got this gig the old-fashioned way too. Since you didn't pick up any class along the way, that says more about you than me. (Note: *THOUGHT* not *said.*)

Forward-promoting is a staple of what used to be called "personality-driven radio." AM Drive would promote PM Drive and vice versa, taking advantage of the day parts with the most listeners. WABC was no different. While we had a set number of times we had to mention "Big Dan was back in afternoons," how we said it was up to us -- mainly up to me. Because he had been such an asshat, I tailored my "forward-promotional" comments accordingly:

> *If you've noticed we don't sound anything like Dan Ingram, that's because we're not! Dan has moved back to his old three to six show here on WABC, so catch him on the way home while you're parked out on the L-I-E (Long Island Expressway).*
>
> *Good old Big Dan is getting his required amount of sleep again now that he's back doing afternoons, three to six, here on WABC.*

It only took a few of those before the PD met me at the control room door after the show, specifically to tell me: stop referring to Dan as "old" or "back on afternoons."

Why? Shouldn't we be forward-promoting his old/new time slot?

As I recall, the answer was that Dan doesn't like being called "old" and "back" sounded like he couldn't cut it in AM Drive.

Not one to give up…

> *Well, he is old – ten years older than I am. PM Drive is his old show time, and didn't Imus whip ass in the AM Drive ratings? Isn't that why we're here?*

I was met with an exasperated request to just stop with "old" and "back."

> *Sure. You bet! No old/back. Got it.*

I wondered whether Ingram had actually said those things or if the PD was just afraid he might have to deal with it.

Hmmmm… little sensitive there, Dan? Gutless management, Mr. PD? Dan should never have gone to AM Drive. Not exactly in those words, he would admit it in an interview several years later.

So I changed direction:

> *BW: Dan Ingram this afternoon at three on New York's Radio Station WABC! Ya know Ross, Dan Ingram has been here so long and has done so well, dominating the afternoon ratings, WABC can't afford to pay him anymore!*

> *RB: What? Really? What are they gonna do?*

> *BW: They've started giving him chunks of the ABC Building here on Sixth Avenue. It's true! Right now he has the lobby and all of the parking garage. This week he gets the cafeteria and half of Howard Cosell's office. The guy's incredible! Big Dan this afternoon at three on WABC!*

Or…

BW: Remember to join Big Dan Ingram this afternoon at three here on WABC – that is if he makes it in this afternoon.

RB: Wha – Whaddaya mean "if" he makes it in?

BW: I guess you didn't hear the news, Rossie – Dan hurt his back yesterday when he came in to pick up his paycheck!

Back at the Control Room door again with another directive from the PD -- Dan doesn't want you talking about how much money he makes.

Oh really? OK.

Dan had two big reputations among the NY ad agencies for which he did a ton of commercial work. One, he was a quick read. He could arrive at the recording studio, take one look at the copy, sit down, nail it in one take, grab his bodacious talent check and be out the door in five minutes. Literally. He was that good.

The other reputation involved what used to be called "flirting." Maybe that explained why he had been married several times. Rumor had it the agencies eventually hired "designated representatives" to be at recording sessions to "oversee the production." Dan's leering ways came to my attention several times from "reputable sources." The idea for a nickname came to me.

Hey, Ross! Big Announcement coming this afternoon! Remember what I said the other day about Big Dan Ingram getting paid with parts of the ABC Building? Well, just before his show at three this afternoon, they're changing the name of the building from A-B-C to B-D-I (Beady-Eye)… you know, for Big Dan Ingram! I can't wait!

Almost every WABC sales weasel along with several agency reps called later that morning laughing their butts off. Everyone got the play on words. Even Kiki Hooper, our well-contained board-op, could be heard laughing on the aircheck tape – which promptly disappeared.

May 10th, 1982, "The Day the Music Died;" Musicradio 77 WABC switched to Talk Radio WABC. By then, my opinion of Dan Ingram couldn't go any lower. I resented his petulance about AM Drive and forcing the PD to censor my poking fun about him. The fact that he rarely forward-promoted Morning Drive didn't sit well either. Foolishly, I thought if he had just made a sincere effort, we might have avoided the inevitable. But it didn't matter now. At noon, Dan Ingram, Ron Lundy (a great talent and human being) and the rest of the air staff gave it up for Talk Radio. **Ross and Wilson** stayed, thanks to our new and improved ratings that had beaten Don Imus. Whatever Dan Ingram's personal issues were with me, he was and remains the Greatest DJ Ever.

Years Later

On Memorial Day, May 25, 1998, contradicting most everything about radio programming, WABC started a Memorial Day tradition that would run for about eight years: **WABC Rewound**, excerpts of the glory days of Musicradio 77 WABC featuring airchecks of most of the great jocks who had made WABC every Top 40 DJ's Radio Mecca! Of course, Big Dan was the big feature, helped in large part because WABC and Dan kept a huge library of Dan's shows; almost every show was reported to be on tape somewhere. **Ross and Wilson** -- not so much. I was informed the "tradition" of taping and keeping daily shows became an afterthought shortly after our arrival, due to the perpetually-denied pending flip to Talk. Very little of our WABC work exists except for a select few made on cassette decks, mostly at home by adoring fans, for which I am grateful.*

"Shocked" was more accurate than "surprised" to describe my reaction to the invitation to host 30-minutes of that first **Rewound** show, a Beatles retrospective. At the time, I had a farm in Upstate New York, doing talk shows in Dallas, San Francisco and Baltimore from my in-house studio; the other guest hosts were in Manhattan at WABC. A few minutes into a song during my 5:30 p.m. to 6 p.m. segment, Johnny Donovan came on the IFB to tell me I'd be getting a call from *Dan Ingram*! Dan was working at WCBS-FM at the time. Typical of radio management, the Suits at CBS forbid Dan to appear on WABC under his real name. Not to be denied, Dan conspired to call in as "Not Chuck Dunaway." (Allan Sniffen has the background at his www.musicradio77.com website.)

I started to panic! Granted, it had been 16 years, but who knew what Dan's memories were of that first meeting or trading thinly-veiled on-air insults? Now I would have to tap dance thru some "interview" with him playing like he was someone else. Above all, what the hell were we gonna talk about? Through eight minutes and 26 seconds, Dan was Dan and the consummate professional. It was gratifying to receive mega-kudos from the writers, producers, and critics who gave high marks for how I handled it. But what really made this such a great experience and story came several years later. In a magazine and broadcast interview, Dan was asked about that first **WABC Rewound** and the "Not Chuck Dunaway" interview. After tracing the "Chuck Dunaway" backstory, the host asked, "Who interviewed 'Not Chuck Dunaway' during that **WABC Rewound**?" Without hesitation, Dan said, "That was with Brian Wilson, yeah… Brian Wilson, and I gotta tell ya, he did one helluva job. He was really great!"

Dan's stock went sky-high when I heard that. Had he forgotten those early WABC days? Was he just being a pro? Or did I blow it all out of proportion from Day One and that incident in the hallway?

Don't know. Won't know. But in a business which is super-stingy with compliments and recognition among its peers (except when it means getting a new gig), having the Greatest DJ Ever compliment you like that is unforgettable.

On June 24, 2018, Dan Ingram died at his home in Florida. Accolades poured in from throughout the radio business, toasting Dan as a great person and an even greater talent. On Allan Sniffen's www.musicradio77.com, I wrote:

I never intended to be in radio as a DJ or talk show host. But when I fell into it in 1965 and had no idea what to do when the mic opened, I remembered coming home from high school, laughing and listening to Big Dan Ingram. So I tried to be like him. 15 years later, I was hired to replace him in AM Drive on WABC as he returned to afternoons. Some crazy days back then -- even for radio! Dan Ingram, the Greatest. DJ. Ever.

**Joe Tedd Locastro, an early NYC fan, created one of the biggest collections known and, along with Ellis B. Feaster, was of inestimable value putting audio chunks of these stories together. They can be heard on the 50 Stories Facebook page http://fb.me.50Storiesbook and YouTube channel.*

Story Twenty-Five

THE HOROSCOPES

Sometimes when you least expect it, spontaneous combustion and creativity come together to form something totally unanticipated and turns out stupendously successful. Such was the case on the second morning of the B104 **Brian and O'Brien Show**, July 1984.

The back story ….

I was supremely ticked off having been "shotgun married" to a new partner. The **Ross and Wilson** break-up was still simmering, although a great lesson was learned about working relationships in showbiz. Unlike teaming up with Ross, I had no time to get to know Don, test our compatibility or see if we had the chemistry to make a prime-time AM Drive show work from Day One in a Top 20 market. Baltimore was no Baton Rouge where you could polish your act in front of a live audience first to see if you had what it takes for the Big Time.

The PD assured me Don would be "just fine," but if at any time I wanted him gone, he'd be gone. "Just give it a chance." That didn't take long. By the end of the first show, it was clear to me it was not going to work -- our on-air personalities were not a good fit. At all. Unfortunately, as much as I'd like to, I can't go into all the details. As I saw it, Don's inexperience, lack of formal education, taste in humor and personal issues would have killed any chance of a compelling, intelligent, entertaining show such as the late R&W. At the end of our debut, I went to the PD and explained to him in small words this wasn't happening and why, and I would take him up on his promise to take Don off the show. Instead, he asked me to give it till the end of the week and if it still wasn't working, he would. In short – I did, he didn't. The rest is an ironic and sordid history of what remains *the most successful team show ever* on Baltimore radio. But it came at a big cost.

Back to that spontaneous combustion/creativity thing mentioned above...

By the second hour of our show, I was angry all over again. Set-ups were missed, punchlines were trampled; Don's need for one-upmanship became the order of the morning. The show continued like the proverbial Chinese fire drill.

Shortly after the 7 a.m. news, handled by the very capable Sean Hall, Sean came into the control room waving a sheet of paper and informed us that quite a few listeners had called to complain they hadn't heard the daily horoscopes.

I was appalled!

> *WHAT? DAILY HOROSCOPES? This is 1984! Who the hell does horoscopes anymore? That went out with disco and 'what's your sign' pick-up lines!*

Sean advised that the act we replaced faithfully did them every morning along with the other old DJ crutch, **Today in History**. I couldn't believe it! Had I jumped aboard a time machine back to the 70s? Sean informed me in no uncertain terms -- this audience was *totally* into their horoscopes.

Like totally, man.

There are businesses that offer "show prep" services to DJs around the country. In the 70s and 80s, part of the package in the 70s and 80s was the weekly horoscopes. I'd seen plenty of free sample solicitations; the ones our predecessors had used were among the lamest available. With everything else that was going wrong, I wasn't about to use that crap. Still, Sean's point was well taken. If the audience wanted horoscopes badly enough to call with a hissy fit, I said: "They want horoscopes, I'll give 'em horoscopes!" And with that, I flipped over the syndicated horoscope sheet and scribbled my own version of asinine astrological prognostications.

The following, while not the original 12 from that show (I tossed them as soon as I was done), is typical of what the audience heard every morning for the next four years, complete with a George Harrison sitar riff looped underneath me and Don's intro of **Horoscopes with the Amazing Wilson**:

ARIES: Your chart is in a state of confusion. You will spend 30 minutes trying to get a phone booth to flush.

TAURUS: You're in for a big surprise when you accidentally enter a gay bar and say you'd like to have Jack Daniels.

GEMINI: 75% of your body heat escapes thru your head, which means you can ski naked if you have a good hat.

CANCER: Ask your parents, who has the headache: the bird or the bee?

LEO: Try a simple diet, like putting a speed bump in front of the refrigerator.

VIRGO: Explain to an old person that life in the fast lane doesn't mean getting your picture on a carton of prune juice!

LIBRA: Try something new and exciting this weekend. Give your Pinocchio doll a polygraph test.

SCORPIO: Avoid Tuesdays.

SAGITTARIUS: Your job is really punishment for giving the "thumbs up" sign to Barabbas in a former life.

CAPRICORN: Putting a mirror over your bed won't help. You still need a woman.

AQUARIUS: Explain to the cops you weren't mooning anyone – just letting the ink dry on your new tattoo!

PISCES: You will finally meet the girl of your dreams: a nymphomaniac who owns a liquor store!

The audience went wild! While some true believers were totally bent out of shape and swore they'd "never listen to B104 ever again," the majority of callers were still laughing. If tweets, Facebook "likes" and emojis had been available back then, it would have set a record!

That started the morning feature of unique, custom-made horoscopes that couldn't be heard anywhere else. I wrote them every day, sometimes not finishing until the commercial break preceding them. As the word spread, even people who hated the show or Top 40 music would tune in just to hear them. When I went on vacation, the receptionist had to field phone calls from the less attentive, asking why the horoscopes weren't on.

Like other things that were hip 'n happenin' back in the day, a radio show trying to air these horoscopes today would likely be a total fail! But for four years in the mid-80s Baltimore, the B104 **Horoscopes with the Amazing Wilson** were a *very big deal.*

If you semi-enjoyed the above horoscopes… I happen to have several years' worth languishing on my hard drive. I'll tastelessly sprinkle some throughout the rest of the book. Avoid them at your peril.

Story Twenty-Six

WE HAVE A WINNER!

For most of its existence, which happen to parallel my DJ years, Top 40 radio was famous and great fun on both sides of the mic -- for a lot of reasons besides the great music from the 50s thru 80s. I leave out the 90s because by then, both Top 40 radio and Top 40 music started its downward spiral to Sucksville. With asinine regulatory interference from the FCC, quick-buck attorneys and "socially-conscious" advertisers, owners/managers began mangling DJ creativity that was insufficiently PC. Squeamish advertisers, fearing listener boycotts, threatened their own boycotts of shows or entire stations with personalities who hurt their feelings or contradicted the politics of the earliest Snowflakes that surround us today. National ad agencies actually had a list of programs, jocks and talk show hosts distributed to station owners, GMs and GSMs with instructions *not* to run their client's spots within or adjacent to them. Howard Stern, Don Imus, The Greaseman, Moby, Tom Leykis and others, along with (guess who?) **Ross and Wilson**, **Brian and O'Brien** or just plain ol' **Brian Wilson**, all made the list!

Before all of that began suffocating the "good times," the shenanigans from jocks like us were a great way for listeners to start the day as well as the DJ to earn a paycheck! It took talented, creative, funny and daring DJs to "press the envelope" and "color outside the lines." Call it whatever -- organized chaos, uncivil disobedience or flipping off social convention -- an unpredictable radio Bad Boy would always seize the listener's attention as well as folks from other media who didn't have the opportunity (or guts) to be naughty in public like we did! Invariably, TV and newspapers would indignantly report the "outrageous" stories of how the local Bad Boys of Radio did (fill in the blank) to upset some segment of the audience. What they never realized was how blatantly their envy was on parade; they were the only ones not having a ball! But such is the nature of "news" people, hypocritical politicians and members of the Social Justice Warrior Snowflake Battalion.

Noodling out what to do next to get that "water cooler talk" going was 98 percent inspiration, one percent perspiration and one percent theft (why be creative when you can steal?). The "best of the best" on-air bits were those that spontaneously combusted due to a perfect storm of time, circumstance and twisted thinking. Nothing is more contagious than spontaneous humor. Just hearing someone LOL in honest reaction to a funny bit will make most anyone laugh, even if they didn't hear the punchline. Having a listener say, "I damn near wet my pants when I heard you say…" is just about the highest compliment a DJ can get, at least it was back in the day.

I'm proud of the times I received such kudos. It's more poignant for a DJ since, unlike performing stand-up comedy, you don't know whether you really hit that last one out of park until someone calls, still in tears of laughter. Sometimes you don't find out for days. And sometimes you have a partner in the studio who is just as liable to react as any other listener. My partner, friend and broadcast veteran, Bob Madigan, from our short-lived -- yet award-winning -- **Brian and Bob** AM Drive show on the late WWRC/DC was the best and most dependable for that.

The only problem with a spontaneous dinger is attempting to re-create the moment when writing a book like this! But I'll give it a try…

One morning on the **Brian and O'Brien Show**, we had six tickets to give away to the Maryland State Fair. Some big acts were set to appear in concert, so it was the hot ticket in town. When the time came to give them away, we followed the old "be the tenth caller and win" format. Over a song intro, Don would make the announcement and the five incoming lines would light up. I handled clearing 'em: "B104, you're caller number one," *click* "B104, you're caller number two," *click* – and so on until nine callers had come and gone. Then Don would start the tape (reel-to-reel back then) and I'd punch up the tenth call. After the winner was identified and awarded the prize, we'd rewind the tape, play it back at the end of the song to make it sound as if it was happening in real time, then jingle out into the next tune. Quick and easy. But most often I would take that tenth caller live! Very risky! With no delay in the system, anything could be said… anything could happen! *But Momma… that's where the fun is!* And when it does happen, you are what everybody's talking about!

This was one of those times:

> *BW: B104* ***Brian and O'Brien Show****, hello…?*
>
> *Female Caller: (scream) OH MY GOD! AM I THE TENTH CALLER?? AM I THE TENTH CALLER??*
>
> *BW: Whoa there, sisterhood… who is this?*
>
> *Caller: Sandy… Sandy Sandifer… am I the tenth caller?*
>
> *BW: Hey, hey, hey! Hold on a dad-gum minute there, girl. Who's running this contest, you or me?*
>
> *Caller (with contrition): Oh I'm sorry, you are…*
>
> *BW: That's right, cutimous, and I'm telling you… YOU ARE THE BIG WEINER!*

Cue the screams, giggles, and all the usual hysteria.

> *BW: Sandy, where are you calling from Sandy? Sandy? Where are you calling from Sandy? Sandy, I've asked you twice now, where you callin' from, girl?*
>
> *Caller (giggling): Dundalk.*

BW: Ah! Dundalk! The Overhand Bowling Capital of the World!

(Note: Dumping on Dundalk, a Baltimore suburb, was one of my regular bits whenever I needed a place of appalling mediocrity, questionable intelligence and El Caminos on concrete blocks. Some residents loved it; some hated it. It never failed to get reactions beyond the show.)

BW: Well Sandy, you've won six – count 'em – six tickets to the Maryland State Fair for Friday with seats to hear Fats Mallard and the Blue Grass Dimwits sing their moderate hit, I Want to Whip Your Cow.

Caller: Oh thank you, thank you, thank you! My aunt was a big fan of youse guys.

BW: Your aunt WAS a big fan?

Caller: Yeah, she died last week.

BW: Oh well, it wasn't our fault.

With that line, Don O'Brien -- fortunately off mic -- let out a yell and began laughing hysterically.

Caller: No… no… no… but she really liked listening to youse guys!

BW: Well, isn't that nice! I guess she won't be doing that anymore! So you'll only be needing five tickets then?

This put Don near convulsions…

Caller: Oh no! No! We have a big family. My aunt wouldn't have been able to go anyway.

BW: Well alright then, you can have all six.

Caller: Oh thank you! Thank you! Thank you!

BW: You're much too welcome, Sandy! Hang on so Don can get your measurements…

Don is just starting to regain control…

Don (between laughs): I don't believe you!

BW: What?

Don: The woman died!

BW: So? She couldn't hear me and her niece won the big tickets. Everybody's happy!

Don: I don't believe you!

(Brian and O'Brien jingle into the next song.)

For the rest of the show, we took calls from listeners laughing just as hard as Don did, at how *outrageous* the whole bit was.

One young woman's call we saved and played often: "I think the **Brian and O'Brien Show** on B104 is rude, crude and obnoxious. And I love it!"

For the four years **Brian and O'Brien** ran in Baltimore, she summed it up nicely. That show will always be a part of Baltimore radio history when we put outrageously funny, spontaneously-combusted, culturally contrarian entertainment on the air.

More Brian and O'Brien (1986 Photo courtesy Brian Wilson collection)

Story Twenty-Seven

THE BOYS IN BLUE

Being the Morning Drive Guy for most of my career was *The Best.*

Unlike almost everyone I've ever known, I always enjoyed early mornings: getting up, "taking on the day," seeing what Life had up its sleeve. Even as a kid on the farm, I always was the first one up. Today, there's nothing like being the first one on a lake like glass when the sun is just coming up, trying to coax some monster bass to mistake your lure for brekkie!

Morning Drive never was as calm and bucolic as bass fishing, but bass fishing never paid the rent either! Career-wise, AM Drive is *the* day part to have in radio. Since forever, more people listen to the radio between 6 a.m. and 10 a.m. than any other time of day. Naturally, owners/managers always wanted their "best and brightest" on the air in Morning Drive.

So how does this relate to the "Boys in Blue," the hard-working members of our police departments? Thanks for asking…

In 1987, the third year of **Brian and O'Brien** (B104/Baltimore), I was living in Cockeysville, one of Baltimore's bedroom communities. The townhouse was precisely 15 miles from our new studios on "TV Hill." One morning, something very rare happened: I overslept. I *never* overslept. Never needed an alarm clock either. I just naturally woke up at 4 a.m. showered/shaved, dressed, coffee-d, and hit the road in plenty of time to make the 25-minute drive. Unlike today, traffic heading into Baltimore at oh-four-hundred hours was still sparse; at least enough to slightly bend the 60 mile-per-hour speed limit.

But not *this* morning!

5:09 glared from the clock radio and I came out of bed like a cruise missile from a submarine! Shower? Forget it -- just add more deodorant! Pants... socks... shirt... shoes... car keys... coffee? Ha! Out-the-door-and-into-the-car in about as much time as it took you to read that. To this day, when the lighting is just right, you can still see my vapor trail hanging in the air.

The first couple of miles wound thru sleepy suburban streets. With zero traffic, the 35 mile-per-hour speed limit *wasn't*! No worries. Once I made it to I-83, I would be able to really make up the time to the station's exit.

Sure enough, only a few cars and a distant 18-wheeler were up on the Super Slab when I came roaring down the Padonia Road entrance ramp, pedal-to-the-metal on my Jeep Cherokee. Shortly before the merge onto the Baltimore Beltway (I-695), one of those "few cars" grew a set of flashing red and blue lights and found a perch on my rear bumper. Surely you know the feeling and can easily imagine what was going through my punkin' head: *CRAP!*

I pulled off to the shoulder, whipped out my wallet and grabbed Ze Papers...

In the rear-view mirror, a large mountain strongly resembling a human being in a Baltimore County Police uniform appeared through the flashing lights and strolled up to my open window. Not being my first rodeo, driver's license and registration were already in hand. Why prolong the agony? I thrust them out to Officer Huge just as he said:

License and regis... oh, OK. Do you know why I pulled you over?

What? You mean you don't?

Not really. As a practice, I only *think* intemperate thoughts when facing men with guns.

Was it my new land speed record?

You might say that.

With that droll response, he turned to lumber back to the flashing lights, looking at my "paperwork" as he went. Midway, he stopped dead. Made an about-face and returned to my window.

He took a look at my face, then down at my license, then back to my face:

Brian Wilson… THE Brian Wilson on B104?

Guilty as charged, my Captain.

Wait here.

Do I have a choice?

This created either a Very Good or Very Bad situation. If "Brian Wilson on B104?" translated to: "I'm a listener and a fan," fines and points just might be avoided; I might even make it to the studio on time. If it meant: "So you're that sarcastic jackass on the radio, always knocking my hometown Dundalk," then I could easily be facing a life sentence for Offending An Officer's Sense of Humor, Disturbing His Peace and Molesting Public Airwaves. Over the years, from Baton Rouge to Atlanta to New York, I had learned the hard way: *anything could happen* – and always did.

Mt. Officer barely paused at the disco cruiser, leaned in the window to say something to his partner and made the return trip to my docile, unimposing Cherokee. After handing back my papers, he put both hands on the window, bent down from his eight-foot 14-inch height and leaned in toward me with a big grin.

So you're the Boss Jock Radio Star, huh? I'm Mark Vahlkamp.

Glad to meet you… sorta.

I shook his hand and smiled back. Then he glanced at his watch.

Running a little late for work, are we?

I don't know about you officer, but yeah, I am a tad behind.

And then he said something I had never heard – from Baton Rouge to Atlanta to New York:

Follow me. I can take you down 83 to your exit, but that's the city-county line and as far as I can go. You're on your own from there.

Very cool! Thanks a lot!

And off he went, back to the lights and then away in a cloud of dust, while I tried to keep up.

We hit 80-90 miles-per-hour down the Jones Falls Expressway (I-83 South), making up for our "get acquainted" time. At the exit, the flashing lights went dark as we crossed the line, the Baltimore County Rocket Sled turned left and I peeled right, making the last three miles in record time, not encountering any of Officer Vahlkamp's city brethren prowling the area.

I walked into the studio at 5:58 a.m.; my partner's fingernails noticeably shorter.

Headphones… microphone… music! And it's Showtime!

During the first few minutes, I mentioned how nice it was to have stopped on the way to the studio to chat with one of Baltimore's Finest, Officer Mark Vahlkamp, keeping Baltimore Countrty streets safe for mankind and guarding us against those reckless drivers who had become a plague upon our highways and byways!

A couple weeks later, damned if it happened *again* -- I overslept! Up to then, some 23 years of mostly AM Drive, I had come close to being late just twice. Now, this! Was I getting old? Did I require the Senior Alarm Clock w/Extra-Loud Klaxon Wake-Up Noise? Hell, I was barely 40. Or so…

Once again: no shower… no coffee… flying shirt… pants*… socks… shoes… car keys, vapor trail out the door. *(*Yes, I still wore underwear back then.)*

And as I turned from locking up -- BAM! Twin spotlights hit me from across the parking lot.

What the…?

Those disco lights flashed for a second as two County Mounties pulled up behind the Jeep. In the lead car, my new large friend, Officer Mark Vahlkamp, was grinning at me.

> *Running late again, Mr. Wilson?*
>
> *Not really. I just like a challenge!*
>
> *Since my partner and I pulled the night shift, we decided to keep an eye on you, just in case. C'mon, follow us. Same drill as last time.*

I walked into the studio at 5:58 a.m.; my partner damn near apoplectic.

For the rest of the B104 years, and on subsequent stints on Baltimore's WBAL, WCBM, WOCT-FM, and WQSR-FM, I would occasionally be Mark's "ride-along", a civilian cleared to go out on actual patrol. Those "tours" included everything from routine monotony to running radar to a high-speed pursuit a la **Grand Theft Auto**… until the "Lead Sled," the ancient patrol car Mark was driving, pooped out on I-83 just as we were about to nab the bad guy! How embarrassing! I made certain to mention the incident on the show the next day, berating the Baltimore County Governing Royalty that the "Boys in Blue" should not have to deal with such unreliable equipment when chasing down perps. While state troopers went on to apprehend the new felon, what if it had been shoplifting -- or worse?

I'd like to say my on-air comments resulted in a whole brand-new fleet of patrol cars for the county cops! I'd *like* to say that – but it didn't. It only got Officer Vahlkamp a few hi-fives from his fellow officers.

I told Mark this experience was just prepping him for a career in broadcasting.

Now, 30+ years later, Mark is retired, enjoying a new boat and cruising the Chesapeake Bay. On too rare occasions, we meet up back in Cockeysville to consume vast quantities and recall the Glory Days.

That's what old friends do, right?

Story Twenty-Eight

THE SING-ALONG

Do you remember the 1984 David Lee Roth hit, **Just a Gigolo**? Regardless of whether or not you were born yet, have a lousy memory or were listening to Classic Willie Nelson Rap at the time, it's still a great tune! It only made it to #25 on **Billboard** but developed its own cult following.

We helped it along on B104.

Maybe because Roth's arrangement was just so damned infectious, you wanted to sing along with it anywhere, anytime you would hear it – even in public! Always looking for ways to please the listeners, beat up the competition and goose the ratings, we began a Friday ritual of inviting listeners to call in and sing along, live on the air. Unlike Talk Radio, Music Radio was still in the glory days of "no delay," which made the real-time sing-along possible. In addition, there was a local controversy about some of the lyrics. Did David Lee sing "bozey bozey bop, tiddy bob" or "bozey bozey bop, titty bop?" "Sad and lonely" or "Fat and ugly?" And at the break, was that: "Homily bibbily zibbly boobily homily biddily zippity bop?"

The controversy raged on from week to week!

As selected listeners were punched up on the air to do their thing as best they could, I did my best to derail them with distracting comments. If they lost it, they were gone! Survivors generally received a big prize – like a **Brian and O'Brien** genuine plastic fly swatter! Whether you were on hold, ready to sing, listening to the mayhem in the car or singing along in the shower, it was as good a time as radio can provide!

The YouTube channel we have to go with this book contains the very best example of one of these Friday sing-alongs. In fact, this actual aircheck is so good, certain GMs, PDs, consultants and other professional radio vermin didn't believe it had been recorded *live*, with no post-production edits. That would have been impossible anyway because I was among the worst audio editing DJs who ever disgraced a production booth! Razor blade or digital, I remain one of radio's all-time klutzs when editing audio! OTOH, that means this recording is a reflection of my absolute genius in spontaneous performance with a listener. Shamefully, the Radio Hall of Fame doesn't have an award for this!

Go to the **50 Stories** Facebook page http://fb.me/50Storiesbook or YouTube channel and listen!

Go ahead. I'll wait on the next page…

Brian and O'Brien in their natural habitat (1984 Photo: Brian Wilson collection)

Story Twenty-Nine

IMPOSSIBLE TRIVIA

Radio changed a lot over the five decades I haunted the studios of some of America's heritage stations and some of the peanut whistles, too. By the mid-70s, as technology led the way, those of us in the biz focused on Reagan's Deregulation: ownership changes, the FCC scuttling the Fairness Doctrine opening the door to Talk Radio, air talent moves throughout the country and other "inside radio" stuff.

A much more subtle change came in the way programming was being treated; specifically, how management treated the creative efforts of air talent. For those of us trying to make names for ourselves by pressing the envelope with our on-air treatment of popular conventions, the change was not welcome. At all. It was constricting, stifling, condescending, cowardly and mostly unnecessary.

It worked like this:

During a show, you would do something spontaneous, original and generally harmless -- also funny, entertaining and compelling. Maybe it had a hint of blue, maybe it didn't. After the show, the PD or GM would call you on the carpet and chew you out for (insert perceived offense here). In most every instance, the "offense" was a matter of taste. Humor being totally subjective, not every joke is going to get a laugh from everyone who hears it.

Try MC'ing a CPA Convention. Not everyone thought George Carlin, Sam Kinison, Abbott and Costello, Bill Cosby, Chris Rock or SNL were all gut-busters. Inept, incompetent management-types who had never been on-air talent were too-often motivated by their own envy or fear of hearing from clients complaining because they didn't get the joke. Program directors and consultants suffered from a near maniacal need to *control the talent*! Big egos can be so insufferable! Next thing ya know, with all that popularity and rating success, they'll be wanting raises and benefits and stuff! OMG!

Yeah, it's tough having a wild 'n crazy morning show with #1 ratings in the important demos!

Here's a true story and perfect example.

I called it **Impossible Trivia**.

Thanks to the 1981 debut of the Trivial Pursuit board game, by the mid-80s trivia was everywhere; it was the *next big thing*. In homes, on campus, in bars and, of course, on the radio. The broadcast treatment was generally treated like **Today in History**, a nugget of infotainment rather than a contest.

Not us. As **Brian and O'Brien** on B104/Baltimore, we started using it to give away whatever goodies might have been loitering in the prize closet: movie passes, concert tickets, station T-shirts, my partner's mug shots, etc.

The game was easy enough to play. Be the tenth caller and answer the trivia question of the day. Right answer wins; wrong answer gets an embarrassing verbal drubbing.

This all worked well enough for a while. But, like most structured comedy bits, without some new and different content other than my wrong answer put-downs, it was getting stale.

Enter **Impossible Trivia**.

The promo went like this:

> *Join the mentally challenged Brian and O'Brien Show tomorrow morning for radio's largest and fastest growing game -- Impossible Trivia! Give the correct answer in ten seconds or less and win all the money in the jackpot, which right now stands at $100,000! For every incorrect answer, we add another $100,000 until we get a winner! It's the largest cash giveaway game on radio ANYwhere! Play Impossible Trivia with Brian and O'Brien, tomorrow morning on B104!*

Listeners quickly discovered why we called it **Impossible Trivia**. With only ten seconds to come up with the answer, even if you had it, giving it in ten seconds was virtually impossible.

Like this:

> *Alright, here we go! This is the moment you've been waiting for! Yes, boys and girls and whatever those creatures are in Dundalk… it's time to play Impossible Trivia! Be the tenth caller at 410 104 104 and you'll get a shot at all the money in the Impossible Trivia jackpot -- $100,000!*

Commercial break then **Hooray for Hollywood** intro music.

> *Alright – here we go – it's Impossible Trivia! Let's get our tenth caller…*
>
> *BW: B-104 -- You are caller number ten -- who's this?*
>
> *Caller: (sounds of screaming and yelling…)*
>
> *BW: Hello? Hysterical person? We only have so much time for this…*
>
> *Caller: Ohmygawd! Ohmygawd! I can't believe it! Yes-yes-yes I'm ready…*
>
> *BW: I'll bet…What's your name?*
>
> *Caller: Martha.*
>
> *BW: Martha what?*

MM: Martha Mertz.

BW: Martha Mertz… how's Fred?

MM: What? Who?

BW: Never mind… this isn't looking good already. Where ya calling from Martha?

MM: (giggle) I'm from Dundalk!

BW: AH! Well, that explains everything! OK, Martha Mertz from Dundalk… I'm going to ask you our Impossible Trivia question. You'll have ten seconds to answer… if you get it right, you'll win all the money in the Impossible Trivia jackpot which, right now, is $100,000. If you get it wrong, you'll just be another Big Loser from Dundalk and will blend right in. Remember – TEN seconds -- the decision of the judges is final and I am the judges!

OK, Martha Mertz, for $100,000 Hey! Even after taxes, that would be enough to move out of that God-forsaken hell hole! Are you ready?

MM: (more giggling) Oh no – I was born here and I'll die here…

BW: Right…Probably a lot sooner than you think…in fact, this whole bit is starting to die so let's get on with it! Here is your chance to win Impossible Trivia: Recite the alphabet… backwards! GO!

MM: What? Backwards? Recite the alphabet backwards?

BW: Seven seconds… Six seconds…

MM: Oh! Uh… ummm… Z… Y… X… W….

BUZZZZZZZZZZZZZ

BW: Oh I'm sorry Martha, times up!

MM: But you said to recite the alphabet backwards! I can't do that in ten seconds!

BW: Correct! That's why we call it Impossible Trivia! Hang on the line, Martha! We have some parting gifts for our losers! Don, see if we have any empty anchovy cans left over from the staff meeting yesterday...

Well, as you heard, we didn't get a winner on today's Impossible Trivia contest, so we add another $100,000 to the jackpot making it $200,000 the next time we play Radio's Largest Cash Giveaway Game, Impossible Trivia!

(Brian and O'Brien jingle out.)

Invariably, after each game we'd get at least one call that went like this:

BW: B104 Brian and O'Brien show... hello?

Caller: Is this Brian and O'Brien?

BW: No, you moron, it's the Mensa Society – and you don't qualify...

Caller: Ha ha ha ha, it IS Brian and O'Brien!

BW: Brilliant! Whaddaya want, Genius?

Caller: I was wondering... what are you gonna do if someone wins the jackpot? They don't really get $200,000, do they?

BW: Are you calling me a liar?

Caller: No! I was ju...

BW: Of course, they won't win $200,000!

Caller: I thought so!

BW: Not if the jackpot has $300,000 in it! What kind of All-American Stand-Up DJs do you think we are?

Caller: All I was wondering was what would happen if someone won?

BW: Can't happen.

Caller: How do you know?

BW: Because it's impossible! That's why we call it Impossible Triviaaaa!

(Commercial break)

With our #1 ratings, **Impossible Trivia** started a lot of talk on the street. So much so, even the GM heard about it. Ordinarily, he and the GSM and rest of the sales weasels spent their time listening to other stations in order to steal any of their advertisers we didn't have, while their sales departments were listening to us for the same reason. Kinda like **Spy vs. Spy**. The last people to know what was happening on B104 were the same people who were supposed to be out selling our show to potential advertisers. Ironic much?

After the show one morning, right about the time the **Impossible Trivia** jackpot hit *eight million dollars*, we were called into the GM's office. He was agitated – which is to say he wasn't happy but wasn't volcanic. Yet.

Our conversation went like this:

GM: What's this Impossible Trivia thing? Who authorized that?

BW: I invented it.

GM: But who authorized it?

BW: What's to authorize? It's just a bit.

GM: You're promising an eight million dollar prize!

The Management Volcano was rumbling now.

BW: I'm promising nothing. The rules plainly and repeatedly state, you could win NOT you will win. Big difference.

GM: What are you going to do if someone does win?

BW: Not gonna happen. In fact, it can't happen.

GM: Why not?

BW: Because it's impossible. That's why we call it Impossible Trivia!

At that, the Management Volcano erupted!

GM: #(**%$#!%!!! (O#U$$$ #!($@*)#))#!

Slowly, using small words, I explained how the questions were constructed to make the answers impossible for an average caller to know, or, even if known, impossible to answer in ten seconds. After the first few games, everyone got the joke but still wanted to play just for the challenge and let their friends hear them on B104. It's really no big deal.

Mount Management started to simmer… but he emphasized that it was a big deal to him and that someone probably would call the FCC or file a lawsuit claiming fraud or some other damn thing. Either way, the risk was too high even if there never was a winner, so the game had to be shut down.

Unfortunately, it was an irrefutable argument. Gone were the fun days of radio. Now there was hair-splitting regulation that stifled creativity and snuffed out humor. We had laws and lawyers and the smarmy litigious people who would scheme to use them – and likely win – at the expense of people who were just out for a good time.

In a rare display of non-confrontational capitulation, I came up with a solution:

BW: OK. I have a way out. It will end tomorrow.

GM: WAIT! What are you going to do?

BW: Trust me. You'll like it.

GM: #**@!#^^@*) !!! #((U)(!#)) $$$!!!!!

The next morning, everything was set and I went into the standard **Impossible Trivia** open:

> *Alright, here we go! Here we go! The moment you've been waiting for! Yes, boys and girls and all you Nerf ball bowlers in Dundalk… time once again to play Impossible Trivia! Be the tenth caller at 410 104 104 and you'll get a shot at all the money in the Impossible Trivia jackpot, which this morning now totals an astounding EIGHT million dollars exclusively with Brian and O'Brien here on B104!*

Commercial break then **Hooray for Hollywood** intro music.

> *Alright! Time for Impossible Trivia and a shot at EIGHT million US government-approved dollars! Let's get our tenth caller…*
>
> *BW: B104 -- you are caller number ten – who's this?*
>
> *Caller: Oh, hey…it's Fred… Fred Fox.*

A pretty low key Fred Fox.

> *BW: Fred Fox… ya don't sound all that excited Fred. Where ya callin' from Fred?*
>
> *Fred: I'm in Cockeysville.*
>
> *BW: Cockeysville, huh? Isn't that where John Holmes is buried?*
>
> *Fred: Gee, I don't know…*
>
> *BW: It's that big pyramid-looking building off York Road.*
>
> *Fred: I don't think I've….*
>
> *BW: Forget it, Fred… guess you don't get to the movies much. Anyway, it's time to play Impossible Trivia. Here are the rules: I'm gonna ask you an Impossible Trivia question. You'll have <u>five</u> seconds to come up with the correct answer. If you do, you'll be the Big Weiner and win all the money in the Impossible Trivia jackpot which right now stands at EIGHT million dollars. If you're wrong,*

you'll be a big loser and get an Official Brian and O'Brien cheap plastic fly swatter. The decision of the judges is final and I am the judges. Are you ready, Freddy?

Fred: Yes, I think so…

BW: I'll bet! OK, for eight million dollars in five seconds: What year is this – in Roman numerals?

Fred: Oh… um… MCMLXXXVII.

BUZZZZZZZZZZZZZZZZZZZ

(A moment of silence…)

BW: MCMLXXXVII IS… EXACTLY RIGHT!

Don hits the crowd cheering/band playing sfx.

BW: Oh my god, Fred! You've done it! You've just won eight million dollars! How did you know the answer so quickly?

Fred: I had four years of Latin in school. And we're Catholic so I…

BW: Well that explains it! Congratulations, Fred! Eight million bux!

Fred: Yeah, that's great. I bet my uncle Jim down there will be really surprised.

BW: Wait… What? Your uncle Jim? Down where? Down HERE?

Fred: Yeah, my uncle Jim… Jim Fox… you know… your boss… he's the general manager.

(Silence)

BW: Well, yeah… yeah, Fred, I know your uncle, Jim Fox, alright – but you know what that means?

Fred: No – what?

BW: That means you aren't getting eight million dollars…

Fred: WHAT? I don't? Why not?

BW: Well, Fred, as the rules for all our B104 contests plainly state, "relatives of B104 employees are not eligible for prizes." I'm surprised you didn't know that.

Fred: Uncle Jim never told me that…

BW: Well… sux to be you, Fred. Sorry. But thanks for playing Impossible Trivia – and the partial heart attack. Hold on, Don will get you your fly swatter.

And that was The End of **Impossible Trivia**. Literally, it was the talk of the town for weeks. And that's what made it such a great bit. And a great example of how laws, regulations and management anxiety began seriously killing off fun and creativity in the "Theater of the Mind" called Radio.

The audience never knew "Fred" was actually our chief engineer. I had scripted the whole thing with him after the "impossible" meeting with the GM the day before.

Still, it was great fun while it lasted!

MORE HOROSCOPES

ARIES: Good news! People your age are coming back in style!

TAURUS: If she says she loves you more than anyone else in the world, it may only mean she hasn't met everyone yet.

GEMINI: Consider it diet time when your loved one gives you a pair of Lard-Ass jeans – extra-large.

CANCER: You meet a guy at a singles bar who keeps pouring drinks over his hand trying to get his date drunk.

LEO: Your grandmother accuses your grandfather of squirting Polident in her girdle.

VIRGO: Don't get your hopes up. Your new love interest is still trying to figure out how to play his shoe horn.

LIBRA: Surprise the rest of the girls and try out for football – although offensive center may not be the best position.

SCORPIO: Avoid a restaurant that serves everything from soup to nuts – all from the same animal.

SAGITTARIUS: Prepare for an exciting weekend! Pour milk on your waterbed and invite your girlfriend over to make butter!

CAPRICORN: Ask your pediatrician how something that cute can smell that bad!

AQUARIUS: You meet a gay army sergeant who keeps grabbing his privates.

PISCES: An epileptic friend lands a high-paying job with the circus as an elephant vibrator.

Story Thirty

RUSH & WILSON

After **Ross and Wilson, The Next Generation** on Z100/NY sadly imploded, it was back to Atlanta; back to Talk Radio -- PM Drive on Jacor-owned WGST. With all the talking and phone bits I had done over the years on music stations plus the three transitional years on WABC/NY, getting back into Talk Radio was exciting. The **Ross and Wilson Zoo** experience proved to me that the creative freedom that once flourished in Music Radio was decomposing into micro-managed mediocrity at the hands of incompetent programmers, consultants and the search for the lowest common denominator for an audience.

When I started my first show on WGST, I was not at the top of my Talk Radio game. But most everyone at the station and in the listening audience still had fond memories of Z-93's wildly popular **Ross and Wilson** show, so content and form weren't all that noticed. For the first few weeks, most of the callers just wanted to say, "Welcome back" and reminisce about their personal favorite R&W story from "back in the day." It was fun and funny – unless you had arrived in Atlanta after our 1980 departure for WABC. Now 12-13 years later, there was a crowd of new listeners in a different format with no clue what a **Ross and Wilson** was. Getting off Memory Lane and onto current issues took some effort but, eventually, my prodigal son status wore off and I was just another horse in the Atlanta Talk Radio stable.

Two very interesting things happened during that brief stay -- one was Rush Limbaugh, the other was **Talk at Nite**, my second journey into TV.

First -- Rush.

WGST was Atlanta's perennial #2 talk station, forever in the shadow of WSB, the 50,000 watt Cox O&O. It wasn't so much that WSB had the better talent than it was WGST had such a lousy signal, even after a frequency change. WSB could be heard in several states. WGST, with a southerly-directed signal, couldn't be heard in some of the northern Atlanta suburbs where all the white-collar Talk Radio audience growth was taking place. Tough to get ratings when your audience can't hear you.

Duh.

The one bright programming light WGST could exclusively claim was the brash, new **Rush Limbaugh Show**, syndicated out of WABC. Still in his early growth phase, Rush did a series of **Rush to Excellence Tour** promotions, airing his show from affiliate studios in markets around the country, followed by a stand-up and Q&A appearance in a venue large enough to hold an SRO crowd of new and dedicated followers. One of those tours brought him to Atlanta and WGST.

The way it was supposed to work: Rush would do his regular show from our studios, take a break from 3 p.m. to 6 p.m., then appear at a local venue circa 7 p.m. How it actually came off in Atlanta was different.

Rush and I met in the studio as he was leaving at the end of his show. He had heard of my years at WABC and we played the "who-do-you-know" game, as radio types always do. I made a half-serious comment: "You ought to stick around for my show; we can call it **Rush and Wilson**." He thought that was hilarious and perfect. And so he stayed -- for the next three hours! Despite being total strangers, the show was superb! We played off each other as well – if not better – than Ross and I did after our first meeting in Baton Rouge 16 years earlier.

When it was over, I drove him to his speech and stand-up show. Traffic gave us an additional 45 minutes to chat about radio, politics, programming philosophy, future plans for the show, etc. Inside, Rush went off to freshen up, long enough for me to get drafted into greeting the house and introducing them to Rush.

On stage, I introduced myself to some very nice applause, got off a few one-liners and thanked everyone for listening to WGST.

> *And now, with half his brain tied behind his back just to be fair, Rush Limbaugh!*

The crowd went nuts! Standing O! Whistles! Yells! Everything except flying panties and hotel room keys! I watched most of the show backstage, then hit the road.

The next morning, perusing the **Atlanta Journal-Constitution**, I noted that one of their liberal columnists had ripped into Rush as well as WGST and conservative Talk Radio in general. Just before noon, I received a call from the PD:

> *Rush wants to know if it would be OK if he did the show again with you today. He's really peeved at what the paper said and he wants to get his licks in, something he won't be able to pull off on his national show.*

Would it be "OK" to do another show with the number one talk show host in the country? Hmmm, lemme think about that for a nanosecond or two.

And so it came to pass: **Rush and Wilson** lived to play and fight another day against the evil forces of the liberal elite media! And a good time was had by all, with the possible exception of a certain **AJC** columnist whose "opinion" was thoroughly shredded from 3 p.m. to 6 p.m.

For my posterity and the historical record, Rush Limbaugh never did another "two-man" show anywhere with anyone after **Rush and Wilson** on WGST. How about that!

Story Thirty-One

THE NIGHT NO ONE SHOWED UP

Along with **Music Notes** at CNN, Emmy Award-winning **Crabs** at PBS and a deplorable basketful of commercials, promos and contests, for better or worse, my mug occasionally appeared on TV. Having the additional dimension to play in spawned a slew of new creativity. But unlike radio, it also brought along gangs of people to contend with while getting that creativity to the screen. The spontaneity of radio was more my thing. Then, in 1991, while doing PM Drive on News/Talk WGST/Atlanta, Hal Gore* called.

Hal, a long-time Radio/TV veteran with a great reputation, invited me to dinner to talk about a late-night talk show on his new WTLK-TV. After steaks, etc. at Atlanta's renowned Bone's Restaurant, he laid out the idea: a one-hour live talk show, 10 p.m. to 11 p.m., Monday through Friday, with a live studio audience, guests and – the kicker – live phone calls from viewers!

That last part was unheard of. You couldn't effectively put live TV audio on a delay, so the danger of someone calling in with obscenities on his mind could colorize the airwaves a dark blue until the phone op could dump the call. Without Talk Radio's seven-second delay and patented Dump Button, such Technicolor vocabulary could be fatal to your license!

My response: Let's do it!

The $$$ were OK but the broadcast day was gonna be a long one – 3 p.m. to 6 p.m. on WGST, four hours until TV show time, then a 90-minute drive back home. Sometime later, WTLK lost the **Sally Jessy Raphael Show** and the extra hour was added to **Talk at Nite**, making my "day" even longer.

In the early 90s, the nagging question was when would WTLK get on cable? Without a cable presence, advertising sales were difficult because the broadcast audience was tiny. No one knew when cable access would come through, it was one of those government red tape things. Whatever, the show pulled respectable ratings, even up against Johnny Carson. That was enough to attract some local Bar-B-Q restaurants, grocery stores, auto repair shops and, of course, the usual gang of PI (per-inquiry) spots for Slim Whitman, Ferrante & Teicher and Zamfir CDs and the never-popular "But Wait! There's More!" Ronco's All-Weather Shoe Horn and other gems of "As Seen on TV" whizbangs and gadgets.

TV has never been done as casually as **Talk at Nite**. While we waited for cable access, we had some great shows! Fortunately, we never did get one of those colorful calls, just a bunch of fans from the radio show and wack-a-doodles who wanted friends to hear their voice on TV! With that little bump in the ratings, we started to get some credibility in the market, snagging some big-time guests, including Heavyweight Champ Evander Holyfield, the Wayans Brothers from **In Living Color**, Steve Harvey, Dannion Brinkley and even a reunion with New Orleans Chef Paul Prudhomme! Not bad for a non-cable local show from an Atlanta suburb!

We even scored our own band! Some local guys were fans of the show and offered to come in on their open dates and be our **Talk at Nite** Show Orchestra!

Talk at Nite had a very loyal in-studio audience! One large guy, "Dave," showed up every night. *Every night.* He'd plop down in the middle of the bleacher seating, clap, whistle and whoop it up through the entire show, both one and two-hour versions. Most of the time, he even brought his wife and always sat in the same spot. When the cameras panned the applauding audience at the beginning of the show, I'd mention "Dave and the entire Dave Section." A veritable cult following was developing!

There are lots of great stories from that show but easily the best of all is: **The Night Nobody Showed Up**.

As the show opening began, not one body was in the bleachers. Zero. Not even Dave. On cue, I made my entrance:

> *Hold it! Hold it! Stop the music! I don't believe this! Well, actually, I do; I knew this night would come eventually. Take a look…*

The cameras did their usual pan of the seats.

> *I knew this time would come. It's taken a few months, but as you can see, the boring, brain-dead mediocrity of this show has finally scared off anybody from coming in – even with free admission! I knew we had our moments but… no one? Not even Dave? I don't know if this is just a tragic confluence of circumstance or a real slap in the face! Regardless, this can't happen! If the Brass sees this, that will be the end of Talk at Nite!*
>
> *No way! Not gonna happen! Not my show! Tell ya what I'm gonna do… I think this is just some strange anomaly! Sunspots! Bad Mojo! So here's the deal: I want you to get your buns out of bed, get dressed and haul your freight down here to the studio. Better yet! Don't get dressed! Just come in your jammies or Dr. Denton's. If you sleep in your birthday suit, grab some patriotic Band-Aids – two stars and a stripe oughta do it -- or a fig tree but don't bother to get all gussied up! There's no time for all that!*
>
> *And here's the deal: if before the show is over we fill up all these seats like we always do, I will personally escort everybody over to the Kennesaw Waffle House and buy coffee for the whole gang! So get moving! Time's a-wasting!*

All this time, a camera held the shot of the empty studio seating area.

> *So that's what it is right now, live as we come on the air. Here's a shot of the clock... at the end of the show we'll take a look and see how we did. Meanwhile, let's go to the phones.*

It took about ten minutes for people to start coming in. Sure enough, most of them were in robes and slippers; some even brought sleepy kids! Dave and Mrs. Dave showed up, all apologetic, "We just thought we'd take one night off!" I swear I thought he was about to burst into tears!

After the final commercial break, I re-capped for the viewers:

> *OK, if you weren't watching when we started, here's a shot of the studio audience about two hours ago..."*

The booth put up the clock and pan shot of the empty seats.

> *As you can see, when we started the show, it was Sitting Room Only -- no one was here. In pure desperation to save Talk at Nite, I told everyone watching to come on down, fill those empty seats to keep Talk at Nite on the air – and if you filled all the seats, right after the show I would personally buy everybody coffee over at the Kennesaw Waffle House. Now, here is a live shot of what has happened!*

As the camera panned the seating area, it revealed a packed house! The audience stood and applauded and whistled and cheered!

> *We did it! S-R-O for T-A-N! Good night everybody! Thanks for watching! We're on our way to the Waffle House!*

It was a great night for the Waffle House and staff! Most everyone went, but not everyone stayed. After all, it was after midnight, pretty late for folks with jobs and kids. Still, we packed the Waffle House and it stayed that way for another hour. While I tried to make good on my offer, the manager wouldn't hear of it. When I went to tip the staff, he told me not to sweat it. He said it was the best publicity they ever had, and the biggest crowd. It turned out everyone had generously tipped all the waitresses too.

A great time was had by all! The local paper gave us a nice write-up and made Hal Gore and the sales weasels very happy!

But not quite "happy" enough.

The cable must-carry rules wouldn't impact WTLK for another six years! Hal never thought cable access would take so long and the expenses became unsustainable. The station's live shows hosted by some other Atlanta-area celebs were cancelled one by one. Thanks to our gigantic ratings, and an actual revenue trickle, **Talk at Nite** was the last to shut down.

That last night was sad. Our little show and its loyal band of merry audience members had become a tight convivial group with viewers at home watching every night. But we had a great run and great fun! I think about it every time I pass a Waffle House! If doing live TV could have been like that all the time…

Well, you get the drift.

**Regrettably, Harold W. "Hal" Gore died August 2014.*

Story Thirty-Two

GENERAL SUTTER'S CHAMPAGNE

Here is the other non-radio story. Two's my limit. Promise!

This one was a lotta fun! Cassie and I still get a smile out of this one because it went so perfectly!

Lititz, PA is a quaint little town near Lancaster that attracts its fair share of tourists looking for the quaint little antique stores and shops one expects to find in quaint little towns throughout the Northeast. We were into antiques at the time and conveniently, there was an outdoor antique festival in progress, so there we were.

As is our custom and preference as mentioned in the other "non-radio" story, we opted for an early dinner at Lititz's premier dining spot, the General Sutter Inn. (Note: I can't confirm it is still premier; we haven't been back since, but the restaurant is still in business.)

But I digress…

Fortuitously, we were seated by the door nearest the lobby. Not our preference, but it was the only two-top available. As we waited for our drinks, we noted – with some dread – a table set for 20 was perpendicular to us, to my right. When I told the waiter we had no desire to be dining that close to whatever celebratory event was about to happen, he assured me the reservations were two hours away and unless we were the world's slowest eaters, we'd be long gone before the multitude arrived.

Oh. OK.

Except he was wrong.

Guests started arriving about the time we were finishing dinner but before ordering dessert/coffee.

I called this to the attention of our waiter with the lousy forecast.

Not to worry. This was a gathering for a woman celebrating her 90th birthday. No kids. Just friends and family. No hats. No horns. Adult Behavior was assured.

OK.

As we enjoyed dessert, the rest of the entourage trickled in; indeed, they were a most genteel, well-mannered group. Two of the party even came to our table to assure us everyone would be civilized and respectful of other diners, especially since we were close enough to have been a part of the action!

Then, the guest of honor arrived. A lovely woman, beautifully dressed, not looking her age at all, navigating under her own power, greeting and hugging along the way to her seat at the head of the table. Notably missing in this gathering of couples was anyone resembling a spouse or partner at her side. And that gave me an idea!

The waiter caught my nod and brought the check. Handing it back, I told him: "Ice down a bottle of a decent champagne and deliver it to the birthday girl. When she asks – because she will – tell her it's from her Secret Admirer and you were sworn to keep the secret!" Fortunately, our waiter was one of the rare ones who "got it" and with a knowing grin, scurried off as a few more couples came in.

By the time everyone had arrived, said their hellos and were seated, our waiter dropped off our amended check, left, then promptly returned with an ice bucket complete with stand. A bright red ribbon was tied around the bottleneck as he set the stand at the head of the table next to the guest of honor and prepared to pop the cork.

She and others seated nearby were visibly surprised. Watching surreptitiously, we saw her puzzled look at the waiter and read her lips, "Who ordered this? Where did this come from?" While we couldn't see the waiter's face as he shook his head, the "shock and awe" on her face, as well as the guests within earshot, was priceless! She and they immediately started asking the other guests at their table, "Who sent the champagne?" With shrugs and puzzled looks in response, they all began scanning the room for a familiar face and a wave.

While all this was happening, Cassie and I stood to leave. As we went out the nearby door, we paused for a look back at the bewildered group still gazing about and just happened to make direct eye contact with the Birthday Girl! I gave her a big wink and a smile. Her jaw dropped in surprise, astonishment and confusion -- who was this stranger? But before she could fully recover and point me out to nearby friends, we hustled out the door and into pedestrian traffic.

I can still see that scene mixed with revelry, astonishment, wonder, curiosity and finally, the bewildered realization on her face, discovering her anonymous Secret Admirer, who just disappeared!

It couldn't have been choreographed better! I hope it became one of those "family stories" that is told every year: "Remember the time someone sent Grandma that bottle of champagne?"

Story Thirty-Three

PAUL HARVEY

A vital component of a great sense of humor is a having skewed view of things. In order to be really, really successful in radio -- with the exception of news, engineering, and bookkeeping -- a great sense of humor is an absolute necessity.

That being said, sometimes a great sense of humor can go downright silly on you. That's not necessarily a bad thing; it just makes explaining funny things difficult.

Here's an example:

If you've never heard of Paul Harvey, stop here and Google him. It will make the rest of the story much more understandable, possibly entertaining, and hopefully, funny. It sure as hell was funny at the time!

I landed the PD/AM Drive gig at WQXY-FM, Baton Rouge's "Beautiful Music" station. Granted, a beautiful music format and Brian Wilson was never a perfect match. But part-owner and GM Ken Winstanley hired me to bring some energy to the morning show and, of course, oversee all the other nitpicking things a PD does (see also: boring parts of the job).

Twice a day, in Morning Drive and again at noon, we carried the incredibly popular **Paul Harvey News and Comment** from ABC Radio. This was unheard of on a beautiful music station. But we were the ABC affiliate with access to certain network features like Paul Harvey. His immense popularity made him eminently sellable to advertisers for premium dollars. And making money is what the business is all about.

Like most stations, we took the feature live in AM Drive. And like most stations, his longer **News and Comment** segment aired at noon, while actually fed by ABC at 11:40 a.m. We would record it and have just enough time to get it cued up and programmed into the automation for playback at high noon.

So much for the mechanics. Here's where the fun starts and why you had to know how Paul Harvey ran his **News and Comments**.

Every Paul Harvey broadcast was compelling and unique. But it was his sign off that was his signature trademark. At the conclusion of his last story, he would say, "Paul Harvey.... Good Day!" It was that pause he put between his name and "Good Day" that befuddled many an air talent because there was just no way to perfectly time when he was going to say "Good Day!" It was never off by more than a fraction of a second, but the precise moment was totally unpredictable. When you're attempting to run the tightest board, a given in any radio format, hitting the nanosecond after "day" was a challenge Monday through Friday.

I took a different view.

Except for AM Drive, WQXY-FM was totally automated, allowing for a few options in running certain programming features. I wondered if the more passive, upscale, beautiful music FM audience (and the boss) would notice if Paul Harvey's sign off was slightly out of sync.

I had to find out.

Starting on a Monday, I ran the Paul Harvey feature at noon as usual. But on Tuesday, before the playback at noon, I would edit in a length of leader tape (blank tape) between the words, "Paul Harvey" and "Good Day!"

That Tuesday, instead of hearing the customary, "Paul Harvey… Good Day," the attentive listener heard, Paul Harvey …….. Good Day!"

It played through without a hitch. I sat at my desk and waited for a call from some listener wanting to know what was wrong with Paul Harvey. This is not as ridiculous as it may sound; Paul Harvey's fans were attentive and rabid. On this Tuesday, the phone didn't ring.

On Wednesday, more leader tape. And listeners heard, "Paul Harvey …………….. Good Day!"

And I sat at my desk and waited for a call. Nothing.

On Thursday, still more leader tape. Listeners heard, "Paul Harvey ……………………. Good Day!"

Desk. Phone. Silence. Maybe Paul Harvey's listeners weren't as sharp as I thought.

On Friday, the leader tape was so long, the time to splice it in and get the program into the system was dicey. On this day, listeners heard, "Paul Harvey…………………………………. Good Day!"

Back at my desk, I sat dumbfounded. Not one call.

Determined to see this through to the end -- whatever "the end" might turn out to be -- I got pretty good at adding more and more leader tape. By Wednesday of the following week, there was a full 30 seconds of dead air between "Paul Harvey" and "Good Day!" And on *this* day, the phone rang! Twice! The first was a concerned listener who was becoming worried about Mr. Harvey's health because it was taking him longer and longer to say "Good Day." I assured him that Mr. Harvey was in perfect health and that in all likelihood the delay had something to do with sunspots or, maybe, his radio.

The second caller was Ken Winstanley. And he was laughing so hard, he could hardly speak. It actually took me a moment to figure out it was Ken on the line!

> *Wilson, you are too much! You are just too damn much! I heard this on Monday and again on Tuesday, but I was too damn busy to call and ask you what the hell was going on! When I heard it again today, what… 30 seconds? I figured out what you were doing.*

It actually took him a while to say all that because, after every two or three words, he'd break up laughing again!

Finally, he got a grip.

> *OK, OK. That was some really funny stuff. Thanks a lot. I haven't laughed this hard in years. Now cut it out. If the sponsors or ABC hear this, we could lose a big account and ABC could even yank the affiliation. So, congratulations, that was a great bit. I'll be sure to tell my grandchildren about it.*
>
> *Click.*

I don't know if Ken ever told his grandchildren the story. If he did, I wonder if they got the joke. It takes a skewed view of the world along with a unique sense of humor to have appreciated a stunt like this! Fortunately for me, Ken Winstanley had it all. This time.

Story Thirty-Four

BLOOPERS

Up until recently, DJs were human beings and, as you may have heard, humans make mistakes. In my business, those "mistakes" were originally called "bloopers." Since the 1950s, other less family-friendly labels have been given to show content that wasn't intended – or just shouldn't have made it – to air.

It should come as no surprise that, over the years, your humble scribbler made a few contributions to this category. I am not referring to the occasional hiccup or mispronunciation. Nope. I'm talking full-blown-bad, the kind of stuff that gets you fired and your station fined mega-bux.

These are my three most notorious contributions.

Radio Silence

My first journey into FCC No-No Land occurred, conspicuously enough, my first day on the air. I had not taken the FCC Third Class License (with Broadcast Endorsement) test yet, so someone with those credentials had to be in the Control Room with me the entire time I was on the air. At this point – day one of my subsequently illustrious career, who better than the dude from the party who loved my voice, Large Pink Bill Loving, to monitor my actions simultaneously training me in proper equipment operation, meter reading, music rotation, etc.

Ten minutes into the second hour of the show, the scheduled commercial on the program log was for Newport cigarettes. I dutifully loaded the cart (tape cartridge with recorded commercial) into one of the two cart machines. At the end of whatever record was playing, I keyed the mic, said something forgettable and hit the machine's start button. Nothing happened. Silence. And in radio, silence = bad. Following Bill's instructions, I hit the red stop button and re-hit the green start button again. Nada. More dreaded silence.

Again I looked over at Large Pink, who was getting a little antsy as he pointed to the #2 cart machine. I transferred the cart, pushed the green-then red-then green buttons again. Still more silence. This had taken all of maybe ten seconds. And in radio, that much dead air is an eternity. With this second failure, I said, "Hey, Bill – this damn thing isn't working!" I might just as well have said, "Hey Bill, there's a cottonmouth crawling up your leg!" and he wouldn't have moved any faster. He rushed the three steps to my chair, reached over my shoulder and flipped a switch. The *mic* switch.

My "this damn thing isn't working" comment had just been broadcast to the entire listening area. And in September 1965, "damn" was not an acceptable expletive one could utter on the public airwaves. Bill fixed the cart problem quickly enough, but for the next five days, we all lived in fear that we'd receive a telegram -- or worse -- a *visit* from the FCC. Had I known then what I know now, I wouldn't have damaged one fingernail worrying my fledgling career was going to die more quickly than it began. Bottom line: nothing happened.

Tongue Twister

Fast forward a couple years. I've been hired for PM Drive on WIBR/Baton Rouge. Even today, part of the job is reading live copy, but mainly as an "endorsement."

Twice a month on Wednesday afternoons, I had to read a spot for Fairfield Cleaners on Plank Road. In the two years I had been there, the copy had never changed. After a couple months, I had it memorized:

All the friendly folks at Fairfield Cleaners up on Plank Road, want you to know about their weekly dry cleaning specials! Featured all this week: short sleeve sports shirts – three for three dollars, sports coats – seven dollars, men's suits – ten dollars and ladies blouses – three for five dollars. Yes, all the friendly folks at Fairfield Cleaners want you to know they appreciate your business and blah blah blah…

Then came this fateful Wednesday. Something had changed. The paper in the copy book for Fairfield Cleaners was fresh and clean. OK. Whatever. A quick glance indicated fresh paper was the only real change. Here is what the audience heard:

All the friendly folks at Fairfield Cleaners up on Plank Road want you to know about their dry cleaning specials. Featured all this week: short sleeve sports shits…

SPORT SHITS! OMG! If "damn" was a problem, "shits" would lose the license! But never let them see you sweat, right? I didn't miss a beat and kept right on reading as if "short sleeve sports shits" was what everyone wore!

Remarkably, no one noticed! No one at the station came running in, no listeners called. Crickets.

Some great lessons were learned that day: Always double-check your copy for human error. And whether running a show or advertising a business, if you want the listener to really hear your message, you better do something more noticeable than just say "shit" on the air! I made both a part of my everyday programming philosophy! A few years later, when I opened my own ad agency, a great deal of the success my clients enjoyed was based on writing ad copy with "short-sleeved sports shits" in mind!

The Grand Daddy of Them All

1988 – 20+ years later. Baton Rouge, Houston, Atlanta and New York all are in my rear-view mirror. While Atlanta (Z-93) and NYC (WABC) provided fertile territory for innuendo, double entendre and other word games, I was careful to kinda-sorta sanitize my air work. Societal changes no longer gave the occasional "hell" or "damn" an audience double-take or a "stern warning" from the FCC. Still, that was about the limit for on-air "profanity" on "family-oriented radio stations."

In July 1984, I landed in Baltimore as half of the **Brian and O'Brien Show** on B104, WBSB-FM. At this juncture, it is fair and accurate to say that, chiseled in Baltimore Radio history, no AM Drive show on any frequency before or since has been more outrageous, scandalous, notorious or successful. Our contentious relationship was the basic and biggest reason for our success.

At this particular juncture in our "partnership," Don had been suspended or fired. I had been doing the show solo for some weeks. John Nolan, one of the most talented board-ops in the business, was running the board, playing the spots and occasionally commenting from the main control room. I recorded listener calls, mangled live commercials and played whatever on-air games and giveaways from my separate smaller studio in line-of-sight of John; we communicated by intercom.

One of our regular features was B104's **Bear in the Air** traffic reports, radioed in from a helicopter. The reporting recently had been taken over by an attractive young woman, which gave me all the reason I needed to change the AM Drive reports to B104's ***Pair*** **in the Air** traffic. At that time, Baltimore society hadn't gotten all that wrapped around the PC nonsense and Barb played right along, not being so tightly wrapped herself, she got the joke.

This particular morning was not one of Baltimore's best. Gray, overcast but no fog or rain. Our first traffic report was logged within the 7 a.m. news. At 6:10, while I was ramping up the opening hour, Barb called in to tell John she'd have to do the show from home; the chopper was down due to mechanical issues. After giving me the news, I informed the audience that our **Pair in the Air** would be our **Pair on the Ground** that morning, but not to fear, we would still be on top of things – so to speak.

Immediately, I got a call from a guy who said he owned a helicopter with all the right radio frequencies and he'd be happy to take Barb up in return for a mention of his company. He'd prep the chopper and meet Barb at the airport.

I relayed the good news to John who called Barb. She was not happy, believing she'd be spending the morning in bed, John told me over the intercom.

> *Well, tell her to get her buns outta bed; this guy is gonna be at the airport to meet her in 30 minutes.*

I went back to the phones and tunes and bits.

Five minutes later, Barb called the control room again. John signaled there was a problem -- Barb doesn't think she can get dressed and meet the guy in time.

> *Tell her it's no problem. We'll have 15 minutes to spare. She can fake the first report from the ground if she has to.*

John relayed the message and I went back to the show.

Around 6:35, Barb called again. This time, she was worried the radio frequencies wouldn't match.

> *Tell her I've already covered that with the owner; everything is A-OK.*

John relayed the message and I went back to the show.

Minutes later, just as I finished a bit on the air, I saw John pick up the hotline again. It was getting closer to the 7 a.m. news and Barb was still calling with "issues." I hit the intercom:

Is that Barb?

John nods.

Now what?

Barb's just now ready to leave and she doesn't think she can make it to the airport on time.

I lose it.

Look. Tell her to get in the fucking car, go to the fucking airport and do the fucking traffic. Now!

John passed along my order (sorta) and hung up. The commercials were still running, so I hit record on the tape deck and went fishing for a decent caller. Just then, I noticed the hotline blinking. This would be about the right time for my son to call before he left for school.

Hi son!

Hi Dad.

You about ready to hit the road?

Yes sir, all set. Say, Dad… do you know what you just said on air?

No, wha…

Looking down at my control board, sure enough -- my mic light was still bright red. I punched it off and hit the intercom:

John! Didn't you take my studio off the air after that last bit?

John looked at the main board and turned white. He punched his intercom.

Oh crap!

My little expletive-laced directive to Barb had been broadcast to the largest morning radio audience listening to any Baltimore station.

> *Well son, thanks for mentioning that! Have a great day at school. I hope I'll still be employed when you get home.*

He laughed.

> *Love ya Dad!*
>
> *Love you, too, son. Be careful driving.*
>
> *Yes sir, I will.*
>
> *Click.*

While not all that unusual, I noticed all eight of the other incoming lines were blinking.

Gee, I wonder why…

> *B104, Hello…*
>
> *HA-HA-HA HEY WILSON! DO YOU KNOW WHAT YOU JUST SAID ON THE AIR? HA-HA-HA-HA*
>
> *Click.*
>
> *B104, Hello…*
>
> *HEY, WILSON! YOUR MIC IS OPEN! HA-HA-HA-HA-HA!*
>
> *Click.*
>
> *B104, Hello…*
>
> *I want to speak to the manager. I was just listening to your station and the man on the air just used the most obscene language! I want to register a complaint!*
>
> *Yes, ma'am… please hold for just a moment.*

Five minutes later the hold light stopped flashing.

And so it went for the next dozen calls until I just stopped answering. I needed to get thru the rest of the show and prepare for the coming confrontation with the GM who would be screaming for me to come to his office the moment the show was over.

Amazingly enough, that didn't happen. In fact, no one in the station said a word about it. Not the sales weasels, engineering, office staff, receptionist – no one. I hung around looking busy for a while, then left as I normally did. Hey! Maybe I dodged a bullet! Or three bullets!

The phone was ringing when I arrived home.

> *Hello.*
>
> *Hey, Brian – it's Steve McKerrow at* **The Baltimore Sun**.
>
> *Hey – what's up? (as if…)*
>
> *I understand you taught your audience a few new words this morning!*
>
> *Gee, where did you hear that spurious rumor?*

He laughed.

> *Are you saying you didn't say it?*
>
> *Say what? "It"? I say "it" quite often actually.*

He became semi-serious.

> *I didn't hear it myself, but everyone at the paper was talking about you saying "fuck" on your show this morning; in fact, saying it three times while you were yelling at someone about a traffic report or something. I'm calling to confirm whether or not it happened.*
>
> *Yeah, it happened.*

I gave him the thumbnail version from my side. He laughed, said something about the perils of technology.

> *So are you going to apologize to your audience tomorrow?*

> *Apologize? Why? I seriously doubt my dozens of loyal fans would be shocked and amazed to know I occasionally employ that word; apologizing would only draw negative attention to the station, the show and me. Unlike your newspaper that stays around long enough to housebreak puppies, radio is like a rifle shot. If you are in front of the bullet at the time, you're gonna get hit. A second early or a second late and you have no clue what just happened.*

> *For me to apologize would mean first having to explain to everyone who missed it just what happened in order for the apology to have any effect. So, in a word, hell no, I'm not apologizing. If someone registers a complaint with the FCC, I'll explain the circumstances and take the punishment, if any. Otherwise, if no one actually complained, I have nothing to apologize for. As my former attorney said: "A crime hasn't been committed until somebody screams." It's an adult show for kids. The music keeps the kids happy and the adults get off on the big words. Until I hear otherwise, tomorrow is just another day, just another show.*

The next day, along with one of the menacing pictures of me **The Sun** kept in its files, was the headline, **Regrets, not apologies, for open-mike [sic] outburst**. The story was a reasonable facsimile of my conversation with McKerrow. This time, before the show was even over, the GM slammed my studio door open and yelled:

> *GET INTO MY OFFICE AS SOON AS YOU'RE DONE!*

The GM's love of drama was exceeded only by the genius of his personnel management technique; I took my time getting there. After screaming a third time over the paging system:

BRIAN WILSON -- BRIAN WILSON -- TO MY OFFICE IMMEDIATELY!

I strolled in.

Good morning -You bellowed?

SHUT THE DOOR!

He held up the paper with the screaming headline… not to be outdone, he screamed himself.

WHAT THE HELL IS THIS ALL ABOUT?

Well, if you listened to the show now and then instead of monitoring the competition to see what advertisers they have that we don't, you might have heard it. To **The Sun***'s credit, they've got the gist of it right.*

WHAT DO YOU MEAN YOU'RE NOT GOING TO APOLOGIZE? YOU SURE AS HELL ARE GOING TO --TOMORROW MORNING. TWICE.

By end of the sentence, he looks apoplectic. And purple. I had seen this act before.

I remained calm.

No, sir, I'm not – and here's why. Has anyone called to complain? Has the FCC called to inquire? Has any sponsor called to cancel their ads?

THAT'S GOT NOTHING TO DO WITH IT. YOU CAN'T GO ON THE AIR AND USE LANGUAGE LIKE THAT –

And I didn't. To my knowledge, my studio and the main studio were both off the air. Thanks to Barb's constant calling and paranoia about flying, which distracted both John and me, the proper buttons didn't get pushed. In a civilized society, it's called an "accident" and, like shit, it happens. To apologize, I'd have to

> *explain what happened off the air. Think about that. You know as well as I, certain sponsors would be calling immediately demanding some "consideration" for your obscene ad rates, or they'd cancel. Should someone call at this late date, you or I can deal with it on a case-by-case basis. For all the people who weren't listening at that moment, let them hear it second-hand. If they're amused, we win. If they're pissed, they'll listen to hear if it happens again.*

Silence.

> *Get the fuck outta here.*

> *Now THAT'S funny!*

And that was it.

But there was an amazing P.S. a few days later, thanks to engineering pulling the aircheck tape – just in case.

In the offending moment, a commercial for a new Baltimore hotel was playing. With nautical music, ship bells and seagull sound-effects, the soft-voiced announcer gently intoned something like this:

The management of the fantastic new Rambilicus Inner Harbor Hotel would like to welcome you to our newest luxurious accommodations. Grand views of the harbor; great rooms and suites. And right now, as a thank you and welcome to the people of Baltimore, we are offering a special weekend celebration, with special rates on rooms for just $199. Relax in our whirlpool tubs… enjoy world-class room service… and dine in any one of our four-star restaurants! All for just $199 per person. Call for your reservations right away. Come and enjoy the New Rambilicus Inner Harbor Hotel at Baltimore's fabulous Inner Harbor.

But here's what the listener heard:

The management of the fantastic new Rambilicus Inner Harbor Hotel would like to welcome you to our newest luxurious accommodations. Grand views of the harbor; great rooms and suites. And right now, as a thank you and welcome to the people of Baltimore, we are offering a special weekend *celebration, with special rates on rooms for just $199. [GET IN THE FUCKING CAR] Relax in our whirlpool tubs, [GO TO THE FUCKING AIRPORT] enjoy world-class room service [AND DO THE FUCKING TAFFIC] and dine in any one of our four-star restaurants! All for just $199 per person. Call for your reservations right away. Come and enjoy the New Rambilicus Inner-Harbor Hotel at Baltimore's fabulous Inner Harbor.*

Since my unabashed comments fit so perfectly within the announcer's pitch, there were those, like the GM, who actually thought I had pre-produced the spot *just for that moment.*

Bloopers! Better than TV! Stranger than reality!

Story Thirty-Five

WALT DISNEY WORLD

Funny things happen in this business. Funny things happen in every business. But the funny things that happen in your business -- assuming you're not in radio -- are rarely broadcast to the entire free world. Additionally, like all forms of humor, funny is subjective. It takes a special blend of skewed perception to see, create and bring ordinary things to a show and make them funny enough for the audience to laugh.

It was Walt Disney World circa 1993. I was happily teamed with Bob Madigan, one of the truly great talents in radio. We were hosting AM Drive as **Brian and Bob** on WWRC/Washington DC. Like **Brian and O'Brien**, Bob and I had been magically paired after I left WGST/Atlanta, making room for some whippersnapper from Alabama named Sean Hannity. WWRC management had been searching for a change in their current morning show, **Mornings with Rita and Bob**. As a team, they had virtually zero positive chemistry between them. Put simply -- the show was a big snoozer. Management got word from friend and former colleague John Nolan I was available, and the rest is history.

See **The Reader's Guide** for details of how **Mornings with Brian and Bob** came to be. Suffice to say it was not typical of the way people normally get hired in radio. This just happened to be one of the fortunate times I was on the *hired* side. It was also fortunate that it turned out to be a marriage made in heaven. Even at our best of times, **Ross and Wilson** would have struggled to hold a candle to the rapier wit, experience, chemistry, intelligence, content and mutual respect heard daily on **Mornings with Brian and Bob**. And that was just when Bob was talking!

On this particular occasion, Walt Disney World was running its annual promotion. Disney would fly in top Morning Drive shows from the Top Ten markets across the country to do their shows live from inside the park. By the time **Brian and Bob** got the call, I had already been there several times with the **Ross and Wilson Z-Morning Zoo** and the B104 **Brian and O'Brien Show**. It was a brilliant win-win marketing ploy by Disney and a great promotion for the stations and shows. We were flown in on The Mouse, Disney's private Gulfstream, and put up in private rooms at the newly-opened Grand Floridian Hotel. We also were each issued the Magic Kingdom tag. When wearing this tag, you had access to everything in the park -- food and drinks included -- all at no charge! In return, all we had to do was the same show we would do back home, except much of our content would feature conversations about Walt Disney World. So Disney received four hours of advertising on the top-rated AM Drive shows on the top-rated stations in the top ten markets across the country. A plane ride, a hotel room, some food, and booze was a small price to pay for such a package, even with the way some of those other guys drank!

So here we were, early one morning, in the dark, empty park. The only people around were other morning shows doing their thing and Disney grounds crews sweeping, cleaning and wiping stuff down for another exciting day in the Magic Kingdom!

Each morning show was assigned a Disney representative; invariably an attractive young woman decked out in the Disney uniform du jour. Her job fell somewhere between hall monitor and concierge. Whatever we needed -- coffee, doughnuts, orange juice -- she would make it appear. She would also make guests appear: stars within the Disney firmament who went from show to show promoting their latest picture, album or TV appearance. She would also summon the appropriate personnel to deal with any non-radio issues like the dangerously-tilting giant umbrella covering the table where we made our magic happen – before it collapsed.

The second day of our broadcast week, Bob and I had been chatting merrily along, relating to the audience back in DC what an absolutely fabulous time we were having at Disney World and encouraged everyone listening to immediately make plans to come down for their next vacation or holiday -- make sure to see the Disney World this; don't forget the Disney World that; take the kids to experience this new Disney World feature. The show was good; life was good. During a commercial break, Cindy, our official Disney assistant, came to the table for an unscheduled chat.

Unbeknownst to us, certain Disney World officials monitored the shows every morning to make sure absolutely accurate information was being broadcast to the folks back home. Cindy informed us that we had been guilty of an egregious error in our programming content. How could that be? Well… Cindy informed us that we – especially I -- had been consistently and incorrectly referring to our location as Disney World. *So what?* You see, the proper name for the Orlando property is *WALT* Disney World; Disneyland is in Anaheim, California. Orlando, Florida is the home of *WALT* Disney World and we were told we must refer to it as such accordingly. Of course, she was very nice about it, almost apologetic, but she made it plain this was not a subject for debate.

I debated it anyway.

What did the Suits think was going to happen? Was there some other Disney World in the area? Could someone see a mouse or a duck toy on someone's lawn and think the swing set in the backyard was Disney World? Bob found the exercise in logic amusing; Cindy found the discussion uncomfortable. Of course, it was a distinction without a difference but she had her bosses and, for the moment, they were ours, too.

By now the commercial break was just about over and my conversation with Cindy ended unresolved – for me, anyway. So we're back on the air with this nonsense hanging over the table like a wet Mouseketeer beach blanket. Not being long on self-control, I couldn't let this pass:

> *Good morning, everyone, Brian and Bob still pretty much live from Orlando. Before we get on with our award-losing, high-energy, New York-style morning show, I need to stop here for a moment and offer a sincere apology to our hosts as well as a clarification to those of you listening back home. On behalf of the Brian and Bob Show, I would like to apologize to the officials of Walt Disney World for possibly misleading you in the audience into thinking we were somewhere else called Disney World. We need to clarify that, in fact, we are broadcasting live from Walt Disney World.*
>
> *Another reason I need to make this clarification is that we were advised during the commercial break that a competing Disney World has opened three miles down the highway. Now, granted, even a casual observer would immediately notice the substantive differences between the two. First, the competing park is actually called FRED Disney World and is no relation to the late WALT Disney. Secondly, Fred Disney World only has a merry-go-round, three bumper cars, a Tilt-a-Whirl and a food concession featuring Polish sausage – frozen, not fresh -- lemonade, and day-old cotton candy. Oh, and they also have a pony ride. But, hey! Even with that, it cannot hold a candle to the glory and splendor here at WALT Disney World.*
>
> *So as you make your vacation or holiday reservations with your travel agent, don't make the same lame mistake your Brian and Bob Show made thinking everyone knew there was just one Disney World when, in fact, there is only one WALT Disney World. Be sure your travel agent books you and your family into WALT*

Disney World. You don't want a car full of crying, heart-broken kids when you pull into the parking lot and see FRED Disney World.

Now that we've got that cleared up, let's get on with the show.

Bob had just made it back to the table, having scooted away a few moments into my little rant, laughing so hard he was afraid it would go out over the air.

It was a brief but great moment in **Brian and Bob** Radio History.

The next morning, I asked Cindy if there had been any repercussions from my little monologue about Fred Disney World. She giggled and said her immediate supervisor was definitely not pleased but the vice president of promotions heard the whole thing and was still laughing when he came into the morning staff meeting.

Mission accomplished.

Bob Madigan (second from left) and Brian Wilson (right) appear on Talk Radio panel (Photo: The Heritage Foundation)

Story Thirty-Six

A KING AND HIS TAXES

Not so deep down inside, every talk show host who keyed a mic wants to see results from his work. Eventually. Whether opening minds with compelling information, positive reactions to new information or correcting a bad situation.

This Story accomplished all three!

During the halcyon days of **Mornings with Brian and Bob**, then WWRC/DC GM, Radio Legend Dick Rakovan, nabbed two syndicated programs to fill our night-time programming: Talk Radio pioneer Bruce Williams and perennial-talker Larry King. It was such a big deal, the station threw a rare reception for the two hosts, to celebrate our mutual good fortunes as well as score some promotional coverage from the DC media.

Larry King was at the top of his broadcasting game: a CNN show, syndicated **USA Today** column and published author. **The Larry King Show** aired from midnight to 5:30 a.m. and was the lead-in to **Brian and Bob**. As a result, I was able to hear the "open phones" segment of Larry's last two hours while driving to the palatial WWRC studios in the overly-pretentious World Building in Silver Spring from my meager hovel in suburban Columbia, MD.

Despite the ginormous income earned with his CNN and syndicated radio shows, newspaper columns and book deals, Larry complained a lot about taxes. Not about *paying* taxes. But that too many people weren't paying enough; a typical left/liberal complaint I found personally and politically offensive. Like most people, I worked my ass off for what I got paid and I resented various levels of government appropriating larger and larger chunks of that paycheck to fund federal and state boondoggles designed to keep them in office rather than performing government's essential responsibilities: preserving freedom and protecting rights. Whenever "taxes" came up during the show, I would rant "Taxation is Theft!" and rail about how a *free* country would not send Men With Guns to seize you and your property if you failed – or refused – to fork over whatever the IRS demanded! While not nearly as strident as I, my beloved partner, Bob Madigan, himself a noted figure in financial matters, would at least support the logic of my podium-pounding. Other than the occasional altruistic caller, no one successfully challenged the "Tax is Theft" charge.

But I digress…

The redundancy of hearing Larry boo-hoo about how "too few people were paying too few taxes" grew increasingly irritating -- enough to spark an idea, which I promptly put to work.

Explaining the issue to Bob and the audience, noting the absence of any logical or sustaining "pro-tax" argument, I implored anyone listening who also had earlier heard Larry do his thing to call him and say something -- something like:

> *Hey Larry! I've been listening to you here on WWRC and I've got a question. You've been saying we don't pay enough taxes, not just the rich people – but all of us don't pay enough. Here's my question. I saw a recent* **USA Today** *article about you; it said with your TV and radio shows, books and newspaper column, you were knocking down around $17 Large a year. If that's even close to accurate, I'm certain you pay your CPA's to make sure you cough up the <u>least</u> amount of taxes possible, right? So why don't you just*

personally send in an extra million or two? There's no law against sending in more money than you owe, right? What do think, Larry?

You get the idea. The caller's question didn't have to be verbatim, but simply point out that someone making more in a year than you and I will make in a lifetime could send in as much as he wanted, rather than complain about *everyone* paying too little. It's not illegal and no one would stop him! Hell, they might even say it's patriotic!

This went on every few mornings for a week or two. Every time Larry went off on "too few taxes" on his show, I'd make my little speech later on **Brian and Bob**. Then, I'd listen on the drive in to work the next morning to see if a **Brian and Bob** listener got through.

About a month and a half-dozen rants later, after my usual routine: dress, drive, stop for coffee, drive, etc., I hopped in the Jeep just in time to hear:

Silver Spring, Maryland, hello…

Hi Larry! Thanks for taking my call. Listening to you on WWRC and I have a question. You've been talking a lot lately about taxes and people not paying enough or their fair share or something like that. I've read that you're doing pretty well with your TV show and this radio show and your books and all; ***USA Today*** *says you're making around $17 million a year. So I was just wondering after you take all your legal deductions, why not just set a good example and send in a few extra million of your own?*

The dead air lasted seven or eight seconds, an eternity in radio. At last, King spoke:

I will when everyone else does. Biloxi, Mississippi… hello?

How *lame* was that!

John Nolan, our ace board op, had grabbed the aircheck tape and pulled off the segment by the time I got in. He knew immediately the replay would be a big part of the show. And it was!

I never met the caller from Silver Spring but, if you're reading this sir, a very belated thanks for your perfectly executed effort, making a great contribution to the **Brian and Bob Show** and an unforgettable **Story** for this book!

Story Thirty-Seven

AFFIRMATIVE ACTION

Dr. Walter E. Williams, Ph.D., is a professor of Economics at George Mason University. It's *slightly* possible you may not be familiar with Walter. If that's the case, I'll pause here while you Google him.

>>>>>>>>

Now you know something about the genius of the man.

One morning, while working with the erudite Bob Madigan on **Mornings with Brian and Bob** on WWRC/DC, I came across Walter's syndicated column in **The Washington Times** concerning Affirmative Action. Contrary to most pundits, especially those who also were African-American, he was against it on many levels. As the esteemed Senior Economics Professor at George Mason University, he had first-hand knowledge of how the program had negatively impacted both students and schools.

With a market as thoroughly liberal as Washington, DC and this talented professor/writer who obviously wasn't liberal at all, I had to get him on the air for listeners who might otherwise have missed the piece! Our esteemed producer, Shelia Jaskot, set it up.

At first, Walter was understandably tentative. Considering the market and subject matter, it was logical he would be locked and loaded for "opposition." I hurried to remind him of my libertarian credentials; that we had first met several years prior when he was the featured guest speaker and I was the MC for the Georgia State Libertarian Convention in Atlanta. The on-air atmosphere improved immeasurably.

Essentially, Walter's position was – and remains – Affirmative Action is a bad deal. It lowers the bar of qualifications for minority students simply because they are… minorities! The lower expectations of university admissions departments results in less qualified students taking the seats of more qualified students. It's a disservice to everyone, including the Affirmative Action students who subsequently flunk out in great numbers, since they are totally unprepared for the academic work required at a university level. It all made perfect sense.

I asked Walter if he'd be up for taking some calls:

> *WEW: Sure. Let's go.*
>
> *BW: Joe's up first… hi Joe, it's Brian and Bob with Professor Walter Williams on WRC.*
>
> *Joe: Yeah, I've been listening to this guy for the last 20 minutes. And as an African-American, I can say he doesn't have any idea what he's talking about. Affirmative Action is one of the best entitlement programs we've got. Thousands and thousands of students wouldn't have gotten into college without it.*
>
> *WEW: That may be true, but they also fail and drop out at nearly the same number.*
>
> *Joe: You know what your problem is, Williams? You don't hang around with black people enough. You need to get out more, meet people in the black community. You might learn something.*

While I didn't know Walter very well at the time, I knew something was about to happen. And it did.

> *WEW: You know, Joe, you must be a teeny-bopper or something. I've been black for a looong time. My brother and I were raised in*

> *the Philadelphia projects by a single mother who made sure every day we took a bath, wore clean clothes to school and did our homework. These Affirmative Action kids can hardly read and write, much less pass a college entrance exam.*

Because Walter was on the phone at his office at George Mason, he couldn't see Bob and me laughing or hear us pounding on the counter. It is one interview I'll never forget!

It also set the stage for countless other interviews I did with Walter. Because he was so damned good explaining economics, race relations and commenting on social and government policies, all under the bright light of Freedom and Liberty, I would have him on every station where **VRINK** booked me.

One time, introducing him on WBAP/DFW, I failed to mention among his credentials his former chairmanship of the Economics Department at George Mason. He called me out for it and "suggested" I repeat the intro. That soon became an audience favorite as the intro grew longer and longer with each interview.

Here's the intro from his latest visit:

> *BW: Ladies and Gentlemen, it is my honor and privilege to welcome back to the show, a man who needs no introduction but is assured to get one anyway. Professor of Economics and former Chairman of the Economics Department at the prestigious George Mason University, best-selling author of more than 17 books including his autobiography,* **Up From The Projects***, syndicated columnist, speaker, occasional guest host on the Rush Limbaugh Show, personal friends with Dr. Tom Sowell and Supreme Court Justice Clarence Thomas, noted epicurean and renowned wine connoisseur, expert marksman and collector of fine sporting devices, marathon bicyclist and winner of the Uppity White Woman Marathon, the living image of* **GQ** *and sex symbol to women worldwide, father and now, grandfather, my close, warm, personal friend, Professor Walter E. Williams.... how was that?*

WEW: I think that might have been OK. Did you mention wine connoisseur?

BW: Of course! I wouldn't want the audience to think any friend of mine or guest on this show would be swilling Boone's Farm Frozen Concentrate! Occasionally, I have to remind people you won't even lower your standards to pull an artificial cork!

WEW: Well, that's better than the last I time, I guess. OK, what do you want to talk about?

And so it goes... Space won't permit telling all the stories with my friend, Walter. Visit Walter's page at George Mason University (http://econfaculty.gmu.edu/wew/) and receive his free gift: "Proclamation of Amnesty and Pardon Granted to All Persons of European Descent," suitable for framing.

WHAT? EVEN MORE HOROSCOPES

ARIES: You will make a fortune selling life-size Shake & Bake bags to cannibals.

TAURUS: A blind man explains to you why his favorite color is corduroy.

GEMINI: Consider polygamy – if they all have good jobs!

CANCER: Explain to a senior citizen "wash and wear" doesn't mean "at the same time."

LEO: Tell your blind date that her braces don't bother you, but her smile reminds you of a '56 Buick.

VIRGO: Sex will not cure pimples, but it will give them something to smile about!

LIBRA: Your Shrink announces a major break-thru in your therapy since you no longer wet the couch.

SCORPIO: You know it's over when she hangs a picture of her ex-husband over the bed.

SAGITTARIUS: It's diet time when your tattoo becomes a mural.

AQUARIUS: Your girlfriend likes your new car's tilt-steering wheel because it gives her more head room.

PISCES: Remember we are born naked, wet and hungry… and then it gets worse!

Story Thirty-Eight

YOU'RE FIRED!

If "security" is a high priority on your career choice list, *broadcasting* is third from the bottom – just above Nitro Glycerin Juggler and Kamikaze Reenactment Pilot.

To my knowledge, no one has been fired in more creative ways than I have: face-to-face, telegram, USPS, answering machine, fax and "budget." Smoke signals, Morse code and carrier pigeon are the only three that missed me! So far…

Contrary to "normal" businesses, no one can claim having had an actual career in broadcasting if they were never fired. Probably several times! It's right there in the job description:

Radio -- *Work your ass off. Ridiculous hours. Slave wages. Undependable equipment. Lousy work environment. Worst. Management. Anywhere. No holidays. Vacation subject to change and cancellation with minimal notice. Termination any time on the whim of management (Christmas included). Experience required. Send resume, aircheck, 8x10 glossy, education transcripts, blood type and no less than 20 notarized references. (We WILL check each one of them.) Your Glorious Career In Showbiz Awaits You! Looking forward to having you join our team!*

Right.

But you will be ON THE AIR – IN SHOWBIZ!

Actually, there was one occasion I was terminated for good reason -- the first time.

It was a few months into my first gig. I don't recall the exact situation, but I remember that the office manager, Mabel, gave me an order to not do something wacky on the air. Feeling quite full of myself, I told her *she* wasn't my boss and went ahead with whatever it was; when the GM came in, *he* could give me the order if he was so inclined.

A little while later, after speaking with Mabel, *he* was very much inclined and I was immediately among the unemployed.

There also were some not-so-good reasons…

The Telegram

A few years later, I was doing a remote broadcast from Polk Chevrolet, a big Chevy dealer in Baton Rouge. The guy who owned it was one of the city's heavies; his ad budget was the envy of all the other car dealers. Of course, he and it were cherished by my station management, looking to get as much of it as possible.

For this occasion, a riser for the broadcast equipment and me was set up in the middle of the showroom to draw people inside and into the clutches of the awaiting sales weasels. About an hour into inviting "everyone to come on down and meet all the friendly Polk Folk," a showroom door flew open, followed by a loud scream and the blur of a 20-something female dashing across the floor. She jumped me standing behind the control board, wrapped her arms and legs around me and planted a big kiss.

Undoubtedly, the girl was a fan. A big fan. She breathlessly told me she had been out of the country for a year on some college venture, had just gotten back, heard me on the radio and zoomed right over. I kinda/sorta recognized her from some previous appearances but that was it. I was married – with two children. What could happen? I know what you're thinking – but fuggetaboudit.

She babbled on for some time about herself, Europe, herself, where she'd been, herself, ad infinitum. She was a supreme distraction; a remote broadcast is just as much work as being in-studio. I was getting paid a decent talent fee to get people in the door and long-term yapping with a fan wasn't part of the strategy. The owner had taken notice of the situation and was not pleased. Using a couple of movie ticket giveaways, I finally got her to leave without tossing her out the door -- although the thought had occurred to me.

As soon as the remote was over, I left on a week's vacation to Dauphin Island with the wife and kids.

All R&R'd, we returned home on a Sunday afternoon. Stuck in the door was a yellow Western Union telegram envelope. WTF? Telegrams weren't all that popular even pre-Internet and cell phone. This had to be something, and probably not good. Before I unlocked the door, I ripped open the envelope.

> "Please be advised effective this date, your employment at WIBR Radio, Community Broadcasting Company is terminated. Report to the general manager's office Monday morning to claim your severance check and remove any personal belongings.
> Robert Earle, President."

What the hell was this? Why? No cause was given. And what great timing, having just blown over $1,000 to rent a house, food, gas, entry fees and trinkets for the kids. And now SUS -- Sudden Unemployment Syndrome.

On Monday at 9 a.m. sharp, I walked – no, marched – into Earle's office. Nonplused, he looked up from his desk, picked up an envelope and tossed it to me and said dismissively:

> *Do you have all your stuff?*

I needed some details.

> *Hold on. What is this all about?*

You made a spectacle of yourself at the Polk remote. Mr. Polk called threatening to cancel his entire ad budget, including payment for the remote because of your conduct with some woman in the middle of the showroom. I told him we do not tolerate such conduct and you would be terminated immediately.

I was really pissed.

So I don't get to tell my side of the story?

Putting on his "I'm so bored" face, Earle leaned back in his chair and said, dripping with sarcasm:

Sure. Go ahead.

I laid it out exactly as it happened.

Did you bother to speak with any of the people who were there? She came flying in and jumped me. What was I supposed to do? Punch her out? Call the cops? If Polk was so pissed, why didn't he tell her to leave? Why didn't his agency rep tell her? Why didn't Ed (our sales rep) tell her? They were all standing right there. How did I know she wasn't there to buy a car?

From his body language and facial expression, it was obvious Earle hadn't known or considered any of that. It also was obvious he now found himself between the proverbial rock and hard place. He couldn't afford to lose a big chunk of Polk's ad dollars but also realized he really had no grounds to fire me.

He took the envelope with my final paycheck back, told me to sit down and left the office. He returned a few minutes later.

Here.

It was the severance check.

I asked Ed about what happened and he confirmed your story. But you're still fired; I can't afford to lose the Polk account. I've doubled your severance and will give you a good reference for your next job.

Three years into showbiz, already fired twice. I was getting a quick and unpleasant education.

Story Thirty-Nine

YOU'RE FIRED! AGAIN

U.S. Mail

I'm at WQXY-FM, Baton Rouge's "Beautiful Music" station, taking my radio pal George Bonnell's old gig as PD/AM Drive host. While the format was obviously not my shtick, it was a gig with a paycheck and bennies; Owner/General Manager Ken Winstanley was nothing like WIBR's Bob Earle! Ken was a cool dude. He knew what was hip 'n happenin' in town, in the culture and in the radio biz. His brilliant stroke to launch a beautiful music format covering a growing Baton Rouge Metro got WQXY piped into the offices of every doctor, lawyer, accountant and hospital within 50 miles, surprising the other radio geniuses with ratings they only thought possible by "Playing TEN in a row!" with screaming jocks and expensive promotions.

It was an easy gig. My workday started with a music intensive/low comment show from 6 a.m. to 9 a.m., then commercial production, paperwork, record and edit **Paul Harvey News and Comment**, take ABC network news at noon and… head home!

Around 11:45 one morning while recording Paul Harvey, the studio hotline lit up. Everyone in radio knows, one must always answer the hotline.

Studio…

Hi Brian, it's Mrs. Winstanley. Is Ken back there somewhere? He's not answering his office line.

No, he's not. He's taken Libby (our receptionist) out to lunch for her birthday today.

Oh, OK. Well, I'll call him later then. But if you see him before you leave, would you please ask him to give me a call?

Absolutely.

Great. Thanks, bye.

Mrs. Winstanley was a nice lady. I'd met her a couple times at the station. Libby, our receptionist, was a stunning young woman: mid-twenties; strawberry blond hair, pretty face, nice fuselage, great sense of humor, intelligent, perky, a well-spoken Southern lady. Everybody liked Libby. I left the station before they returned from lunch but dropped a "While You Were Out" slip on Ken's desk, advising him of his wife's call.

The next morning, I showed up for work as usual and greeted my friend and award-winning newsman, Jules d'Hemecourt, who would later go on to do great things in broadcast journalism. As he prepared the morning's news, I pulled records and tore the AP wire for appropriate tidbits. At some point in all of this, Jules came into the control room.

Hey, would you do me a favor and stick this in the mailbox?

The building had one of those central mailbox conglomerations in the lobby. Except for packages and Special Delivery, the mail guy only had to make one stop and all 24 offices were covered.

Sure.

Would you mind doing it right now?

Huh?

It's 5:45, Jules. The Pony doesn't ride until 10-ish, give or take an –ish.

I know. Indulge me. Would you please take it out right now?

Yeah. Sure. OK.

Hmmm, Jules is a tad weird this morning.

So out I went to the building lobby and the wall of mailboxes.

Just as I was about to insert Jules' envelope in the outgoing slot, another envelope blocked the way, half inserted, half-out of the slot. The return address was showing the WQXY-FM logo. That was strange. How and why was that here at this hour? Upon closer examination, I noted "d'Hemecourt" above the station logo and then noticed the letter was addressed to ME! What the…?

Naturally, I ripped open the envelope.

Dear Brian,

You are likely wondering what this is all about.

When Ken Winstanley comes in this morning, he is going to fire you.

I was here when he returned from lunch with Libby; he saw your note and called his wife. She went crazy, having long-believed he and Libby were having an affair. The "birthday lunch" you told her about convinced her this was just more proof. Their conversation lasted quite a while and not sotto voce. When it was over, Winstanley was supremely pissed at you for telling her about the lunch and said he was going to "fire your ass tomorrow." He made me agree to not say anything to you about it – so I'm honoring his request.

I'm sorry this will be our last show together. You are a great friend and one of the most talented people I've ever met in this business. I know it will ultimately turn out well for you.

Warm regards,
JdH

I was stunned; appreciative of Jules' cleverness but not surprised. Jules was one of the most intelligent men I have ever known. It was a huge part of what made working with him so enjoyable. Yet, there I was facing another termination.

After the show, I answered Ken's page. Before saying a word, he handed me the dreaded envelope, saying he actually admired my skullduggery; he wished he was as good at it as I was.

I just looked at him.

> *I have no idea what you're talking about.*

He said he was aware I was trying to torpedo his marriage, probably because I had the hots for Libby and, while he understood that, he couldn't allow me to continue working there.

I was aghast.

> *What the hell are you talking about? I have a wife, a son and one on the way. I have no interest in Libby or what, if anything, you're doing with her. Your wife called and asked where you were. You never told me to not say anything about taking Libby to lunch or that your wife has a problem with the two of you. I'm not a mind reader but you are one crappy manager and a miserable human being.*

And I walked out.

Some 20 years later, Ken literally bumped into me outside the New Orleans airport! Honestly surprised, he laughed, "Brian Wilson!" When I didn't immediately recognize him he said:

> *Ken Winstanley! This is my wife. How have you been? I hear you made the big time!*

I was thoroughly surprised and flashed back to that day in his office, which made his jovial "Hail Good Fellow" greeting even more baffling. Not to mention, "...and this is my wife." THAT wife?

Fortunately, we were all in a hurry to go somewhere so the entire encounter was fast and furious. He was a retired radio exec in Florida; I was on the air in New York, yak yak yak...

Good-to-see-you-again-yeah-right-same-here-good-luck-bye.

Radio – what a business!

Story Forty

YOU'RE REALLY FIRED!

Answering Machine

It started in September 1983. Ross was fired from WABC/NY, ending our incredibly successful run as **Ross and Wilson**, and programming began its serious slide down the razor blade of ratings. Everyone at every level of management believed they had the answer to fix everything, from **Brian Wilson and Company** as the new name for AM Drive to starting a sports talk show at 6 p.m. It was radio's answer to the blind leading the stupid. Only the new PD, Mark Mason, had a firm grip on what needed to be done, but lacked the unilateral authority to make it happen. The empty Suits upstairs wouldn't stop tinkering, adding elements that could be sold rather than letting the show breathe, attract new listeners and grow the ratings. Morale was subterranean.

But the paycheck still cleared and vacation time was still on tap! So, as an April birthday present to myself, I took my fiancé on a Caribbean cruise; one of those "43 islands in five days" specials! We returned just before the start of the dreaded spring Ratings Book. As we walked in the front door, mail was scattered all over the floor. Damn! Forgot to notify the post office. Scattered among the envelopes were a couple of those green Registered Letter notification cards. Knowing there had to be messages, I checked the answering machine, and *4* blinked at me.

The first message was from my sometimes "agent," Ralph:

> *Hey Brian, welcome back. Please call me as soon as you get in.*

Second message, Ralph again:

> *Hey Brian. We need to talk as soon as you get in, so gimme a call, OK?*

Third call, who else? Ralph:

> *Brian, call me right away. Please.*

Fourth call – not Ralph.

> *Hi Brian, it's Mark Mason. Hope you enjoyed your cruise. Listen, don't be in a hurry to come in tomorrow. The decision has been made to take the show in a different direction. But do come in when it's convenient to pick up your personal stuff and we can talk then. Sorry to bring you this news and at this time but I know you know this business. See you Monday.*

And so, the Great WABC Adventure had come to an ignominious end. What was supposed to be the pinnacle of every DJ's career sadly ended in a goofy pile of dumb programming stunts and, in my opinion, incompetent management.

Still, for all it's insanity, getting The Call, replacing Dan Ingram in Morning Drive, spending nearly four years on the legendary WABC, doing the run-up to the historical "Day the Music Died" and flip to Talk, I'm happy to be among a very select group of radio talent who have *WABC/New York* on the resume.

My only regret is filed under "If only…"

FAX

After WABC, it was B104/Baltimore, back to Z100/New York, back to Atlanta at WGST and WTLK-TV, up to WWRC/DC, then WCBM/Baltimore, finally landing at the "new B104," WOCT-FM "The Colt" back in good ole Bal'mer!

With all due respect to you, Dear Reader, the insanity that infected my brief stay at "The Colt" will not be recounted in its entirety here. It would take too damn long just to get through the backstory needed to set up each stomach-turning episode. Suffice it to say that the seven months I endured there was a mere shadow of my Abnormal Psychology Lab in college when we would ride out to the "state farm" and observe the behavior of "guests" incarcerated there "for their own good." Yes, it's a compelling, somewhat entertaining and very insightful story –but not worth the lawsuits it would be sure to engender.

But I can tell you this…

Once again, it was vacay time: just a few days to enjoy a deer hunting trip with an old friend down in Georgia. Despite our best efforts, Bambi was never threatened but it was a good time. Nothing like getting out of that mind-boggling environment and into clean, clear Georgia mountain air; harvesting some venison was a very distant second place.

Sure enough, upon my return: USPS -- nothing but bills and bull. Email -- nothing. Voicemail -- nothing. But on the fax machine was this one page:

> Your services are no longer required at WOCT-FM, The Colt. Your severance is being mailed to your home address on file. If you have any personal items you wish to claim, call Security to make arrangements to retrieve them.
>
> (Name Obliterated), General Manager.

Fired by FAX – another first! It actually was a huge relief to be out of such a toxic environment. It was an even greater satisfaction a few months later to deposit the very nice settlement check the company had to write after my successful lawsuit for Breach of Contract.

Story Forty-One

YOU'RE FIRED, FIRED, FIRED!

I was "fired" two more times before declaring myself retired; each time it was for "budget reasons," which actually was poorly disguised ageism. Air talent with my resume easily commanded a hefty salary, something for which I was eternally grateful. Adding up all those years of experience rightfully added to the total compensation package, which created a load for employers from San Francisco (ABC) to Toledo (Clear Channel).

Buying the equity of a 60-year-old major market talent, even with WSPD's "three-fer" of program and news director, put quite a distance between the dollar sign and decimal point on the paycheck. And there were plenty of younger guys who would gladly work for waaay less. Yes, those baby wanna-be's didn't have the panache, maturity, education, experience, legacy and talent as some of us old farts -- but money and profits are number one "with a bullet" to the stockholders.

My age converged with some big changes in the radio industry involving group ownership. The larger companies began "experimenting" with their own version of Vacation Relief – having employees voice track shows on stations in several markets, allowing them to cut the work force and save $$$. For Clear Channel (now iHeart), the savings weren't coming fast enough.

The first "paycheck" call came in January, asking me --*telling* me, actually -- my salary would be reduced by $50K; was that OK with me? BWAHAHAHA… management has a sense of humor, after all!

Wha…? Only $50K? Sure… no problem-o! I'll just fire the pool boy and cut back on my vintage wine collecting.

Six months later, the second call followed the old script, "Umm… we have to make some changes… going in a different direction…"

Translation: the company is losing its ass due to brain-dead management, homogenized programming and bloated payroll at company headquarters, reflected by iHeart's stock price and pending bankruptcy.

This happened in markets all over the country: the older experienced guys with big ratings, legendary content *and* making the big bux were sacrificed on the Altar of the Aged. Three or four almost adequate hosts could be paid with my salary alone. No, the kiddies didn't bring the inestimable value of all that seasoned experience, but short-sightedness has always been the greatest talent of empty Suits.

Sadly that's why, from coast to coast, today's AM and FM radio has lost the programming and advertising revenue battle to new technology, replacing talent and entertainment with non-stop streaming music, music, music. But radio's compelling entertainment in the "Theater of the Mind" is closed forever. Insert heavy sigh sfx here.

Story Forty-Two

VRINK

Looking at these 50 years, it's personally and professionally gratifying to recall some of the significant events I was part of in "the business." Some are among the **50 Stories** in this book: the startup at CNN, **The Day the Music Died** (WABC's switch from Music to Talk) and others. Here is one of the big ones. It didn't make national news like CNN or cause a great tremor in the broadcasting business like WABC. But it did have a significant impact on how talk stations handled a difficult time running their new popular programming: finding qualified hosts to fill in while the Regular Guy was on vacation. In the business, it's called "Vacation Relief."

This was never a big deal for music stations. They would just shuffle some jocks around from Afternoon Drive to Morning Drive or bring in some dude from the weekend for middays with instructions to play more music and not try to do "funny stuff."

For talk stations, it was a lot different. Not so much in small markets where management would do essentially the same personnel shuffle music stations did; some would bring in a local politician for their name recognition and the gift of gab. This didn't work so well for medium and major market stations. Talk hosts there wouldn't be there if they didn't have the talent and brains to deal with current events.

Major market program directors often would bring in celebrity talent from other major markets. These were generally other hosts who were "on the beach" (unemployed). The station and the audience would enjoy a superior, experienced talent for a week or two with little disruption of their regular standard of programming.

There were two downsides to this arrangement. One – even temporary major market talent was expensive. Besides whatever talent fee was negotiated, the host also had to be brought into town, put up at some hotel, fed, watered, and provided transportation. Number two -- the threat to the vacationing host. What if the new guy was really, *really* good -- even better than the guy on vacation? What if the audience really, *really* liked the replacement more than the regular dude?

In major markets, that second part wasn't a big deal since the hosts had contracts that would be too expensive to break and quite frankly, it wasn't necessary; most major market management was happy with their lineup. But that didn't mean they wouldn't notice a positive response from the audience while Regular Guy was with his family at *Walt* Disney World for a week.

VR funds were management's biggest concern. Fortunately for me, "Necessity is the mother of Invention," "Be in the right place at the right time" and "Opportunity knocks" all happened at once!

Here's what happened:

Driving home after a WBAL/Baltimore interview with Ron Smith about my book **the little black book on Whitewater**, I heard the commercial that changed my professional life for the next 20 years – and a large chunk of Talk Radio with it.

It was a Verizon spot pushing the latest high-speed residential Internet connection available to computer owners everywhere: the ISDN (Integrated Services Digital Network) telephone line.

Up until then, ISDN lines were only available and affordable to radio and TV stations and the government. Now that Verizon was making a version available the common man could afford, an idea hit me right up 'longside mah punkin' hay'ed!

What if I had one of these lines run into the house? With the appropriate equipment (modem, control board, microphone), I could offer myself as Vacation Relief host at any station anywhere with an ISDN line. And that meant all of them! Only the smallest peanut whistle in the smallest market wouldn't have an ISDN line. Of course, it wouldn't have a need for a major market talk show host either. With the Internet, I could access the local paper and TV station web sites to catch up on all the hot local issues, learn names and as much local "inside stuff" that was fit to print.

As soon as I got home, I kicked it around with Cassie. As a kid, she had worked on radios with her dad and was more up on the technical stuff than I was. I also put in a call to a computer techie I knew for guidance on hardware, installation and who he knew at the local phone company.

All the lights started blinking green: Verizon confirmed ISDN service was available at my house, the hardware was affordable and, between the IT guy, Cassie and me, installation and operation were just a week away.

With all that good news, I called Tyler Cox, then program director at ABC O&O WBAP/Fort Worth-Dallas.

Sidebar:

Tyler was the PD who, just a few years earlier, hired me to team up with Bob Madigan for **Mornings with Brian and Bob** on WWRC/Washington, DC. Unfortunately for me, several months later, Tyler accepted an offer from ABC for the WBAP PD gig. His first hire before leaving town was Mark Davis, the very talented guy who followed **Brian and Bob**. I later found out from Tyler, he originally planned to take *me* to Texas with him. But I had a contract with WWRC.

That afternoon, Tyler answered the phone -- one of the few major market program directors who did such a thing -- and a gabfest ensued. After several minutes of catch-up, I said: "Tyler, I've come up with a great idea. I'm calling it VRINK, Vacation Relief, Inc." I gave him the short version of how it worked -- anytime he needed a fill-in for Mark or anyone else, all he had to do was gimme a call, book the time, dial up the ISDN number, and pay my terribly reasonable talent fee.

Tyler was almost as excited as I was! Not only did he agree it was a brilliant idea but asked why I hadn't come up with it sooner! Mark had just returned from a week's vacation and for "vacation relief" Tyler had to fly in, house, feed and pay former WWRC mid-morning host, Joel A. Spivak Speaking – $X,XXX!

I hadn't determined what my rates were going to be, but if Joel A. Spivak Speaking could command $X,XXX, I could be a very happy VRINKER!

Tyler didn't even ask about rates. All he said was, "Sign me up! I will be your first and best client!" And over the next 12 years, he was.

Over the next few weeks, I worked out the format for how I would communicate with the producer/phone screener/board op at the client station. There were several software programs that would mirror of the station's phone screen on my computer so I could see the name of the person calling, where they were calling from, what they wanted to talk about and any other messages the phone screener needed to send.

With only limited technical control at my end, I set up a template for the board op so he would get my verbal cues when to bring the caller on the air, when to dump him, when to go to a commercial, news or any other break. The PD provided the station liners they were using, live copy, intros/extros, call-in phone numbers and all that jazz!

If you had spent serious time in radio, this wasn't that complicated. Many functions and elements of a radio show that require a board op, phone screener, news anchor and traffic reporter are done audibly, without visual contact anyway. Whether the board op was ten feet or a thousand miles away, the cue to go to a commercial break was the same. The ISDN line provided the on-air audio quality to the listener to sound as if I was right there in the same studio as the vacationing host. This was a source of constant amazement for listeners not familiar with this latest technological wizardry when they discovered I was hundreds if not thousands of miles away.

Right about the time all the technical details were in place, Tyler called. Mark was going in for a root canal the next day --- was I available?

Hell yes!

And so it came to pass, Vacation Relief, Inc. had its maiden voyage in America's fifth largest market. Much to everyone's surprise and amazement, including mine, the show went off without a hitch. The WBAP phone screener and board op handled everything that like the pros they were. We had zero technical problems. With Mark's exceedingly large audience, a result of his talent and WBAP's 50,000 watts, the phone lines stayed lit for all three hours! Despite broadcasting from WBAP's double-secret studios "just outside the logic-free zone of Washington DC," the audience got the joke as well as my libertarian take on current events, philosophically different from Mark's conservative positions. Nevertheless, this was the start of a beautiful, long-term relationship and subtle career change that made "going to work" a challenge and a real pleasure again.

About the time WBAP's check arrived, Jeff Beauchamp called, asking if I could do a one week fill-in for Ron Smith; since I was in the Baltimore area, I could come into the studio. In fact, that was his preference. It would give us a chance to visit before the show started.

Things were starting to look very good for my little brainstorm!

Story Forty-Three

VRINK
Part Two

With such enthusiastic reception from Tyler and Jeff, I decided to take advantage of the benefits of promotion and advertising. I took out a big ad in the industry paper, Radio& Records. With Cassie's help, we designed one ad briefly describing what VRINK did, and how:

> *Brian Wilson, Major Market Talk Show host available on your station via ISDN when your Host is on vacation, needs a root canal, quits, retires or been fired! Call Vacation Relief, Inc. pronto! Just one hour's notice (or less!) required. Clip and Save this ad! You'll need it eventually!*

We put in a fresh head shot for the hell of it! (No radio personality has ever been hired for his good looks.)

After running that ad for a few weeks, **Radio & Records** held a Talk Radio convention in DC. Of course, I had to be there! Cassie and I drove down and immediately upon entering, talk hosts and PDs who recognized me from the ad surrounded us with congratulations on the idea, along with "how do you do it" questions and "here's my card." At one point, the waters parted and Jack Swanson strolled into the inner circle. Jack was PD of the two most successful talk stations in the country: KGO and KSFO/San Francisco. He didn't need to introduce himself – but he did.

Brian – Jack Swanson… good to meet you.

Thanks. Good to meet you, too, Jack…

I've seen your ad in the paper. Helluva idea! How did you come up with it?

I gave him the condensed version, ending with a mention of clients -- the notorious Jeff Beauchamp at WBAL and Tyler Cox at his own ABC sister station, WBAP.

Impressive! Really. And I liked your ad, too. Clipped it and have it in my desk.

WOW, I thought, how great is this?

Then he blew me away when he said:

I'd never hire you, but I did get a kick out of the ad. Good luck!

And off he went.

What the…? I have your ad in my desk… but I'd never hire you?

Two weeks later, Jack Swanson called.

Could you fill in for Michael Savage for the next two days?

Ya think?

That fill-in, followed by several others for Lee Rodgers, Jim Eason, Geoff Metcalf and Michael Savage lead to a contract and seven years on KSFO, some of the best broadcast years of my life. Great station, great people and a fantastic audience. Even though it's been over a decade since Jack had to replace me for "someone cheaper and there," I'm still in touch with Melanie Morgan, Officer Vic and listeners like La Vonne Bauder in Napa, Bruce Gammill, now in Colorado, Denis Laws in San Diego and Richard Arrowood at Amapola Creek Winery. Aside from several week-long visits to Meet & Greet clients and listeners, I never lived there one day! But I got to know that "City by the Bay" as well as most anyone who was there 24/7/52.

Fighting the Good Fight in San Fran (2001 Photo: Brian Wilson collection)

VRINK grew nicely and quickly. Signed to do 90 days of AM Drive on KCMO/Kansas City while management searched for a new host turned into an entire year. By then, they gave up the search and offered me a contract -- but it required moving there. Time and circumstances wouldn't permit that, so management signed someone who could and we all said fond good-byes. The **Kansas City Star** media columnist wrote a very nice piece about my "temporary one-year stay" and how amazing it was I could discuss Kansas City issues from an in-home studio a thousand miles away and no one could tell "he wasn't right down the street." During that year, the station changed program directors which is how I met Bill White, who later took command of heritage station WBT/Charlotte. At WBT, Bill had me fill-in for local legend, "Charlotte's Most Beloved" John Hancock and other air staff as well. As of this writing, Mr. C.M. Beloved is still killin' 'em in PM Drive.

But the single most remarkable VRINK experience came in December 1999.

I was still doing AM Drive on KCMO/KC. Jack Swanson had me booked on KSFO/SF. Tyler Cox always signed me up to fill in for Mark Davis around Christmas time. And this particular year, Jeff Beauchamp had me on WBAL for Ron Smith.

Not being the best record keeper, it semi-suddenly dawned on me what I had done. Starting in the mid-December and for the next three weeks, I had committed to do:

Morning Drive 6 a.m. to 9 a.m. Central Time on KCMO

Middays 9 a.m. to noon Central Time on WBAP

Afternoon Drive 3 p.m. to 6 p.m. Eastern Time on WBAL

Evenings 7 p.m. to 10 p.m. Pacific Time on KSFO

Four stations, three time zones, three weeks!

Many have asked: Just how in the HELL did you pull that off? How did you keep the call letters straight? The time? The market? The news?

Answer: I have no clue. By the last couple days, it all became a blur. Fortunately, with the Christmas holidays, New Year's Eve and all the football games, I'd like to think the audiences didn't notice much! At least my producers never mentioned anything!

What I do recall is how after the last show of the last week on KSFO, I swore I was quitting radio forever! I swore I wouldn't give another station break for the rest of my life! Burn Out's new poster child was B. Wilson!

Ultimately, I edited that oath down to "for the rest of the month."

Having totaled up the checks that would be coming in for this marathon performance -- at special holiday rates -- I threw a pair of socks and a toothbrush in a suitcase, grabbed Cassie and hit the road! Wandering the backroads of Maryland and Virginia, we somehow wound up at the Inn at Little Washington for some hard-earned, well-deserved R&R – not to mention excellent meals, a wine list that came in chapters, and glorious accommodations. Actually, I think Cassie specked all this out while my mouth was running the Holiday Marathon!

VRINK has joined me in retirement. During those 20+ years and the blossoming of Talk Radio, I hosted shows on some of America's heritage radio stations in Seattle, Portland, San Francisco, Los Angeles, Sacramento, Denver, San Antonio, Austin, Dallas-Fort Worth, Minneapolis-St. Paul, Kansas City, St. Louis, Atlanta, Charlotte, Richmond, Harrisburg, Trenton, Washington DC, Baltimore, Philadelphia and New York.

It was a good run! Ultimately, my little idea was copied by others and I suspect they made some decent bux with it – even though they undercut my rates and delivered an inferior product!

HA! I'm only serious!

Someday I'll send Verizon a thank you note for running that commercial!

Contact Brian Wilson, very much alive, at VRINK:

888.300.5006

DEAD

Yes, dead air is the last thing you should worry about when one of your stars is out. That's why Brian Wilson, major market talk show vet shown here with his best professional smirk, established VRINK, Vacation Relief, Incorporated.

From his ISDN studio just outside the Logic Free Zone (Washington, DC), Brian can fill your air with intelligent, compelling and even amusing conversation until your Regular Dude get back. And, thanks to the Internet, Brian can be as local as you are.

WABC, WBAL, WBAP, KSFO, KFBK, KCMO and others know Brian is as near as the phone. Keep the number handy. You wouldn't want to be caught dead without it!

Some sent flowers! (1995 Photo: Myrmidon, LLC)

Story Forty-Four

GOING NATIONAL

Nothing confirms the old radio adage: "You never know who's listening" than hosting a nationally-syndicated show. Sadly, such an achievement eluded me most of my nomadic career. However, once VRINK achieved industry-wide notoriety, several opportunities to paddle around in those listener-rich waters came my way. On several occasions, Laura Ingraham, Jim Bohannon, the late Art Bell, Michael Smerconish and ABC's Sirius/XM **Live from 125** entrusted me with their huge audiences. Along with callers from coast-to-coast and Socialist to Statist to Anarchist, at some point a surprise would be at the other end of the line!

One day, waiting for a call begging VRINK to come to the rescue of some host in distress, the phone rang! I was pleasantly surprised to hear Laura Ingraham's producer asking me if I would be available to fill in.

> *BW: I hope so! What days do you need me?*
>
> *LP: Actually in 30 minutes. Can you handle it?*
>
> *BW: 30 MINUTES? Oh sure. I'm not doin' nuthin'…*
>
> *LP: Sorry for the short notice. Laura's two regular subs can't be reached for some reason. You were recommended by one of her consultants.*

BW: How quaint! OK, I'll fire up the equipment. Email the format clock, liners and anything else and we'll do a line test in 20 minutes. How's that?

LP: Twenty minutes.

Click.

So much for small talk. Oh well, when you're the third choice…

Everything went off like a nationally-syndicated show should. Laura's politics are a bit conservative for me, but not so much I couldn't treat the day's events in a libertarian context that satisfied the producer.

On the call screen, the next call up was "Joe in New Jersey."

BW: Back to the phones and over to the Garden State of Nueva Jersey, where only half of it smells bad, Joe is on the line and on the Laura Ingraham Show…. hello, Joe, whatcha know?

JH: Hi there, Brian, it's Joe Hannan.

BW: JOE HANNAN? THE Joe Hannan? Hey everybody, it's my sixth grade teacher from Packanack Lake Elementary School in Wayne, New Jersey! Good morning, Mr. Hannan!

JH: It's OK, Brian – you're old enough to call me Joe now.

BW: HA! OK! Thanks… Mr. Hannan! Wow! It's only been, what? 70 or 80 years since you held me back from seventh grade?

JH: (laughing) Well, it has been a few years but your listeners need to know you were never held back!

BW: So you're not going to spill the beans about sending me to the principal's office either?

JH: No… nothing about the principal's office either! But I will tell you I wrote a book and you're in it!

BW: Wow! Really? What's the title – Wilson Flew over the Cuckoo's Nest?

JH: Close! **Never Tease a Dinosaur: Tales of a Man in a Woman's World**. *It's about my years teaching elementary school back when things were a lot different from today. I have a story about you in there, about the commotion you caused during a fire drill. Do you remember that?*

BW: Commotion? Me? Fire drill? What is the statute of limitations on this? I don't remember causing any… guess I'll have to read the book!

JH: Great! Why don't we have lunch the next time you're in town?

BW: Super idea! Hang on, Mr. Han… Joe… give Kathy all your contact stuff and I'll get in touch!

Mr. Hannan was second on a short list of the greatest teachers I ever had. A month later, we had our reunion, a wonderful lunch and the story in the book was just as I remembered it!

Without telling me, Mr. Joseph F. Hannan died in 2009.

One winter night, while filling in for the great Jim "Jimbo" Bohannon on Westwood One, a guy from Tempe, Arizona started his call with the classic:

MP: Hi, Brian, it's great to hear your voice! I'll bet you don't remember me!

Oh boy.

BW: Well, let's see… you're not an old girlfriend…

MP: (laugh) Not hardly!

BW: Didn't think so. I don't know that any of them are living in Arizona. Ah! I know! It's Furd Burfal, my retired CPA! How ya doin', ya lyin', cheatin', thievin' bandit?

MP: (more laughter) No, no, no – not your CPA.

BW: Well look, this is only a three-hour show, so maybe you better let me in on the secret!

MP: It's Mike Pasqualetti!

I was blown away!

Back Story:

In 1969, Mike's wife, Jennifer,* was our secretary at WAFB-FM/Baton Rouge. The station was brand new, not even on the air yet. It was to become the first Top 40 FM station in town. I was working with an old radio pal, George Bonnell, who had tipped me off to the new gig. I jumped on it and it jumped on me. These were exciting times -- something actually *NEW* happening in stodgy old Baton Rouge radio!

Jennifer was an amazing person, fun, funny and beyond capable! Her husband, Mike, was doing graduate work in Geography at LSU so the three of us and our spouses were all around the same age. My wife was pregnant; George's wife and Jenny were "trying." A good time was being had by all!

Just before the station officially signed on the air, Mike graduated; he and Jenny left for a quick vacation to see family in Upstate New York. Four days later, Mike called to tell us Jenny wouldn't be coming back to work; she had died. Some disease had moved so quickly, she was beyond help by the time Mike got her to the hospital. I hadn't spoken with him since that call, but had heard he left Baton Rouge to accept a teaching job at Arizona State.

Under the circumstances, I was at a total loss for words. I couldn't come up with a way to tell the audience why this call was special and I didn't want Mike to think he had some obligation to fill what had become a big chunk of dead air.

BW: Mike, it is so great to hear your voice again. I never had the chance to tell you we named our daughter Jennifer.

Dead air again. It was Mike's turn to be surprised.

> *MP: Thanks, thank you, Brian. That's quite an honor. I'm certain Jenny would be thrilled.*

With the audience in the dark, this was getting difficult.

> *BW: Mike, I'm going to put you on hold. Please give the producer whatever number and time are best. I'll call you tomorrow and we'll catch up.*
>
> *MP: That would be great.*
>
> *BW: Standby…*

After the commercial break, I told Mike and Jenny's story to the audience and moved on.

Once again, you never *really* know who is listening.

Easily the *most* traumatic national moment came three hours into my first night subbing for Art Bell. Just being on **Coast To Coast** with that show's history and audience was a rush in itself! Far from being an authority on Area 51, flying saucers, space aliens, or anal probes beyond the annual prostate exam, I remained terminally curious about those uniquely-Art Bell topics, happy to let guests and callers educate me, answering my kindergarten questions.

As they always do during "open phone" segments, challenging subjects drift from the sublime to the ridiculous. Punching up calls with no knowledge of who was there other than he or she was "West of the Rockies" or "East of the Mississippi" or on the "First Time Caller" line. This tends to center your attention like nothing else – with the possible exception of a full bladder and how long to a commercial break!

> *BW: East of the Mississippi line, Hello -- Brian Wilson in for Art Bell…*

Grumpy Caller: Yeah, hello! Question for ya… did you ever live in a red house in Baton Rouge, Louisiana?

Oh-oh.

BW: Hmmm, maybe… could be… I did go to LSU there.

GC: Yeah, I heard you mention that at the beginning of the show. It was a red Cape Cod on Bluebonnet Road, right on the corner.

Whoa! It had been over 30 years since I lived there! What the hell?

BW: Oh… ummm… yeah, red house… Bluebonnet Road, right on the corner. Big oak trees, carport, no garage – that one?

GC: Yeah, that one!

BW: OK… is there something special I should know here?

GC: I was your landlord! It's Bill Wylly!

BW: Damn, Bill! My abacus tells me that was over 30 years ago! Do I owe you back rent? Did the dog ruin the carpet? Are you having trouble with aliens?

GC: (finally sounding friendly) I'm a huge Art Bell fan. Listen every night at work. When I heard "Brian Wilson" and "LSU" I figured it had to be you. No one else with that name went to LSU and became a big radio star and was a tenant of mine, too! So I figured after your guest left and you went to open phones, I'd call to test your memory!

BW: Well you caught me on a good night! Adrenalin is a great memory enhancer! How's the house? Still making you money with your horrendous rent?

GC: (chuckling) It's gone. Been gone for years. One of the hurricanes that came through blew down two of those big oaks in the front yard and crushed that sucker flat!

BW: Damn, Bill! Sounds as if we got out just in the nick of time! That could have put a serious dent in my budding radio career!

GC: (big laugh) HEY! You're right! I never thought of that!

BW: Figures… typical landlord!

GC: (another big laugh) We still miss you here in Tiger Country, Brian! Any plans to return?

BW: Thanks, Bill! But as well as LSU has been playing since I left and now with no decent rental property, I don't think that would be a wise move! Plus you have me in Baton Rouge right now!

GC: That is correct, sir! Hey - thanks for taking my call, Brian. I'll enjoy the rest of the show.

A great surprise – and relief! You really never do know who's listening!

* *Jennifer took the call in the* **Suicide** *Story.*

Brian and Ann Coulter finally meet at CPAC after five years of on-air interviews! (Photo: Cassie Wilson)

Brian and Jim Bovard team up at CPAC (Photo: Cassie Wilson)

Story Forty-Five

THAT OLD TOP 40 TRICK

In 1994, WCBM/Baltimore became my newest Vacation Relief (VRINK) client when I received a call from PD and AM Drive Host, Sean Casey. My mission – should I choose to accept it – was to fill in for midday host, Alan Keyes who, you may recall, started a short-lived run for president that year.

Alan is a talented, articulate speaker, Harvard graduate and nice guy. Had his show been on WBAL, Baltimore's dominant talk station, he likely would have done well in local radio.

I always tried to listen to at least a few minutes of whomever I was relieving – it was part of my prep. I wanted to get a sense of the host's style, quirks, how he ran the show, handled callers and to hear if he was doing anything I could improve upon -- I didn't want to sound like some cheap imitation just filling time. The way I saw it, every vacation relief gig was an audition for a job; ya never knew what might happen behind the scenes! If the station liked my work well enough to sub for one of their regulars, maybe they'd like me well enough to become one!

Listening to Alan, I noticed he had one bad habit. Regardless of the day's news or a caller's topic, Alan always brought the conversation around to abortion. For him, it was *the* singular, most important subject of the hour, day, week, month and year. Over the four days prior to his leaving to speak to a Republican campaign event, I never heard him fail to make his anti-abortion position the centerpiece of his show.

In my experience, this simply was bad programming. Imagine listening to a music radio station that played the same song or the same artist over and over and over. No matter how big a fan you were, eventually you burn out, and the repetition would certainly kill off any in the audience that didn't share your devotion. But this was Alan's thing. He based his presidential aspirations on it. Every show was a campaign stop.

I didn't share Alan's programming philosophy. Airing my personal opinion about abortion on Alan's show was irrelevant. Constantly banging on one subject non-stop not only wasn't my thing, it was bad, boring, redundant radio.

But I wasn't the PD; just the VR dude. So, how do I run Alan's show with this conundrum?

Here's where that old Top 40 trick comes in…

Back in the day, when a certain artist (The Beatles) or genre (disco) saturated the playlist, some aspiring PD came up with the brilliant idea of a "No-Beatles Monday" or "Disco-Free Wednesday." All Beatles or disco would be stripped from the playlist for that day. At first, it generated a lot of reaction and publicity, but eventually was considered to be one of the dumbest stunts ever pulled. On those days, competing stations quickly counter-programmed with "Home of the Beatles" or "Your Disco Inferno!" and sucked away the alienated Beatles or disco lovers from the offending station.

Before settling in behind the mic the first day for Alan, I had decided to borrow a version of that old Top 40 trick. After introducing myself to the audience, explaining Alan was off pursuing his presidential hopes and dreams, I announced a slight change in programming:

> *By declaration, namely, mine -- today is officially "Abortion-free Friday!" Here is how it works: we will take no calls or comments about abortion today. Don't even think about it! Your on-air life will be "aborted" otherwise.*

Why was I doing this?

Having listened to Alan's show, it was fair to say he had said everything there was to say about the evils of abortion. Several times over. Regardless, there was no indication of any listeners changing their minds as a result. Everyone against it remained opposed and solidly anti-abortion; everyone believing it to be a matter of a woman's body/woman's choice remains pro-choice. No one was converted. What else could be said that wouldn't paraphrase what Alan had been saying? The only other indisputable fact was, in Talk Radio, abortion was a surefire way to light up the phones.

Personally, I believed the debate was proven fruitless long before Roe v. Wade. When abortion was illegal, they were still performed all across the country. Regardless of who, how, where or with what, women wanting an abortion found ways to get one; Roe v. Wade just made it easier, more affordable and possibly sanitary. Even if Roe v. Wade was repealed and abortions made illegal again, women wanting one would simply go back to the "old way" pre-1973. So why continue the debate? After a certain point, any argument becomes redundant. And the last thing I wanted to be while subbing for Alan was redundant.

> *Anything else that's on your mind is fair game! Guns, the mayor, the governor, the president, the economy, bad drivers, the Orioles... well, not the Orioles. They're on another station! But anything else... let's get started. Welcome to Abortion-free Friday! Here's the number if you'd like to be part of the action..."*

Long before I finished my little spiel, all five incoming lines were flashing. This could be really good or really bad. After giving the call-in numbers and email address, I went to a commercial break and checked with the phone screener: What's the reaction?

Good and bad.

Should be fun!

And it was. Alan's biggest fans called for my head on a platter; everyone else appreciated the chance to talk about other things.

A while into the show, a call to the newsroom was answered by Carol Anne Strippel*, the midday WCBM news anchor. During a break, Carol Anne came into the studio to tell me that a very agitated *Mrs.* Alan Keyes had called – not once, but *three* times -- wanting to know just who I was and what I was doing to her husband's show. Carol Anne reported that Mrs. Keyes had instructed her in no uncertain terms to tell that "man on the air" to stop saying "Abortion-free Friday" *immediately*. This was not a request; it was an order.

Each time Mrs. Keyes called, Carol Anne told her the news department had nothing to do with programming and yes, she had passed along the "message." The fact that I didn't obey orders did not sit well with the potential First Lady. Carol Anne politely told Mrs. Keyes that if she had a complaint, she should call the program director. That call was never made.

Regardless of any agita I caused Mrs. Keyes, my fill-in work for Alan continued that day and beyond as he went off around the country, hot on the trail of the Oval Office. I subsequently was offered – and accepted – a newly-vacant daily show.

As noted elsewhere, sometimes a VR fill-in morphed into a full-time gig.

And that's showbiz!

**As if by magic, a few years later that news anchor, award-winning broadcast journalist, Carol Anne Strippel became Mrs. Cassie Wilson and continued winning awards for the rest of her career.*

Story Forty-Six

MEETING BRIAN WILSON

At this point in the book, you've read how some people have mistaken *this* Brian Wilson for the Beach Boy. The least likely place for that to happen was Baltimore, where so many people listened to **Brian and O'Brien**. But a caller looking for advice from the *other* Brian Wilson opened the door to my meeting Brian Wilson. By now, you know this is the one **Story** Brian didn't write!

A small lobby greeted you when you entered WCBM, where I was working as midday news anchor. Usually Judy, the receptionist, was the only one there. This particular day, several other people were buzzing about. The activity was unusual.

> *What's going on, Judy?*
>
> *He's here! This is so exciting! I never saw him in person!*
>
> *He who?*
>
> *Brian Wilson, you know… from Brian and O'Brien! I listened to those guys every day! Take a look! He's in the newsroom!*

A heavy air-lock door with a small window led from the lobby to the newsroom. I peeked in and saw a man leaning back in a black, faux-leather chair with his eyes closed, his briefcase resting in his lap.

Nothing too out of the ordinary, but the folks at the radio station were acting more like fans than employees. Someone was saying something about "*loving* the sing-along they did…"

I'd never heard the **Brian and O'Brien** show. During their heyday, I was working as a reporter in Atlanta.

But time was wasting; newscasts had to be prepared. Before I could head for the door, Judy handed me a pink "While You Were Out" slip.

> *Would you take that in to Brian?*
>
> *Can't you give him the message?*
>
> *Me? No! I couldn't even say "Good Morning" to him today! I'll be tongue-tied if I go in there. Please, take him the message!*
>
> *OK.*

The heavy door squeaked, but the noise apparently wasn't loud enough to disturb the guy in the chair. His eyes remained closed, his briefcase didn't budge. Curious about the message, I took a look.

> *I'm a big Beach Boys fan. Have been writing my own music. Uncertain about some chords. Please call 321-3210 I'd like your help.*

Hmmm… obviously Judy – and everyone in the lobby – knew that Brian Wilson "Radio Host" and Brian Wilson "Beach Boy" were not one and the same. This note was silly, clearly a "mistaken identity." Not wanting to appear an idiot, but figuring a message is a message… I walked up to the chair.

Brian remained in the same position -- not one muscle moved. Tentatively, I handed the note his way.

> *Hello?*

One eye cracked open a bit.

Yes?

Judy asked me to give you this message.

OK, thanks.

The pink slip disappeared into his briefcase, sight unseen. He resumed his position in the chair and closed his eyes again.

This is the guy filling in for Alan Keyes this week? Normally Alan would busy himself with "show prep" in the main studio while the Morning Drive news anchor finished up. There wasn't much time left to get to the studio and set up for the show.

At precisely 9:03 a.m., with two minutes to spare, Brian opened his eyes, got up and walked into the studio – as if he magically knew the time! For the next three hours, we each were busy with our respective duties. During my noon newscast, at 12:03 p.m. exactly, Brian Wilson left the building.

The next day, there was a similar crowd in the lobby but this time, Brian was entertaining the group. Running late, I headed straight to the newsroom. Three hours flew by. I was hoping to catch him on the way out to ask a question about a news opening at the radio station in DC where he had previously worked. Any inside information might be helpful.

Once the show was over, just as he did the day before, Brian exited the building at exactly 12:03 p.m. – in the middle of my newscast. Two minutes later, I dashed out to the parking lot. Brian was wrapping up a conversation with one of the station's account executives.

Excuse me… hey Brian, we weren't really formally introduced. I'm Carol Anne and I do the news for Alan's show.

I noticed that.

> *Anyway, I was wondering… I'm thinking about applying for a news anchor's position at WWRC. Anything you can tell me about the station that might help?*

His answer came with a hint of sarcasm and a slight grin.

> *I'm not going to say.*
>
> *Oh! OK, well, sorry to bother you…*
>
> *Well, I'm not going to say… HERE.*

Hmmm… perhaps there was a problem at the station?

> *If you're really interested, I can tell you more about the station and the news director… but it would take too long to discuss in the middle of a parking lot.*
>
> *When is a good time?*
>
> *How about for lunch tomorrow after we get off the air?*

A lunch "date" was made!

There's more to tell, but that's best left for another **Story**. Thousands of miles, several states, many, many houses, more than a few jobs, four Golden Retrievers and 25 years later – apparently something special happened at that lunch.

Story Forty-Seven

MY GUARDIAN ANGEL

Twice in my life -- but only once in my career -- I was convinced I had a Guardian Angel.

Ever have one of those moments when something happens to you in direct contradiction to what should have happened, despite the forces of nature, physics, logic, gravity? The fact this story took place in the heart of the Logic Free Zone (Washington DC) makes the event even more astounding.

Here's what happened…

When Alan Keyes left WCBM/Baltimore in 1996 to run for president, I was offered his midday timeslot. Still able to run Vacation Relief (VRINK), I readily accepted a full-time gig with benefits! Talk Radio is Talk Radio regardless of audience size. While bigger stations with bigger audiences did materialize, the best thing to come out of the WCBM gig was meeting AP award-winning News Anchor, Carol Anne Strippel who later would make the dubious decision to become Mrs. Wilson. However, that's not where the Guardian Angel comes in!

WCBM was invited to attend an event in Washington at the United States Capitol; it probably was called "Talk Radio Day" or something similar. Selected talk stations from around the country were invited to send one of their shows to broadcast from inside the Capitol Building. Of course, just being in the building wasn't the draw; the invitation came with the guarantee that congressmen and senators and other political "celebrities" would be roaming the halls, available for interviews.

Probably due to my years earlier as the Brian in **Brian and Bob** on DC's WWRC, I was selected to make the trip. Frankly, by this time, 30+ years into my career, I had grown weary of remote broadcasts. At best, they were plagued with technical problems, weather issues and over-adoring fans. At least broadcasting from inside the Capitol Building might circumvent some of those issues.

All the technical arrangements were made with the engineering department. For me, it would just be a matter of getting there, plugging in my headphones and grabbing some unsuspecting public servants to grill about the issues of the day. The "grabbing some unsuspecting public servant" part is where the future Mrs. Wilson came in. Because of her bodacious broadcast news experience, it was decided she would accompany me to spot, draft and prep the highest profile politicos she found prowling about and deliver them to the WCBM broadcast booth.

Everything was set: technically, logistically and geographically. The chief engineer would arrive early to get our incredibly expensive and highly-sensitive electronic broadcast equipment set up, wired, plugged, tested, connected and ready for broadcast. Carol Anne and I would arrive in a timely manner prior to airtime and prepare for three hours of high-energy, New York-style Talk Radio.

We made the trip by choo-choo from Baltimore to Union Station and the short walk up to the Capitol.

To fully appreciate the next sequence of events, I need to provide this brief sidebar:

Due to the nature of Talk Radio, the generally aggressive in-your-face way I did it and the markets I did it in, experience taught me that it was a really swell idea to carry some means of self-defense.

As a result, despite being against Maryland law, I carried a Para Ordinance .45 in my briefcase to and from the studio every day. Maryland's strict firearm laws paled by comparison to the ones in your nation's capital. At the time, the mere possession of a handgun carried a two-year *mandatory* jail sentence. No bail. No plea bargains. No letter from your congressman or high school sweetheart. Two years in the pokey. *Period.* It was rumored the cop car you were in didn't even stop at the courthouse; just straight to the Washington lockup. Even state policemen coming into DC for legal purposes were required to "check their guns at the border." Every gun owner in Maryland, Pennsylvania, West Virginia and Virginia knew this by heart and conducted themselves accordingly, including Yours Truly.

Prior to leaving the house, I switched briefcases, leaving my personal protection device safely within the confines of la Casa de Wilson. If Miss Strippel and I ran into any DC riffraff bent on harming our corpus delectables, we would be SOL because when seconds count, police are only minutes away. But it was gorgeous that day in the nation's capital. When the show was over, there would still be plenty of daylight and normal people walking the sidewalks back to Union Station.

And now, back to our story…

We arrived at one of the many ground-level entrances to the Capitol Building. Remarkably, there was no crowd milling about, standing in line or any of the other joys one usually deals with when entering any federal building, most certainly this one. Not that we were complaining. Being efficiently processed through metal detectors and X-ray machines was always a good thing.

As we entered with absolutely no one around, we were greeted by two of the Capitol's Finest, operating the security apparatus. One large round officer was leaning back, holding up the wall to our left while the smaller, thinner one cheerfully welcomed us to the Capitol. We knew the drill: place your belongings on the belt to be scanned, enter through the metal detector, gather up your belongings and be on your way.

Everything went as smoothly and efficiently as anyone could ask. The officers were affable as we all chatted about the weather and why we were there. "Oh! You're with Talk Radio?" and other blathering was going on when I stopped in midsentence, frozen in mortal fear: the X-ray's monitor above the belt was crisply displaying a perfect picture of my .45, resting comfortably inside my briefcase. The briefcase switcheroo I was positive I made safely back home, hadn't happened. Somehow, probably in my haste, I grabbed the very one I meant to leave behind.

I was speechless. All I could think of was handcuffs… Capitol Police… squad car...and a cellmate named Sweetness.

First came the understatements.

The skinny cop in charge of the X-ray machine followed my look of panic to the monitor and said with a slight air of surprise:

> *Why, that's a gun…*

> *Yes, I know…*

Officer Skinny turned to his rotund partner.

> *Hey, take a look at this; it's a gun.*

Despite the possibility the wall could collapse, Officer Large took a few steps forward to better see the monitor and, amazingly, concurred.

> *Yep, that's a gun.*

Then he looked at me.

> *Is that your gun?*

Despite the foregone conclusion of my upcoming prison sentence, I felt compelled to whimper a response.

> *Yep. That's mine. I thought I transferred it to another briefcase before I left the house. But obviously, I didn't.*

I put my hands behind my back waiting for the cuffs.

Officer Skinny said:

> *Well, you know guns aren't allowed in the District.*
>
> *Yes, I know.*

And that's when the Guardian Angel arrived, taking over the body of Officer Large.

> *You know, if I were you, I'd get that thing out of here right away.*

I couldn't believe my ears! But I wasn't about to call for an audiologist! Faster than a speeding bullet, I gathered up the briefcase and Miss Strippel, thanked the officers for their time, and left a vapor trail out the door. Even today, if one looks carefully, traces of burning leather from my shoes can still be seen at that particular entrance.

Once outside, my problems weren't over. It was 30 minutes to Showtime. We had to get to the broadcast booth -- wherever that was -- which now required ditching an illegal firearm somewhere geographically convenient to the Capitol Building!

In growing desperation, I actually considered one of the nearby bushes, but they weren't sturdy enough to support the weight of a loaded .45. Of course, there were the ubiquitous security cameras monitoring every blade of grass -- and every grade of ass -- on the property. Tree? No. Flowers? No. Dig a small hole? *Really*? If we only had a car. Hey! That was it! The station engineer setting up inside had a parking permit that allowed him easy access to the building just for this occasion. I asked Carol Anne to go inside, find the booth and our engineer, explain the problem and get his car keys to stash the piece until the show was over. Brilliant! And off she went…

Things were getting tense. Not only was I standing there, hopefully not looking like someone packing illegal weaponry, but it took the better part of ten minutes for Carol Anne to return. And while she was jangling the engineer's car keys in her hand, she wasted no time telling me he was really, really, *really* pissed off:

> *This makes me an accessory to a FELONY if that gun is found in my car!*

Carol Anne's powers of persuasion, along with the only other choice of three hours of dead air, moved him to hand over the keys.

We found his car quickly enough and headed back to the entrance with a little better than eight minutes until air time. Moving briskly along the sidewalk, who should we encounter but a very alert looking Capitol cop.

I had to know I wasn't dreaming this.

> *Excuse me, officer, could you settle an argument for us, please?*

> *I'll try…*

I motioned toward Carol Anne.

> *We were just having this discussion. What happens to someone who gets caught with a firearm, like a pistol, here in the district?*

> *Jail. Two years mandatory minimum sentence. No bail. No plea bargain.*

Triumphantly, I triumphantly turned to Carol Anne.

> *See? What did I tell you?*

Not that she had ever suggested anything different!

> *Thank you, officer. Have a great day!*

And off we went.

We got to the booth just in time to sit down, plug in and start the show. The timing couldn't have been more perfect in that it prevented the chief engineer from chewing my ass off.

The show went pretty well, too, thanks mainly to Carol Anne's years of experience in the field grabbing fleeing politicians trying to avoid her news microphone. Catching members of the Maryland contingent was easy enough. Nabbing Chief of Staff Leon Panetta, Senator Jesse Helms and Representative Pat Schroeder took "veteran expertise." House Majority Leader Dick Gephardt was predictably rude in his refusal; Representative Barney Frank was rude, crude and hysterical as fled to the men's room in response to Carol Anne's simple, polite, professional invitation to be on the show, yelling he was going to:

> …*Have you thrown out of the building if you don't stop harassing me.*

After hearing that, I would have really loved to have had him on.

But overall, I'll always remember that day as the day my Guardian Angel showed, kept me out of prison and preserved another 20+ years of my radio career!

Story Forty-Eight

THE CHESTERTOWN EXPERIENCE

“If you can't lick 'em, join 'em!"

For Millennials, this old saying means "if you can't lick 'em, join 'em!" (Note to Publisher: Not to worry. Millennials don't read anything that has complete words or exceeds the character limit on Twitter.)

After the turn of the century and discovering the Y2K phenom was not going to return us to the Stone Age, Cassie and I decided to do something radically different: buy our own radio station.

Why?

Why not?

We had worked at small to major market stations, moved all over the country and were done, done and done with the prospect of more of the same. That's the way it is in radio: you are a nomad (except for sleeping in the sand with camels and Maria Muldaur); the radio station is an oasis. A lifetime career at one radio station is as rare as finding a credible newspaper in Toledo.

With our decades of experience in Music and News/Talk, including healthy doses of sales and even some minor engineering, station ownership would be a slam dunk! No more empty suits and incompetent program directors ruining the day. With our experience, we could run management, programming, and sales ourselves; a chief engineer would already be there. Any additional air staff and office help could be hired as needed. During my 12 years in Baton Rouge radio, I also started an advertising agency, opened an insurance agency, bought into a real estate agency and built a skateboard park! Together, we knew more than enough to be dangerous, even if we weren't "seasoned business pros." And for that, we knew people...

It wasn't as if we hadn't wandered down this path before. We almost jumped on a couple stations in Corning, New York. Great little town -- Corning Glass, solid economy, lots of tourists… but I couldn't rob enough banks fast enough to close the deal. Then there was Casper, Wyoming. Great station but a lousy market, devastated by the end of "the boom" brought on by the Jimmy Carter oil embargo. As long as it lasted, things were going great until the embargo ended and the oil companies left as quickly as they had arrived. They should have re-named it "Casper the Friendly Ghost Town." One night in October still checking out the station, a former program director called to tell me he wanted to re-unite **Ross and Wilson** at Z100/New York. So much for Casper and buying a radio station.

But I digress…

It didn't take long to find just what we were looking for – WCTR in Chestertown, Maryland. A small station, a one-thousand watt daytimer at 1530 AM in a small community (pop. 5235 or 6) at a relatively small price. Started by a gentleman with some above-average radio experience, WCTR had been a small market success story, tapping into the local news, events and people, right down to leading the 4th of July parade and broadcasting the local obituaries. A nice little operation – until the gentleman had the temerity to unexpectedly die. The station fell into the stupendously incapable hands of his widow, Jody, a former elementary school teacher. Her bodacious radio experience amounted to voicing an occasional commercial, showing up at select station promotions and sleeping with the owner. Without going into all the unpleasantries that resulted from her counter-productive attempt at ownership and management, to put it simply: she ran that sucker into the ground – where we stumbled over it. By then, Jody had re-married, finding a prominent Chestertown man who was his own bank. Owning and running a radio station became a pesky inconvenience, preventing the newlyweds from enjoying his money, her inheritance and their time together squandering it as they pleased.

With the ad listing WCTR for sale in-hand, I contacted the owner and arranged for a visit and tour of the facilities. We were to meet at the WCTR "broadcast tent" where the station was booming from the annual Kent County Fair. Driving over from the Maryland mainland, we finally got in range of WCTR's signal. A woman's voice – assumed to be Jody -- was yammering away about the fair, encouraging everyone listening to stop-by the WCTR broadcast facilities. Then she went to a commercial break.

Listeners heard a locally-produced spot for the area's John Deere dealer. As the WCTR announcer read thru the copy, he paused – *burped* – and continued reading. At first, we couldn't believe what we heard! But we chalked it up to happenstance, knowing that things can sometimes get weird with live copy at a remote broadcast. As we closed the gap, we heard another commercial break with the same John Deere commercial. Amazingly, the burp was still there! OMG! It wasn't a live spot, it was recorded *WITH* the burp left in! Whoever recorded the spot had failed to either edit out the burp or record another take. But no! There it was! Same time, same burp!

After we arrived, introduced ourselves and made some small talk, I mentioned to Jody that she was running a John Deere spot with a burp in the middle. She laughed it off. "Yes! That's Russ, my husband. He doesn't have any radio experience; he was just helping out."

Helping out? How does a burp in the middle of a spot "help out," unless the client is the Flatulent Order of the Drooling Uncouth? That was our introduction to WCTR Chestertown Quality Control!

That should have been sufficient warning.

The physical plant was just as off-putting as the Deere-burp commercial. To say Ms. Jody was a slob would be more of a compliment than a put-down. The station grounds hadn't been mowed or landscaped in weeks; the shrubbery was about to consume the entire building! Inside was worse. Square footage was sparse. Filing cabinets, partitions, unnecessary dilapidated office furniture made for severely cramped quarters – and ugly ones at that. The thought of clients coming by was unimaginable! The studio was a joke – and a bad one! Music came from several sources: two worn-down turntables of questionable shape and speed; one Radio Shack dual cassette deck and two racked reel-to-reel decks supporting ten-inch reels with **Music of Your Life** labels. The soundproofing was from the formerly fashionable Black Egg Carton collection and was peeling off the walls and ceiling. Cups and food wrappers -- fallout from previous McDonald's cuisine -- littered the area. The station's morning man and self-appointed PD took up every available inch of the chair at the ancient control board. The rest of the station was equally horrid. Oblivious to it all, Ms. Jody shoved a few things out of the way and invited us to sit.

After more getting-to-know-you chit-chat, we got down to the business of how much, what terms and how soon. This led to a dinner invitation at her mansion-on-the-Bay with Mr. Megamillions, the famous burping radio talent, and more buy/sell negotiations. The owner's knowledge of radio broadcasting and the radio business wasn't quite deep enough to drown a hamster. However, she did agree to forward WCTR's P&L's, financial statements and tax returns to my CPA.

At the end of all the conversations, Q&A, Due Diligence and the all-important report from the CPA, we settled on a purchase price considerably lower than Jody's lofty notion.

It was a bit awkward having to school Jody in the ways of real radio, but we got 'er done and got her out of the building. We found a nice place on the Chester River and moved in, prepared to raise the broadcast quality standards of WCTR to the benefit of the audience, the market and our bank account!

Or so we intended.

The events that filled our term of ownership could fill a book all its own.

WCTR Studio after our renovations and upgrades!
(2005 Photo: Riverside Communications)

To generalize in the good news/bad news template: first the good news.

Overall, it was a great, albeit traumatic, learning experience. Most such learning experiences tend to be that way. We each learned how stifling local, state and federal regulations are; how they strangle the entrepreneurial spirit, squander time and money with senseless, meaningless reports and fees, using their regulatory power to force you into obedient compliance no different than indentured servitude. This was "good" because we got to see all its tawdriness up front, close and personal. Not pretty but a great lesson.

Also: we tried some programming ideas that had been rejected by management at other stations only to discover that they WORKED! At least for us. At least in Chestertown…

We tried some advertising/promotion ideas with similar success for both station and client…

We raised the awareness level of listeners regarding some unattractive stunts the Board of Supervisors had been pulling on the market to the detriment of people and businesses…

We made some friends, consumed vast quantities of excellent Cream of Crab soup and got a local cheese shop's recipe for an appetizer that Cassie later perfected!

The bad news:

It was disheartening to learn not everyone who listens to the radio is concerned or even appreciates quality programming. Small town stations tend to sound like small town stations because they have small town talent running them; anyone with real talent potential will quickly move to a bigger market. Long-timers come to expect the comfort of mediocrity; generally, it's the local standard.

Similarly, it was frustrating to deal with business owners who preferred *their* marketing and advertising opinions over experience, facts and results. When their ideas were incorporated – and failed –somehow that became our fault too.

Essentially, we learned small markets are no different than grade school cliques with favorites and popularity contests and typical hypocrisy from the Old Rich People. Just like some larger markets, the local paper was cozy with the political element and established businesses, which made advertising sales difficult. They were made much worse when we discovered Ms. Jody's historical lack of integrity with her ad rates -- written on a Magic Slate. Little did we know up-front that the station did not come with very much Good Will.

There were lots of victories but enough failures to put out the For Sale sign and hope to break even. Faster than I imagined we would, we did. The few dollars we lost were chalked up to tuition fees at the Hard Knocks College of Radio Knowledge and Experience.

Our WCTR logo 2005

And that really was the great worth and lesson of the story. From that point on, in any assembly of radio people in which we found ourselves, we were among the few – most often, the only – who could speak from the position of ownership. And that merit badge trumped any PD, GM, VP or CEO drawing a paycheck but without skin in the game.

True, it was a one-horse station in a one-horse market but the only functional difference between WCTR and WABC was the power of the transmitter and the number of employees. Everything else was pure Radio.

Story Forty-Nine

SURVIVOR!

The CBS hit TV show **Survivor** debuted in May 2000 while I was hosting my evening show 7 p.m. to 10 p.m. (PT) on KSFO/San Francisco from the farm we owned in Upstate New York. By the end of its first year, **Survivor** was all the rage. Like a precursor to **The Apprentice** with contestants getting "fired," **Survivor** was all about who would be the *Sole Survivor* at the end of the season and win major bux. On the day of the big finale, everybody on radio and TV chat shows were all atwitter about who the winner might be.

It's important here to remind you how intensely competitive radio is. Or was. On-air personalities in all formats jealously guarded the audience we had and would do anything to keep them listening. Similarly, we would do anything to create a buzz that would attract new listeners. As for **Survivor**, this was not a show I ever would have watched. Just another nonsensical evening soap opera with a vacuous plot and questionable "talent." Sorry, not for me.

After listening all day to this nonstop yammering about who might win, I decided to do something about it. On the East Coast, **Survivor** ended before it began on the West Coast and, like the rest of the country, everyone in the Bay Area was talking about rushing home to watch and see who would be the Big Winner!

During the first hour of my show, I mentioned the nationwide excitement, even taking a few calls from listeners stuck in evening traffic and how they were hoping to make it home for the start of the show.

Little did they know they had nothing to worry about.

I had arranged for my wife, Cassie, an accomplished journalist and veteran reporter, to give me the name of the Big Winner as soon as the show ended on the East Coast.

As we came to the top of the hour and the break for ABC News, this is what my audience heard:

> *Before we get to ABC News here on KSFO/ San Francisco, for all of you speeding home to catch the grand finale of* **Survivor**, *please drive carefully. There is no need for speed… because… Richard Hatch is the Sole Survivor! The show just ended here on the East Coast, so you can say you heard it here first! Now you can calm down, drive friendly, listen to the news and, most importantly, be back here for the next hour of our helpful little show!*

According to my producer in San Francisco, the phones exploded with fire and brimstone from listeners supremely pissed off that I had made the Big Reveal ten minutes before the show started and a full *two hours* before the Big Moment on the West Coast.

From a public relations perspective, it didn't help matters that I laughed at the incendiary comments. Frankly, I could not -- and still cannot -- begin to imagine how any sentient being could get so emotionally wrapped around the axles of a mere TV show, and I said so on the air. I also explained that I had a moral obligation to KSFO, ABC and myself to maintain the highest number of listeners possible. Now that there was no need to rush home, everyone could stick around listen and participate in *this* show. I saw it as a win-win-win situation: listeners didn't have to risk life and limb barreling home through evening traffic while the company, the station, the audience and I won by having them stay tuned for another exciting hour.

The stunt caused such a stir, it was written up in the local newspapers. Of course, I was excoriated by one and all for being so inconsiderate.

Only my boss, Jack Swanson, congratulated me for a job well done!

Story Fifty

THE DAY THE MUSIC DIED

In **Two Dans**, my adventures at WABC/NY with radio legend, Dan Ingram, I wrote:

On May 10th, 1982, "The Day the Music Died," Musicradio WABC switched to Talk Radio WABC. By then, my opinion of Dan Ingram couldn't go any lower. I resented his petulance about AM Drive and forcing the PD to censor my poking fun about him. The fact that he rarely forward-promoted Morning Drive didn't sit well either. Foolishly, I thought if he had just made a sincere effort, we might have avoided the inevitable. But it didn't matter now. At noon and the end of the last music show, Dan Ingram, Ron Lundy (a great talent and human being) and the rest of the air staff gave it up for Talk Radio. ***Ross and Wilson*** *stayed, thanks to our new and improved ratings that had beaten Don Imus. Whatever Dan Ingram's personal issues were with me, he was and remains the Greatest DJ Ever.*

What I didn't elaborate on was the atmosphere around the station as the end of an era arrived. Of course, all the NYC papers and TV stations ran stories, mostly historical perspectives; WCBS-TV did a nice piece with film from inside 8A, you might still find it on YouTube. What they all failed to capture were the gloom clouds that hung over everyone, not just those doing their last show. People who had been there through the "glory days" of 1960 to 1982 knew for months this day would come and WABC's reign would go into the radio history books. Fine. Nice to be a part of history – but the grumbles in the halls on the eighth floor never made it to ink or tape.

It wasn't so much that "The Music Died" as "*Why* the Music Died?" Studies showed perception on the street indicated WABC still was the number one station in town. While actual ratings didn't support that, "perception is reality" and upper management just didn't know or care to do whatever was necessary to preserve Musicradio 77 WABC and its legacy. That might have been assured with the nationwide launch of Super Radio, scheduled for July 4th, but the Suits pulled the plug *literally* the night before the launch. What a waste.

Lots of self-anointed radio wizards speculated other alternatives woulda – coulda saved the day. The most popular was moving the WABC call letters to WPLJ-FM and take the WABC DJs along. But WPLJ was doing really well with its AOR format and laid-back jocks like Jim Kerr, Pat St. John, Tony Pigg, Carol Miller and a bunch of others. So much for that idea. Surrounded by musically-superior FM stations and lacking the managerial stones to go up against WNBC's Imus and Stern, there weren't many other viable choices. Actually, there weren't *any* viable choices for WABC other than Talk.

Since its format flip from Musicradio, Talk Radio WABC has never come close to achieving the market dominance it enjoyed from 1960 to that fateful day in May, 1982.

While I was certainly happy **Ross and Wilson** survived the cut, the next two years were among the worst of my 50 years in Radio.

Our first **Ross and Wilson** AM Drive "Talk" show the morning of May 11th was the stuff nausea is made of. We muddled through somehow (hopefully there aren't any tapes of that show anywhere!). No one in management had a clue what to do or what direction to give us – unless the wimpy – "no issues crap" we put on the air actually was the plan. It was as if management was embarrassed about the loss of the legendary Musicradio 77 and didn't know how to provide a replacement with that typical NYC personality and attitude. AM Drive sounded more like some saccharin medium market station, trying to be all things to all people.

Ross & Wilson Morning Team's Custom Salute to Management on flipping to Talk (1982 Photo: Brian Wilson collection)

Although the mandate was to push *Talk Radio* WABC, we were instructed to play two tunes per hour. Why? Without taking on the big issues of the day, except possible weather events, 6 a.m. to 9 a.m. was a boring jumble of news, traffic, weather, sports, financial news, a tune, a call, repeat. The highlight of the show was the 9 a.m. hour – an entire 60 minutes to chat with an eclectic group of special guests booked by our producer, Cathy Weinflash.

While the show provided those magic moments to stock my growing library with autographed books and to see every Broadway show without waiting eight weeks for nose-bleed seats, going to work was not the thrill it first was or should have been.

Management's lack of leadership and direction made the show more focused on filling time rather than providing building blocks for ratings. Ross and I celebrated five years together with the **Ross and Wilson Fifth Anniversary Bash**, a live performance in my hometown of Wayne, New Jersey.

Ross and Wilson Fifth Anniversary Bash (1983 Photo: Brian Wilson collection)

We featured everyone from the show: Art Athens (news), John Maher (news), Steve McPartlin (sports), Joe Nolan (traffic), "The Coach" Ed Smith, and Rasa Kaye (weather) plus a couple hundred adoring fans and the **Kissing Contest** from our old nightclub act.

In September 1983, Ross was fired and **Ross and Wilson** was over. In a brilliant stroke of genius, the new show was dubbed **Brian Wilson and Friends**. A few weeks later, the talented Mark Mason took over programming.

But, like the station itself, the show was doomed. In the face of falling ratings, management larded up the four hours with commercials and targeted "features" to generate revenue, not to attract a new audience. The Suits upstairs saw the station as their play toy, making occasional visits to the eighth floor to give orders, tweak decisions and otherwise mess with programming that didn't originate from the West Coast affiliates.

Returning from vacation at the end of April 1984, two registered letters and an answering machine message from Mark Mason advised that I didn't have to "hurry in" to do the show the next morning!

A shock at first, it actually morphed into relief. My WABC "dream job" had come true – a least for a while. It ended with the destruction of **Ross and Wilson**, assorted frustration and resentment; I could be glad it was over. Of course, I would have preferred a 20-year run like Dan, Ron and Johnny Donovan had, but my CV says I made it. Brian Wilson: Last of the WABC DJs; First of the WABC Talk Show Hosts. From Baton Rouge to the Big Apple in 15 years. And I came back to New York three more times for shows on Z100, WABC and WOR before retiring the headphones.

Not too shabby.

P.S.

THE ZOO

Prior to **50 Stories** going to press, I was asked why I had written so little about **Ross and Wilson, The Next Generation,** Z100 Z-Morning Zoo. Returning to Gotham to replace Scott Shannon and re-unite the **Nearly-Famous Ross and Wilson** – wasn't that a high point of my career? Aren't there a boatload of "Zoo" Stories?

Good question!

The short answer is "Yes," but…

As noted in the Introduction, despite some necessary personal tidbits, this book was not my autobiography. I chose these **50 Stories** for their unique fun and funny times with some radio history and human pathos sprinkled throughout.

Getting the call to be the new "Zoo Keeper" and all that entailed was great – on the surface. But inside the station, the details and memories of the R&W break-up at WABC hung in the air and it was not pleasant. Painful issues remained unresolved even six years later despite Management's assurance before I arrived everything concerning those matters was A-OK.

It wasn't.

It was obvious to me grudges held by certain individuals poured cold water over the spontaneous combustion that had made R&W

magic and so successful back in the day. The tension and resistance to getting the act rolling again were palpable from the first show. I saw it, felt it – but didn't want to accept what was happening. The Zoo offered too great an opportunity to squander on old resentments, insecurities, butt hurt and power trips, but the show was doomed from the beginning despite some indescribable flashes of that former greatness in-between.

Stated clearly, I could not honestly write even good Zoo stories without the likelihood of certain individuals calling their lawyer yelling "Slander!" "Libel!" "Dandruff!" "Whiplash!" and suing for billions and billions. I wouldn't want that to happen to this little collection of great memories. Or to me either! And, above all, I didn't want this little trip down Memory Lane to end in a bowl of sour grapes.

Prof. John Bell, Ross and Wilson, Claire Stevens
(1989 Photo: Malrite Communications)

There are some great Zoo videos and airchecks on the **50 Stories** YouTube channel that will bring back some happy thoughts of those special but rare times. Give 'em a look and listen.

And thanks for asking…

-BW

ROSS & WILSON

Ross and Wilson publicity shot (Photo: Malrite Communications)

ACKNOWLEDGEMENTS

Over 50 years, ~~a car load~~… ~~truck load~~… ~~train load~~… ~~boat load~~… hundreds of amazing people left a mark on my career. It's a small measure of appreciation to acknowledge them here.

Dick Rakovan – Vice President, Radio Advertising Bureau (Retired). Among his many distinctions, Dick is the only GM to fire me and remain close friends! Not only is he The Ultimate Radio Person in all of American Broadcasting, inducted into two (at last count) Radio Halls of Fame, he also has managed more stations for more broadcast companies than anyone in the biz! There are few in radio who are as well-known and admired as Dick, for all the right reasons. His friendship and guidance have been of inestimable value since we first met and worked those raucous years at WWRC/DC!

Tyler Cox -- Tyler Cox Consulting. Tyler is the Programming Genius who put **Brian and Bob** together, guided Texas radio giant WBAP/DFW to greatness and was first recognized the potential and value of my Vacation Relief (VRINK) idea in 1995, hiring me to fill-in for Mark Davis and later, Hal Jay. While we were never able to forge "the deal" to get me to WBAP permanently, Tyler was my longest-lasting "client" and among the few rare friends I'm privileged to have in this business.

Bob Madigan – Newsman Extraordinaire and **Man About Town** (Retired). After our brief but ecstatic run on WRC/DC's award-winning **Mornings with Brian and Bob**, Bob Madigan became wildly famous as WTOP's **Man About Town**. His adventures literally take up dozens of Wikipedia pages.

Robert Publicover – Official Brian and Bob Laugh Track (Retired). Robert didn't fare quite as well as Madigan. While best of friends, Publicover's subtle Canadian influences, stylized linguistics and deep appreciation for literature from the Permian–Triassic Extinction Event held him back from enjoying the loftier success Madigan enjoyed. Nevertheless, despite his reclusive Jacobinism, he eschewed Bob's media shadow for the small yet indelible impression he left on squalid subsets of Washington society. He is best known for donating to the Smithsonian his vast collection of erotic wicker furniture.

Judge Andrew Napolitano -- Senior Judicial Analyst, FOX News. The Judge and I "met" when he was a guest on my show in 2010 and he was hosting **Freedom Watch** on FOX Business. We had such a great time sharing parallel libertarian political beliefs, he returned again and again, leading to the creation of **Judging Freedom**, a 20-30 minute podcast chat-fest about current events, available on my **Libertas Media Project** website. Eight years, annual dinners and a growing friendship later, a variety of circumstances brought **Judging Freedom** to a halt in January 2018. But by the time you reading this, **Freedom Watch** should be back on FOX, educating and entertaining as only the Judge can do! I know, it's confusing. Welcome to showbiz!

James Bovard – Writer. I first interviewed Jim at WWRC with the publication of his tantalizingly-titled best seller: **Lost Rights: The Destruction of American Liberty**. A Talk Show host couldn't beg for a better subject or more superlative treatment of the subject. This was the beginning of a mutual-admiration relationship that led to more interviews as his books appeared, joint appearances at broadcast events, an Ohio Libertarian convention and several low-profile DC bars where Jim attempted to school me in the finer points of beer and cigars. Despite those failures, we continue to be pals up to today. While tomorrow may change that, it was this notorious writer and modern-day H.L. Mencken who encouraged me to write columns for **LRC.com** and later, my first novel, **Watercolor Memories: The Story of Lauren**. If you enjoy any part of this book, it's partly due to earlier threats from Jim. If you have any objections, you can blame

Jim on Facebook, Twitter, **USA Today** and in better bookstores everywhere.

Bud Polacek – General Manager, Z-93/Atlanta. It was Bud's decision to come to Baton Rouge, listen to and hire the budding talent festering in the fertile creativity of the **Nearly-Famous Ross and Wilson Show**. Bud's been gone for a while, sadly among those who have checked out too early. Along with unlocking the door that opened my career to major market success, he was a great pal and decent racquetball partner. I only wish he had stayed around a little longer.

Mark Mason – Vice President CBS/NY. We didn't have that much time working together, but Mark's class-act upon becoming WABC PD took a lot of the sting out of the tragedy that should have been the high point of anyone's radio career. He went on to do great things at WINS and CBS. We lost touch but I always admired his professionalism and kindness during those depressing times at the end of my days at WABC.

Jack Swanson – Swanson Media. Not only will I never forget our first meeting about VRINK in DC when he said he'd never hire me, I have Jack to thank for the seven subsequent years working for KSFO/San Francisco's stable of great Talk talent: the inimitable Lee Rogers, Melanie Morgan, Officer Vic, Sherry Yee, Geoff Metcalf, Jim Eason, Michael Savage -- and all from 3,000 miles away! A unique challenge and a high point for VRINK. And me. Jack also distinguished himself as one of two PDs to terminate my services with truth and grace!

Phil Boyce – Senior Vice President, Salem Radio Network. I only had one chance to "work" for Phil – he was program director at WABC at the time. I took part in the first WABC **Rewound**, which spawned one of the "great moments" in radio, the "Not Chuck Dunaway" interview.

At the Talk Radio Seminar in Atlanta, Phil was discussing the need for new talk talent and how Music Radio might provide future

Talk Radio hosts. As he began addressing some of the difficult hurdles for DJs transitioning from music to talk, he made this acknowledgement:

> *I only know one person who went to bed a DJ and woke up a Talk Show Host, and he did it on the biggest Talk Radio station in the world, WABC/New York – and that's Brian Wilson. I think Brian is in the audience... are you here Brian?*

Totally surprised, I kinda half-stood and waved to Phil. And that room full of legends and wanna-be's broke out in applause. I had never thought about it that way. I was honored Phil did.

Doug Erickson – President, Erickson Media Consultants. I've never had a good thing to say about "consultants." The ones who "consulted" stations I worked for perfectly fit the old cliché, "If you can't do it, consult..." Except Doug. Doug actually likes and respects Talent and maintains a unique ability to communicate with behaviorally-challenged people who play behind the mic, creating ulcers for the Suits. He recognizes and advocates the importance of Talent to the success of a radio station, a foreign thought for many who hold the future of on-air folks in their hands. I have known Doug so long, I can't remember when or how we met. We had a close mutual friend in Denver, the legendary Steven B. Williams. Doug "consulted" me through some difficult times dealing with testy situations in the biz with some who were not among my biggest fans. A unique talent in this dicey field, one of the few for whom I have admiration and affection. Occasionally, he even returns my calls!

Steven B. Williams – Denver Radio Star. **Steven B and The Hawk** were Denver's version of **Ross and Wilson**. Remarkably, Steven and Don *also* split up for avoidable reasons. In 1988, as Steven was "converting" to a single act on KXKL/Denver, I was exiting B104 to pursue the future and my Breach of Contract suit. Steven called me at home one evening to chat about the vicissitudes of radio. We had never met or spoken before, but we spent four hours yapping about our various adventures with different partners, even about the possibility of teaming up someday. Since I was leaving shortly for Casper, Wyoming on a separate business opportunity, we arranged a slight detour to Denver. In the middle of his Saturday show when I arrived, Steven brought me into the studio and introduced me as his "visitor from the East." We spent the rest of the time having one of those rare spontaneously-combusted and hilarious shows. The aircheck tape became a collector's item! Two months later, I stopped in again. And again, hilarity ensued! While we never got the two-man show we craved, we became great friends over the next 18 years with his trips east and our visits west. In May 2006, our mutual friend, talk show host, Rollye James called with the news that Steven had been murdered, his body found floating off Catalina Island, a bullet in his head. Eventually, the bastard who killed Steven was caught in Montana and is now enjoying life without parole. Not the sentence I preferred. Fortunately, I have some great pictures and wonderful memories. But I still miss my friend.

Rick Sklar, Johnny Donovan, Dan Ingram, **Ron Lundy** and **Pat Pantonini** – New York Radio Legends. While Rick left shortly before I arrived, he was instrumental in the decision to go with **Ross and Wilson** in AM Drive. Johnny is the only surviving member of this group of outstanding radio giants with whom I was able to work at WABC before things got crazy. He was a cool head in the radio storm of those days of transition from music to talk; one of the *truly* decent guys in the business. I've written all I can about Ron and Dan; anything more would be redundant. Pat was the genius in the Promotions Department, a wonderful and brilliant guy, as wacky as the air staff! He personally rescued me from too much sake on a brutal NYC winter night. How he got me back to the Waldorf, I will never know!

John Nolan – Afternoon Drive, 95.9 the Fish, Los Angeles. John was my board-op at B104, WRC and WOCT. Each time was a better experience than the last one -- except for the last one, which was a radio obscenity. As a board-op/producer, John's prescience and perception could make a good bit *great*. What began to emerge as far back as B104 in 1987 was John's own on-air talent. After the WOCT abomination, John blossomed in DC, and now is in the Big Time: PM Drive in L.A.! Great guy, great wife, and righteous dude! You can hear John play the perfect straight man off-mic during a live commercial aircheck on the **50 Years** YouTube channel.

Bill White – Program Director KFBK/KSTE Sacramento. Bill inherited me at KCMO/KC from departing PD John Butler who had originally contacted me through VRINK to fill in for "90 days" while he searched for a new AM Drive host. A year of futile searching later, John headed to WMAL/DC and Bill White stepped in. (Confusing ain't it?) When we were unable to consummate a deal to become the permanent AM Drive host, Bill found someone else and my 12-month (to the day!) "temporary" fill-in ended. Bill subsequently left for heritage station WBT/Charlotte. Over his years there, he gave me the opportunity to fill in for Jason Lewis and "Charlotte's Beloved" John Hancock!

John Gehron – Chairman, AccuRadio. Of all the GMs I ever met, John Gehron is the one I never worked for but would have walked over burning coals (more like very warm briquettes) for the opportunity. I had it once. John flew me up to Boston to interview for the morning gig at Oldies WODS. It was a great time! I left with the distinct feeling a move to Bean Town was in my immediate future. After a few days of deafening silence, I called. Unlike most other GMs in the biz, John took calls – even from Talent! Upon further consideration of my aircheck tape, the PD thought I "sounded *too* Top 40." I was floored. "John, I work for a Top 40 station. How else could I sound? If I sent some of my WABC tapes, would I sound <u>too</u> talk?"

John calmly explained while I was his choice for the job, he paid the PD to make those decisions and despite his disappointment, he had to support his PD. You have to respect a man who tells you what you don't want to hear in a way that you can accept it without the ego, vanity and bullshit that unnecessarily permeates so much of the biz. John has moved on to even greater radio accomplishments and it's unlikely an opportunity like that will come again. Still, even those warm briquettes wouldn't keep me away from working with someone with the class of John Gehron.

Dean Thacker – Executive, Malrite Communications. In November, 1988, Dean occupied the GM chair in the front office of Z100 when I was brought in to replace Scott Shannon. Within days, the news broke that Dean was promoted, handing the gory details of contract negotiations over to the new GM. While Z100 ultimately turned out to be a bittersweet experience, it wouldn't have happened at all without Dean's initial approval and guidance. Judging from his insight and experience I witnessed in just a matter of weeks, I'm confident that entire episode would have had a happier ending had he remained. Regardless, wherever you are now, Dean, a belated thanks!

Carlton Cremeans -- News Director, WAFB-TV, Baton Rouge. Shortly after joining the minuscule staff of the soon-to-be-launched Stereo 98, WAFB-FM in 1968, the air talent on the TV side decided to unionize under AFTRA, the American Federation of Television and Radio Artists, AFL-CIO. They waited for the new FM staff to get in place in order to generate a greater number of votes to "go union" when the time came. Management was not thrilled when the notification letter landed on VP Tom Gibbons' desk. If you've never been through such an ordeal, consider yourself fortunate. The tension, rumors and skullduggery that takes place do not make for happy times. As news director, Carlton was ineligible to vote. Still, he offered a young, inexperienced whippersnapper like me a place to go to get the straight skinny on what was really happening "inside." My career might have taken a sudden turn for the worse without the cool-headed advice from Carlton Cremeens.

Art Athens, **John Maher**, **Palmer Payne** and **Rick James** – WABC News Anchors. Anyone who heard **Ross and Wilson** on WABC also heard at least one of these news guys every morning. Just for the record, despite my best and incessant efforts, John Maher was the only one I was unable to crack up with some smart-ass intro!

Jeff Beauchamp – Vice President and Station Manager, WBAL/Baltimore (Retired). Once upon a time, Jeff told me how much he enjoyed listening to **Brian and O'Brien** on his way to work rather than his own team on WBAL. Even though we were beating the pants off those guys in the ratings, Jeff would listen and laugh along with most of the other drivers coming down the JFX. After writing **the little black book on Whitewater**, Jeff told me that story when I came in for an interview with WBAL's Ron Smith. Later, when I created VRINK, he enthusiastically booked me to fill in for Ron and Allan Prell, an arrangement that continued for years. During that time, we got to be buds. As much as we both wanted me on staff full-time, it wasn't meant to be. Still, his friendship and loyalty meant a lot to me, my business and career. Jeff retired in 2009 and left one helluva legacy.

"Skinny" Bobby Harper -- 96 Rock, Atlanta. Most everyone knows by now, "Skinny" Bobby was the inspiration for Johnny Fever, **WKRP in Cincinnati**. Bobby wasn't nearly that laid back on or off the air! We would meet accidentally on occasion. Not being direct competitors made it easier to be friends. Professionally and personally, I admired his work. When **Ross and Wilson** left for WABC, Bobby met us at a local bar to give us little going away present. Not surprisingly, it was served on a mirror -- with a straw. To the good times! RIP, mi amigo.

Joe Nolan – Shadow Traffic Reporter. Joe was with **Ross and Wilson** on WABC from Day One. Along with being NYC's most adept traffic reporter, he played a good straight man on occasion. Aside from his embarrassingly lopsided loss to me in the Great Lasagna Challenge, I remember Joe for his lovely wife,

Andromeda, but mostly for his account one morning of "early reports" of near-riots breaking out in Times Square due to "nude kids" seen roaming the area. The "early reports" and the "nude kids" turned out to be the New Kids on the Block pop group in Times Square for a photo shoot. The word spread and the rest was history. No doubt the excitement would have been minimal if nude kids actually were seen around the Manhattan landmark. Joe's talent of knowing when to play and when to shut-up served us both well.

Jim Erwin – News Director, WIBR/Baton Rouge. If it hadn't been for Jim's interest in the story of a budding DJ nearly killed in a hit-and-run accident outside Baton Rouge February 1966, who knows where I may have wound up. After my hospital release, Jim "lobbied" GM Bob Earle to give me a weekend gig, and he did. That turned into a full-time PM Drive slot, which firmly planted me on the Radio Road to everywhere else.

Claire Stevens, Dr. Johnathan B. Bell, Bruce ' Maimzini" Maiman – Z100/NY Z-Morning Zoo Original Cast Members. The Zoo was an "ensemble show," another way of saying "organized chaos." While the **Ross and Wilson** act was the basis for everything, there was this gathering of professional talent along with us. On the closing credits, Claire would be "News," John would be "Sports," and Maimzini would be invisibly providing "Everything Else." But they were so much more than that. Aside from "assigned duties," each one of these people were *air talents* in their own right. Yes, Claire did the news, but also was part of whatever mayhem came before or after. She's currently editing her own book of interviews of rock stars – it's probably available by now. John Bell provided stability – or not -- depending on what boat we were rocking at the time. Bruce Maiman became "Maimzini" for his remarkable production and editing skills, making the finished product like an edited phone call appear "like magic." His "almost" Ph.D. in Music didn't hurt. When we last spoke, he was writing things in Sacramento. Regardless of whose Zoo incarnation it was at the time, the show wouldn't have become the monumental success it was without these three talented, intelligent, principled, wack-o players.

Sean Hall -- B104 News (Retired). Sean "The Round Mound of Sound" Hall handled "all things news" for the rarely newsworthy **Brian and O'Brien Show**. Coming from a family with a legendary news background, the mostly unflappable Sean occasionally lost it to my unceasing efforts to get him to break character. Fortunately for both of us, news credibility was not a high priority at B104 but when the news *did* count, Sean delivered. After the **Brian and O'Brien** implosion, Sean went on to more credible work in DC and multiple network gigs.

Cathy Weinflash, Debbi Iacovelli Kelly, WABC/ NY. After the flip to Talk, Cathy Weinflash was anointed producer of the surviving **Ross and Wilson Show**. Fun and easy to work with, Cathy was a former Playboy bunny at the ill-fated Playboy Club in Great Gorge, New Jersey, which provided a fertile field for adolescent jokes! Debbi could have been a Playboy bunny but the Club had gone south by the time she became "of age." Deb put herself through broadcast engineering school and knocked on the door at ABC. As our board-op, her pure enjoyment of the job and being a part of the show added its own electricity to the Control Room atmosphere. Deb rose to become a TV audio-video editor/producer. These two cuties kept our pace and continuity in-line during those frothy years, and even stuck around after Ross was let go and I was flying solo. I couldn't have done it without them.

Commander Bill Eveland – Air Traffic Reporter, KFBK/Sacramento. I never met the man who did the traffic reports for KFBK from whatever it was he flew, but I always appreciated someone who "got it;" namely my brand of on-air sarcasm and general buffoonery. He did. When filling in for Tom Sullivan, he was a bright spot in the broadcast day. I heard he retired circa 2005. I hope he's living large!

Ross Brittain – Since the legendary **Bob and Ray**, there has never been a radio team as organically spontaneous, creative and successful as **Ross and Wilson.** Ross Brittain's production ability, coupled with his education and engineer's sense of order was the perfect complement to my spontaneity, creativity and willingness to press the envelope. By 1983 on WABC, our potential was immeasurable; tragically, easily avoidable circumstances killed it. Five years later, **Ross and Wilson** was resurrected on the perfect platform, Z100's Z Morning Zoo, with the same boundless potential. Despite blinding flashes of the comedic genius of our original pairing, we were DOA before the first new show. Pride, vanity and ego will forever prevent anyone from knowing why. So sad. We could have been among the greatest ever -- if only.

Don O'Brien – From the beginning, there was little to recommend us working together, other than a manager's wet dream. Unlike **Ross and Wilson**, there were no similarities on any level between us, other than radio. Still, one could say "opposites attract" was the explanation for the now-legendary popularity we enjoyed. While Don was a very capable DJ, he lacked Ross' education, experience, maturity and by his own admission, self-discipline. Overall, that still may have contributed to our success in predominantly blue-collar Baltimore since I was willing to play the "disapproving adult" to Don's adolescent humor. **Brian and O'Brien** also got "another chance" some years later on WQSR. But, like **Ross and Wilson**, it was over before it began. The same issues that plagued the original show returned to haunt the new one. But then, as Don later attested, they were never really gone. There's some truth in the line, "You can never go home again." Don went on to become a local legend on some of Maryland's Eastern Shore stations.

A Special *Standing* O for one "Peter Peroxide," obscure sidewalk surfer somewhere in mid-town Manhattan, Fire Island, or apartment pool. WABC listeners with criminally acute memories will recall Peter's occasional interruptions, calling in to the early days of **Ross and Wilson's** AM Drive tenure.

In actuality, "Peter" is one Joe Tedd Locastro, obscure DJ couldabeen who, instead opted for a stellar career in the IT Department of an anonymous Software Giant. Barely known is his early attraction to R&W, which subsequently resulted in more than 35 years of following us and my other incarnations, including the ill-fated reunion at Z100.

More to the point, JT used his bodacious computer skills to amass the largest collection of airchecks from WABC, B104 and Z100. Conditioning himself to mere minutes of sleep, fueled by copious amounts of unnamed lagers, he is singularly responsible for the majority of YouTube audio clips that accompany this book. Everyone who helped with this project thought it imperative for readers to be able to actually hear the insanity mentioned in some of the **50 Stories**. Without Joe's listening, collecting, recording, porting, editing, burning, uploading and drinking, this added dimension would have been impossible. A fan who became a friend, Joe Tedd "Peter Peroxide" Locastro.

***

There are additional people to acknowledge – in and out of radio. It's likely I've missed a few, while others appear prominently in previous pages. In no particular order:

George Bonnell (WAFB-FM), Robert Collins (WAFB-FM), Morton Downey, Jr., (WWRC), Mark Davis (WWRC/WBAP), John Hancock (WBT), Dr. Don Rose (KFRC), Sean Hannity, Rush Limbaugh, Glenn Beck, Dave LaBrozzi (CBS Radio/Baltimore), Randy Reeves (Z-93), Alan Colmes (WABC), Tom Gresham (Gun Talk), Ron Smith (WBAL), Doug "The Greaseman" Tracht, Joey Reynolds (WOR), Kidd Kraddick (KEGL), Fred Winston (WLS), Rollye James (WWDB), Jim Kerr (WPLJ), "Coach" Mike Opelka (Z100), Carl Carl of the Chicago Carls (WABC), Tim Renew (WOCT-FM), Steve Earle (WIBR), Bill Bresnan (WABC), Kevin Metheny (Clear Channel), Al Brady Law (WNBC), David Bernstein (WOR), Mike Wellbrock (WBAL), Bob Shomper (WBAP), Sean Casey (WCBM), Dom Giordano

(WWDB), Jim Heller (Clear Channel), Perry Michael Simon (All Access), Art Vuolo (Vuolo Video Air-Chex) and Allan Sniffen (musicradio77.com).

Also my thanks to Hugh Turley, Frank Huggins, La Vonne Bauder for their special contributions.

BONUS!

My Award-Winning Chili Recipe isn't the only bonus here!

In case you missed my first novel, **Watercolor Memories: The Story of Lauren**, your luck just ran out! A Free Sample, Chapter One follows!

WARNING: Reading Chapter One can be addictive. You may feel compelled to read the rest of the story and it's Surprise Ending!

That's what Amazon is for!

-BW

ABOUT THE AUTHOR

Brian Wilson is a nationally-known radio and television host, author, speaker and consultant.

In his 50-year broadcasting career, Brian hosted successful radio programs at Heritage stations in the nation's largest markets, including New York, San Francisco, Atlanta, Houston, Baltimore and Washington, DC. As morning drive host at WABC/New York, he was the first DJ to successfully transition to Talk Show Host literally overnight as the ABC powerhouse switched from its legendary Music Radio format to Talk Radio in 1982. In 1988, he was hired as "Head Zookeeper" of the highly successful Z-Morning Zoo at Z-100/New York.

Wilson was also a part of the up-start CNN, hosting the entertainment segment, "Music Notes". Later in a return to Atlanta, Brian not only worked in talk radio, he also hosted "Talk at Nite", a late night weekly live television talk program.

In 1994, Brian founded Vacation Relief, Inc. (VRINK), using digital technology to become the first major-market talk radio host to fill-in for hosts around the country from his home studio. Over the next 20 years, Wilson hosted radio programs at Heritage stations in Seattle, Portland, Sacramento, Denver, Minneapolis-St. Paul, Kansas City, Dallas-Fort Worth, Charlotte, Atlanta, Baltimore, Washington, Philadelphia, San Francisco and New York, as well as the nationally syndicated Art Bell, Jim Bohannon and Laura Ingraham shows.

Wilson is the author of four books – 50 Stories: 50 Years in Radio, Watercolor Memories: The Story of Lauren, The Little Black Book on Whitewater, and A Media Guide for Market-Liberal Organizations.

Born and raised in Wayne,New Jersey, Brian attended both public and private schools on the East Coast. He spent his college years at Fairleigh Dickinson University and Louisiana State University. He lives near Smith Mountain Lake, Virginia with his wife, journalist Cassie Wilson, and their golden retriever, Nellie.

Watercolor

Memories

The Story of Lauren

by Brian Wilson

The Story of Lauren Starts Here

In the beginning . . . once upon a time . . . in a galaxy long ago and far away, it was the best of times, it was the worst of times, it was the age of wisdom, it was the age of foolishness, it was the epoch of belief, it was the spring of hope, it was the winter of despair -- and that was one helluva run-on sentence!

Let's get started. First, everything you're about to read is true. I fell in love with Lauren May 28, 1961, on a blind date to the "Roaring Twenties" dance in our high school gym. At this juncture, a pause for some background may be in order.

In 1961, I'm 16 years old. I had been living away from my home in Wayne, New Jersey for the better part of three years attending one of those "All-Boy-Tie-and-Jacket" New England prep schools, like the one you've seen in Scent of a Woman. My parents had decided the local public school system sucked big time, so they determined my newly-discovered elevated IQ needed cultivation at a superior learning institution. Or maybe they just wanted me out of the house. There is evidence to suggest that may have actually been the primary motive. Hell, I had been surrounded for three years by lots of guys who were there for that very reason!

Skipping over the uncomfortable parts of being shuttled off for months at a time to a boarding school two states away, living with people you didn't know in a place you'd never been, things went along just swimmingly until my father's business hit an economic brick wall in 1960. With tuition rivaling that of some small colleges, prep school was no longer an affordable option. Arrangements were made for me to return to the lobotomizing clutches of the Wayne Township Public School System.

It was awkward.

The kids I had grown up with through elementary school hadn't seen me since seventh grade and, of course, had no idea where I went or what happened to me; rumors ran the gauntlet from "dead" to "prison". (Those were some free-floating imaginations for kids in a small town back then.) My sudden appearance after Spring Break caused a mild stir but the ripples died down pretty quickly. More importantly, during my absence, pre-adolescent affiliations sustained everyone heading into puberty and solidified into various identity circles. Having been in absentia during this social gestation period, I wasn't part of any clique or klatch nor was I invited to be nor did I expect to be.

This was no big deal. Really. I had no reason to anticipate anything else. The way Wayne was laid out back then, social groupings spontaneously generated via geography more than anything else. If you lived at Packanack Lake, not that far from our farm but outside the formal parameters of the "lake community", you were definitely not part of the "lake society". And the "lake society" had some pretty stringent rules, barring anyone not a Resident of "the lake" from participating in any of the social functions sponsored by the "lake society" -- with the exception of Boy Scouts, Girl Scouts and (after some effort) Little League. There were similar communities within Wayne's mostly agricultural 27 square miles: Pines Lake, Lionshead Lake, all with similar restrictive covenants. As New Yorkers made their exodus to the newly-discovered 'Burbs, each area built its own elementary school. But after sixth grade, wherever you lived, everybody funneled into the Anthony Wayne Junior High School and Melting Pot. Here you not only learned the joy of changing classrooms and teachers for different subjects at different periods, more importantly, you discovered there were all these other kids your age who had been living within a few miles of you for the last 12 years! Except for those in your Scout troop or on opposing Little League teams, you had no clue they even existed; that is, unless you were part of a "lake society". If you were raised on a chicken farm, unattached to any identifiable area, you were pretty much on your own.

Or on a tractor.

I mention this now to give you a sense of the social fabric wrapped around me like swaddling clothes at the advanced age of 15 and why, despite being born and raised in one of Wayne's earliest families, it was almost as if I was just as much a "New Boy" as I had been my first year away at prep school.

But I digress . . .

After the initial titters of curiosity and surprise upon my return, things calmed down quickly enough and life became just as big a snoozer as it had been whenever I had come home for the holidays. Living in what was still "the country", both parents working 35 miles away in Manhattan, without serious public transportation, parental transportation, filial transportation or even the distractions of a condensed, self-sustaining "lake community" -- and especially without the coveted all-liberating driver's license -- it was definitely not "the best of times".

I'm a little fuzzy on how everything initially came about but one spring afternoon in May, Rich Lambert, a Wayne High School senior who had dated my big sister a few times (before she determined he was "beneath her"), pulled into the farm when he saw me out mowing on the tractor. His "steady", Ann, was sitting right next to him, his high school ring around her neck, her arm over his shoulder in accordance with the Official 1960's Dating Customs Handbook. After the appropriate small talk, he asked, "Would you be interested in going on a blind date to the "Roaring Twenties" dance in the gym Saturday?" Before I could say anything, Ann jumped in -- the girl's name was Lauren. She lived next door to Ann and they lived just a few miles away (the other side of Route 23, Wayne's outback and gateway to Pequannock, a bedroom community often embarrassingly mispronounced). Predictably, Ann painted a picture of a "very cute" girl, also a sophomore and "a little shy" -- which I took to mean "this is why she doesn't have a date". I remember wondering how could she could live so close, be so cute and I have no clue who she was? That's when I gave myself the 1960s equivalent of today's "face palm". Duh! You've been gone for three years, Genius. Based on how the Township school district lines were drawn, we wouldn't have attended the same school until Melting Pot Junior High, which of course, was right when I left for Preppyville.

So? So . . . what the hell? Why not?

Magic Saturday and 6:30 arrived and so did Rich and Ann who picked me up and off we went to Lauren's place. The dance organizers were serious about the "Roaring Twenties" theme. Rich was wearing a sports jacket with the widest lapels I had ever seen outside of an old gangster movie, a wide, gaudy tie and a fedora that must have come over on the Ark. Ann was in a sleek black sheath "Flapper" number with lots of not-really pearls around her neck. I was totally out of costume in your basic tie-and-blazer; I didn't think the theme meant all this – but it did. Too late now. Even if I had something to change into, we would have been unacceptably late. No need to make a bad First Impression; blind dates are hard enough.

Naturally, this was going to involve enduring the dreaded "Meet the Parents and Squirm" Ordeal. While a tad apprehensive, I was reasonably confident my Amy Vanderbilt-inspired prep school-infused manners would get me through the pending inquisition. And it wasn't as if I had never been on a date before. There was the Dance Class Graduation Dance in fifth grade with Barbara Sasse whose tooth I had knocked out, kissing her on a dare in fourth grade. Such a romantic! What I lacked in finesse, I made up with enthusiasm; a regular Romeo cum Marquis de Sade rolled into one otherwise reasonably well-mannered pre-teeny-bopper package. But that had been years ago! I had matured.

In a 10 -15 minute drive from the farm, we're pulling into Lauren's driveway. Rich and Ann led the way to the front door of a modest green shingle ranch house with tall trees all around. I had ridden past this place on the way to Pequannock hundreds of times. Who could have thought then what was about to happen now, not to mention what lied ahead? A child's playground set was in the fenced backyard; Lauren had siblings.

Prep school manners notwithstanding, I've always hated introductions: the meaningless how-do-you-do's, aimless small talk, dull or pointed questions. But Lauren's mom was a charmer; friendly, warm, pleasant and a great laugh. She promptly confirmed I was the Brian Wilson from the Wilson Farm. Sometime, somewhere, she remembered meeting my mother and that took care of my vetting. Lauren's father greeted me with all the warmth and sincerity of any father convinced my only reason for living was to get in his daughter's pants as expeditiously as time, space and opportunity would allow. Thanks to being cloistered in prep school for three of my formative years, I was too inexperienced to be up on the latest Dating Policies, Practices, and Procedures, but I noodled out that Lauren's conspicuous absence was just a necessary part of the ceremony setting me up for her "Grand Entrance".

I was not disappointed. Even in its simplicity, Lauren's entrance was, indeed, very, very "Grand".

For more, go to:
http://bit.ly/watercolormemories

34199037R00196

Made in the USA
Columbia, SC
13 November 2018